FAMILY UNDER SAIL

FAMILY

ILLUSTRATIONS BY MARY LEONARD

UNDER SAIL

A Handbook for First Mates

by JANE KIRSTEIN and MARY LEONARD

THE MACMILLAN COMPANY

COLLIER-MACMILLAN LTD., LONDON

For Jane,
who died before she saw her book

Contents

〜〜〜〜〜〜〜〜〜〜〜〜〜〜〜〜〜〜〜〜〜〜〜〜〜〜〜〜

Foreword

~~~~~~

W<small>HY SOMEONE WRITES</small> a book is usually not of any interest to the reader. He is interested in the subject—not the author. This book, however, has two authors and I think we need a bit of explaining, because, in a way, it is a dialogue between us.

Mary and I have two great things in common: we both love sailing, and we have both owned the same boat. There the similarity between us ends. Mary is in her thirties and has been sailing since she was a child. I am in my fifties, and sailing began for me at forty. Mary has young boys. I have a grown daughter. Mary has had more racing experience than I have. I have cruised longer and farther than she has. In at least two big areas I can't counter Mary: she has worked professionally, along with the men, in a boatyard, and she is a talented painter of pictures.

We met in the fog-bound harbor of Block Island, off Rhode Island's coast, one summer a few years ago. Our collaboration began then, though we didn't know it. Not until we—the Kirsteins—sold our long-loved, wooden Casey yawl *Skylark* to the Leonards and became friends in the process did Mary and I realize we shared a third thing: wonderment at why so many husbands sailed without wives, or with wives who wished they weren't sailing. After talking it over, we think we know why.

Together, we hope to work a sea change in these wives. A sea change is defined by Webster as "a change wrought by the sea, as in the forming of a pearl; hence, marked transformation, to something richer, and finer." In this book Mary sometimes speaks alone, and sometimes I do. We don't always agree, but maybe our ideas will be helpful. We hope we're not just talking into the wind. We'd like to see more women at sea.

Since we hope that this book may be a step toward learning to sail, we have used nautical terms freely. Those that are not explained in the text will be found in the diagrams and definitions in the glossary at the end of the book. Good sailing!

JANE KIRSTEIN

The Rewards of Sailing

1

IT's PRETTY NICE, at my age, to have men fall in love with me at first sight. It happens often, and the circumstances vary little. The setting is always a boat, and my admirers are always on all-male cruises. Either they row over to our boat, or we are invited to visit theirs, and after the initial exchange of small talk about the weather, the day's sail, and the beauties of our respective boats, they turn to George, my skipper, and say, "You're a lucky man to get your wife to cruise with you." Sometimes they add wistfully, "Mine used to," or, "Mine will for a weekend, but no longer," or, saddest of all, "Mine has never set foot on my boat." It always makes me feel sort of precious and brave, and I sometimes fail to point out that all I did all day long was loll in the sun. They listen raptly to everything I say, and I am not even allowed to mix my own drinks. Once in a while my head is so turned that I insist they stay for supper; then adoration flows like the drinks they are mixing. On one memorable occasion I graciously consented to be *their* guest (they included my consort).

I rate such encounters as a "fringe" reward of sailing. The real reward is the fond look in the skipper's eyes. That look is what got me on a small boat in the first place, but it isn't

1

the sole reason I continue to go cruising. I am now as hooked on sailing as my husband.

Admittedly, my addiction didn't come all in a rush. There were moments in my early cruising days when I agreed with the old saw that sailing is a man's world and wished I had stood at home in bed. One early spring cruise in Long Island Sound stands out miserably. Rewards of sailing, indeed. The most rewarding experience of the whole ten days was picking up our mooring at the end of the cruise. We had looked forward to the opening of the cruising season with eager anticipation, remembering the fine final cruise of the year before and the long, gloomy, boatless winter that followed it. What we got was ten days of unmitigated cold, damp weather and very little wind. We started out with colds and came home with bronchitis. Even our trusty old Shipmate coal stove funked its job of soul- and body-warming, having developed flue trouble the second day out. We had our memories of healthy, happy cruises, but as we coughed and sneezed our way down Long Island Sound, they grew increasingly dim. I tried to be a good sport—I really did—but silently I often wondered "Why am I here? *Is* cruising fun—ever?"

Many a sunny summer cruise after that answered those questions, and I'm glad I didn't mutiny for good. The rewards of sailing, I find in looking back, have grown with each season—despite occasional setbacks like the one I just described. As I slowly learned the rudiments of sailing, learned enough to enable me to ask questions so as to learn more, and as I found how to dress comfortably, to house-keep easily, to relax totally, and to expect a little bad weather with the good, I became ever more convinced that during cruising season, a first mate's place is not in the home, but on the boat. The skipper is allowed—even encouraged— to set out an occasional all-male cruise, but only as a side-trip. He may rally some of the boys for a beer-drinking, free-speaking weekend, but the long cruises belong to me.

That, I think, will be the stand of the average first mate after a successful cruising season or two, for I am an average sort of woman: a housewife who has had a career and children, lived in both cities and the country, traveled some, played a fair game of golf and tennis. A landlubber widow at forty, I married a man—after a winter (nonboating) courtship—who had apparently stepped from his baby carriage into a sailboat and has been there every free day since. He brought to our marriage, as part of his "dowry," a 40-foot, twenty-five-year-old Casey-built yawl named *Skylark* (which we sold to Mary and John Leonard two years ago), and all of his sailing friends shook their heads when we set off on our honeymoon. They knew I had never been on a sailboat before.

"That marriage can't last," they said. "They'll be back—busted up—before you can say Lloyd's Point" (our destina-

tion that night, fifteen miles away). Eleven years and several
thousand cruising miles later, I'm glad they were wrong.
I would have missed a lot of fun—fun that only a yachtsman can have.

Who but a yachtsman can poke into coves in Maine, in-
habited only by seals and herons, and go ashore to discover
behind the beach the hand-hewn granite block foundations
of an early Downeaster farm? A four-lane highway may be
only a few hundred yards away, but no path or road con-
nects it to the heron haven by the sea. Ten days in a resort
hotel on Virgin Gorda in the British West Indies is not without delights, but who would not prefer to move from one
palm-treed white-sand beach to another, in the unsur-
passed cruising ground of the Virgin Islands and sleep on
one's own boat at the end of a strenuous day of swimming
and snorkeling? "Getting away from it all" is only half the
story of the joys of cruising. Going to some new and otherwise inaccessible area and living there in one's own house
is the big other half. The freedom to roam the watery world
is what is given to a sailor.

Freedom to roam has to be cultivated—as does any freedom—if it is to reach full maturity. Sailors new to the helm
may have to spend a season or two in their own back bay,
learning the ways of their boats and the winds and tides,
before they feel ready to go farther afield. The first sortie
into unfamiliar waters takes a bit of courage, a lot of boning
up on marine charts, and some luck to make it successful,
but with each subsequent cruise the feeling of liberation
grows, the itineraries lengthen, and the horizon is the limit.
Just thinking of it is one of the rewards of sailing. Only a
few make it far from home, but there is a ring of excitement
to the very thought that I find enchanting.

Independence. Who but a sailor can even dream of saying,
at least to himself, "I don't like what I'm doing or seeing or

feeling, and I can do something about it. I can pick up my house and go. I won't have to pay rent, or light bills, or plane fares. I can live off the land, and in a bathing suit. I can move in a second if I don't like my neighbors." He can go swimming in the nude at high noon, or howl like a banshee at the moon. He can forego shaving and bathing until he—or his first mate—can't stand it. The world is his oyster, and he is a snail, a blissful snail with his house on his back. He will probably stay right there at his desk, but he can dream. Who but a sailor can?

A two-day weekend or a two-week cruise—not beyond the wildest dream of any sailor—may be a declaration of independence printed on microfilm, but even a Sunday sailor is a liberated man to some degree. For one day, at least, he is his own man. Whatever happens in a day's sail on a small boat, good or bad, directly results from decisions taken by him, with no boss or client considerations to foul up the details. The only "higher-ups" are the weather, the boat's capacity to comply with the captain's decisions, and, perhaps, the wishes of his first mate. Given good weather, a good boat, and a good (in every sense of the word) first mate, the captain of a small boat is captain of his fate—a rare and precious power in this corporate age. He can take sole credit for the good, and he can cope singlehandedly with the bad, in the small world of a boat. If the day's sail is agreeable and the night's anchorage pleasing, he has rigged the right sails and chosen the right spot. If, instead, "it comes on to blow" or fog closes in, he will shorten sail or run the buoys to the anchorage, and he does not have to ask another living soul for permission or advice—not even the first mate—if he doesn't want to.

By tradition, the skipper is the only boss on a boat, and I like it that way. I am not a particularly submissive type, but it's restful to have someone else make all the decisions for a change. I just stretch out full-length in the cockpit and think of the things I don't have to do, the big and little problems I don't have to meet. No telephones or doorbells, no committees to work with, no dinner guests to plan for, and no decisions to make except whether to have peanut butter sandwiches or black bean soup for lunch. There is time for reading and talking, painting and swimming, and just looking off into space. I like that.

I like, too, the tourist aspect of cruising—the beautiful, the historic, and most of all, the offbeat places we can reach only on a small boat.

For instance, Letite. We'll never go back to that village on the Bay of Fundy in New Brunswick, Canada, but we'll never forget petite Letite.

There is one industry in Letite: fog-making. Tiny men with pointed ears sit in the lighthouse on the point, day after day, turning the fog-making machine with one hand and blowing the foghorn with the other. Every year or two a sunny day comes along (the fog-making machine breaks down), but the foghorn never stops—it is the Muzak of Letite.

We had been hearing it for three days while we sat in a dripping peasouper, eating our way through all the fresh food on the boat. Wisps of voices came to us occasionally, in between horn grunts, but never a body did we see on the twice-daily gropings to shore that we made with our 170-pound crew, our Newfoundland dog named Skipper. When Skipper ate the last of his chow, we decided what-the-hell, eased him into the dinghy, and pledged ourselves not to return until we found People—and maybe a store. After a half hour of rowing and listening, rowing and listening, we heard a dog barking not far off. The outlines of a dock, and of a large black and white dog held by a very small Letitian standing on the dock, took shape an arm's length away and high above us. The tides on the Bay of Fundy are as busy as the fog, rising and falling 30 feet, and on that day, at that hour, the tide was low—all 30 feet of it.

Skipper did not like to climb perpendicular dock ladders at low tide on the Bay of Fundy, so we edged the dinghy in among the rotting hulls of derelict boats on the beach, where we were met by a large affectionate dog and a small grave young man. There the procession began (to a store, we hoped), with our hosts leading us from the beach to a grassy road that wound by sea-worn cottages whose doors opened as if our passing had triggered electronic eyes. Silently, women, more children and dogs, and a few weather-beaten men emerged and joined the cortege, falling into step behind us in the order of their appearance. We smiled, and Skipper wagged, but not a word did they utter in answer to our questions, which had become monosyllabic. It was as if we were in a foreign land. "Store?" we said, with warmth and friendship in our voices. "Food?" We made motions with our hands as if we were putting food into our mouths. No answer. We walked on.

And then reality, of a sort, returned. Another door opened and out of it came a man who carried in his hand an enormous conch shell painted bright green. Shining even more brightly were his eyes, whose blueness defied comparison with Spanish summer skies, eyes that had knifed through eighty-odd years of Fundy fog. He spoke, unceasingly, as he came up to us, turning the shell from side to side to shows its wonders, and the spell was broken. Above the babel of voices now surrounding us, we gathered that he would like to sell us his shell, that he had found it (where?) many years ago, that he had painted it green because tourists liked their shells that way, he had heard, but maybe we wouldn't, and that probably we had hundreds of them at home ("down there") anyway. In the midst of the turmoil a car full of staring people swept around and past us, and

before we could gracefully acquire the shell and, hopefully, head or be headed toward food, a car grazed us again.
Soon, as the procession moved along the road, we paid no
attention to the "traffic," merely stepping out of its path
from time to time; the "traffic" was the same car, on another
leg of its sightseeing tour.

Everyone talked now, asking questions. Where did we
come from? How did we get there? Did we have any children? What was the dog's name? Had we ever been to Seal
Island? (It was ten miles away.) We learned that another
sailboat had been in Letite, only two years before, and that
after three weeks or so our man with the blue eyes and the
green shell, who was, importantly, the owner of a fishing
boat, had towed the despondent sailor out of the harbor,
past the foghorn on the point, and into the sunlight—never
to be seen again in Letite. But not a word did we hear
of food.

Just as hope was waning, the group swung in a body to a
bright white cottage on the water's edge. Delicious smells
of fresh-baking-something emanated from it, and we knew
that we had finally made contact with provisions.

The beautiful lady of the cottage had crisp, hot dough-

nuts. And from a secret room in back came *cordon bleu* cabbage, pearly potatoes, and two of the handsomest, liveliest lobsters a starving sailor ever laid eyes on. For Skipper there was a bone from what must have been a local dinosaur, and to top it all off we were presented with a bunch of wild flowers that she must have just picked, knowing we were on our way. What to do? What to say? We never found out whether or not it was a store, and cowardly avoiding the issue, we left money tucked hurriedly into a potted geranium as we backed, bowing to the waist, out of the door.

We ate that night, blissfully ad nauseum, and the next day groped our way via compass course past the foghorn on the point and into the sunlight just beyond. On second thought, maybe we will go back someday when we get fed up with people en masse, as we often do.

People who live by or on the sea are nearly all pretty good fellows, and often more than that. Vestiges of the frontier spirit still exist by the sea; a helping hand is instinctively offered in troubled situations and gratitude is but shyly accepted. "You would do it for me" is the feeling. "Why thank me?"

We weren't in trouble one blustery, early June day in the marble-quarry harbor of Stonington, Maine, but we did have a small problem. In order to stay clear of the busy channel where lobstermen and packetboats carrying workmen from the quarry across the narrow passage from Stonington plied purposefully, we anchored well off shore. Wind, tide, and traffic whipped the sea into a drenching chop as we rowed ashore in our dinghy, and we were watched with both concern and amusement from the shore. Arriving wetly but safely at the dock, we asked an onlooker where ice was obtainable and if the lobsters in the pound at his feet were for sale.

We happened on the right man; he supposed the town's ice machine wasn't working so early in the season, but he had some ice he could spare in his storage locker at home, and yes, he might have a lobster or two that would do. He pointed to his house, high on the hill above town, and then he pointed to his truck at the end of the dock.

"The keys are in it," he said. "Just go along and take it, and tell the woman up there I said you can have ice. We'll make out."

After a few false starts, we rode high in the truck's van through the neat, delightful village with newly painted lobster pots hanging from every other pink, blue, or white cottage wall, and up a low-gear grade to "the woman" and the ice. A lady (wife? sister?) left her ironing to attend to us. She didn't really know what she should charge. She supposed a dollar would do. And back we went to the dock—100 pounds of precious ice clumping about at our backs. Our friend at the dock had two tender-sized lobsters packed in a carton and ready for us in his sturdy motorboat with the engine idling.

"Pretty rough for your dink," he said. "Climb aboard, and we'll tow it out to your boat." Protestations would have been as out of order as elaborate thanks would have been when we reached *Shag*, bucking like a bronco at her anchor. We would have done the same thing for him, was the tacit understanding. A small thing, perhaps, the lobsterman's helpfulness, but his warm gesture was characteristic of people who live by the sea. A week before my skipper had seen a man step on the hand of a ragged bundle of bones prone on a busy New York street.

Then there was the lobsterman in Vinalhaven, Maine, who offered us his mooring (he was leaving for two days) after watching us drag anchor twice over the kelp-carpeted bottom. And the lady in Cape Porpoise, Maine, who drove us to her home from the grocery store where we met, emptied her ice trays, and brought them and us back to our boat. Nice people!

We just like people in general better at sea. Party-haters on land, we do our fair share of socializing on a cruise. Mary and Joe Zilch, in the boat moored next to us, may never cross our paths again, nor will we or they care, but for a brief time we have a lot in common—boats! We enjoy talking about them over a drink. There's no nonsense about what do you do for a living, or whom do you know, or whom you are going to vote for in the next election; just—how long have you had your boat, who built it, and where did you come from—today? Sometimes, the talk goes deeper and the friendship does, too, especially if your paths do cross again. Then you're delighted, as we were with (I'll call them) the Murrays.

Christmas day, 1966, Allan's Cay, the Bahamas, was the time and place, and the weather was lousy—a norther blowing 40 knots and full of cold rain. The day before we had supplied in Nassau's hectic Christmas shopping rush and then snaked our way across the shallow, reef-studded Yellow Bank to the Exumas, with me on the bow calling out the coral heads in our path. Navigating by eye is an old native custom in the Bahamas, because there are no buoys, but I was new to the sport of figuring out by the color of the patch how much water was over it and was mighty glad to see Allan's Cay. The only protected anchorage there is tiny, with respectable coral heads of its own, so it became a cozy community when we added *Shag* to the three boats already there. One, a 55-foot ketch named *Sirius,* was apparently a charter boat, with a busy, happy party of five aboard. We all waved, but the norther was already in and setting up was too much of a chop for socializing in comfort. On Christmas morning there was more blow and more chop, but full of Christmas cheer, we accepted their inviting wave, wrapped a bottle of wine in some leftover present-paper, rowed to *Sirius,* and met, for the first of many delightful times, Chris and Chuck Murray. Sometimes we planned to rendezvous, and sometimes we just happened to pick the same anchorages in the chain of coral reefs that make up the Exumas. Chris, a gourmet cook, made us melt-in-your-mouth conch fritters while Chuck and George pored over charts. We shelled and swam together from deserted pink coral-sand beaches, and we were sorry to say good-bye three weeks later when we headed for the northern Bahamas. One year later, on Christmas day, we were anchored by chance next to each other in a harbor in the Virgin Islands, where we had a triple celebration: our reunion, Christmas, and Chris's birthday. Small, pleasant world.

Any sailor can match tales with ours, of the helping hands offered, the cockpit socializing, the adventure of going to new ports, and the pleasure of returning to old, familiar ones. He knows the joy of standing on deck, still in his city clothes minus shoes, a beer in his hand, looking at the sea and the grubby fishing boat in the slip next to him and finding them all beautiful after having been away from them for weeks. He listens to the news broadcast with only half an ear, until the weather report comes along. Then *cordon bleu* steak and canned onions, reading a bit in the coziness of the cabin, a look out the hatch at the stars, a yawn, knocked-out sleep—that's yachtin'. And that's for Mary and me, as first mates. Join us!

JANE KIRSTEIN

Rewards for All Comers

Why would a woman go to sea? It's wet. It can be cold and uncomfortable. It's unpredictable and often dangerous. Women like the status quo, they like to be in command of

the situation, and they continually strive for creature comforts. They prefer to leave physical labor to the men, and
if there is one thing a woman must have, it's a decent kitchen.
But in past ages, in spite of the aforementioned discom-
forts, women followed their armies, Norse women sailed
with the fleet, and Cleopatra, in an early civil rights demon-
stration, sailed her own barge. The wives of whaling
captains often went along with their men. As I see it,
women want to go "where the boys are." They want to
share their adventures, assist them in their labors, and enjoy
the pleasure of their company. In 1937, Mrs. Harold Van-
derbilt and Mrs. Thomas Sopwith sailed as official time-
keepers on their husbands' America's Cup yachts, *Ranger*
and *Endeavor II*. Those were J Boats—huge and tremendously fast, each with a crew of a hundred men and two
acres of sail, twice as long and twice as tall as our present
Cup contenders and without many of their mechanical
devices and scientific refinements. To race on a machine
like that takes nerve and real devotion! (Am I devoted
enough to face a jibe on a J Boat?)

Where I live 95 per cent of the men and boys have boats.
They may be punts, skiffs, lobster boats, draggers, canoes,
dingies, sailfish, racing machines, or cruisers. No matter,
each one is treated with the same regard. Only one man I
know of was brave enough to call a spade a spade and name
his boat *Mistress*. An eminent artist has claimed that his
biggest disappointment in life is that he can't get his Friendship sloop into his living room for the winter. Obviously,
someone has to break this up! My husband and skipper asks,
"Has it occurred to you that men took to the sea to get
away from women?" That may or may not be, but I'm not
about to let some expensive hole in the water, lined with
wood or fiber glass, take off with *my* husband!

Legend has it that a mistress is a very cooperative and

beautiful creature. The wife of a skipper will have to meet the mistress on her own field and beat her at her own game (no small trick), but if the weather is a certain way and things are going just right, a wife can be a lot more cooperative than a boat and a lot more appealing. Just stay cheerful and helpful through a thundersquall in Plum Gut or when the boat is stranded on a sandbar off Montauk ("Don't give up the ship!"). Once a woman has met her rival face to face, she may find the gal quite admirable and her mode and sphere of operations exciting. She may discover something men found out a long time ago. Sailing is fun!

I started sailing at the age of six with "big boys"—campers and junior counselors at the family camp in Maine. For some reason they were amused by an eager little kid and I was taken along on a great many adventures and a few minor shipwrecks. I never felt that I had to beat a rival at her own game, for the boat we used was the most unlovely and discouraging thing anyone ever sailed. She was reputed to be a "cut-down Cape Cod dory." If she was, someone had made two out of the same dory, and it's hard to believe that any Yankee would make that mistake twice. Of course, no Yankee would let half a dory go to waste. She was without question built for "summer people." The first hurdle (rivalry) being nonexistant, I was free to examine my surroundings and decide whether or not we were compatible. I found we were—I had no fear of the water and was too ignorant to have any fear of the boat. I trusted the "big boys" completely. Our short and often abortive voyages in *Junie* whetted my appetite for further exploration; there were beaches within sight that I had never explored and beaches that I had never combed, and I couldn't get there by walking. (Outboard motors, in those days—and even now, I think—were less reliable than sails.)

When the camp acquired seaworthy sailboats, I discovered the magic feeling of a well-designed vessel moving through the water with the wind. A sailboat is a machine, the product of the science of man, but it is so simple and so in tune with nature that it seems to be a part of nature itself. I greatly admire fishing vessels, tugs, freighters, tankers, ocean liners, and even barges as honest commercial vessels well suited to their purpose, but for sheer pleasure and a sense of compatibility with nature, for exploration and discovery, I want a sailboat. Me, Columbus, Adrian Block, and the rest of the boys!

The childhood sense of romance I felt when seeing a sailboat, a new island, a hidden cove, or a deserted beach was the seed of my future career. I am, above all, a scavenger. I have passed this talent along to my sons. If piracy were still in vogue, they would be apprenticed to a pirate. Buzz has talked of going to work for Moran, Foundation Maritime, or Fisheries Products, Ltd., as the next best thing. Meanwhile, we are well suited, as a family, to the sport of "gunk holing"—exploring remote and undeveloped coves and harbors. By mutual agreement, sailboats and gunk holes go together because good sailboats are dependent upon neither gas dock nor shore power and gunk holes don't have such things. To my skipper, that eccentric lover of peace and quiet, the gunk hole is a retreat. There he may philosophize and commune with nature and his most beloved possession, *Skylark*, or fish for whatever happens to be in the area. The boys and I can leap into the dinghy to explore and scavenge to our hearts' content.

Our knowledge of wildlife beyond our backyard has been increased tremendously by sailing, and I hope that a respect for nature and an interest in conservation are silver spoons the boys will think they were born with. A sailboat is a quiet thing and can sneak up on wildlife ashore or afloat. This can be amusing as well as educational. We ran unnoticed into Block Island Sound's first school of tuna last summer while the sport fishermen were burning tanks and tanks of fuel looking for them (we didn't tell on the tuna, either!). I once saw a cavorting whale at the mouth of the New Meadows River; he was obviously friendly and I was all for getting as close as possible, but the boatyard employee I was with, envisioning scenes such as those used to illustrate *Moby Dick*, voted to head in the other direction as fast as a light breeze would carry us (he had the helm). The porpoise is the traditional friend of sailors, and we often come alongside a shark or seal sunning on the water's surface. Gulls, ducks, geese, and other water birds are seldom disturbed by a sail, and we've watched, without disturbing them, sandpipers and herons, a family of weasels, and a doe and a fawn on the shore. Migrating land birds and butterflies sometimes light on the boat to ride for a while. A sailboat seems to be accepted as one of the gang; it is not a noisy mechanical intruder on the waterways. And we find we need a rack of nature books larger than the navigational department for just a weekend cruise!

I like living on a sailboat. It's very light housekeeping; everything, by necessity, is right where it should be. Clothing is strictly utilitarian and therefore easy to care for. Meals are sensible and simple. Housecleaning is minimal. I even found last summer that I was looking for things to scrub and polish, such was the joy of an orderly household. I had plenty of time to chat with other sailors and the dock boys, paint pictures, read, and write. We had rented our house and were living aboard our boat for five weeks. John was commuting to work most of the time, and coming home to the boat was as refreshing to him as a good gale on the high seas. We took off with our home every weekend and didn't have to move all the gear back and forth, for our home was as portable as a turtle's. It was an adventure and a vacation for both of us.

MARY LEONARD

Choosing a
2   Boat

〰〰〰〰〰〰〰〰〰〰〰〰〰〰〰〰〰〰

No SELF-RESPECTING WOMAN would let her husband choose a new house alone, but legend has conned her into believing that a boat should be the skipper's choice. It began way back when yachts were Yachts, playthings of the very rich, and were sailed by professional crews. The owner took his lady along for the ride sometimes, but she knew her place and it wasn't at the helm. Sailing was truly a man's world and the only concession made to the ladies was maybe an enclosed toilet. Things are different now; the owner sails the boat himself and his first mate is his wife, but the "man's world" mystique lingers on. When it comes time to choose a new boat, the first mate may be given an option between green or blue bunk cushions, but neither advice nor consent in other areas is courted. Her happiness aboard, however, is going to be affected by many more things than meet the eye, so she ought to be cut in on decisions from the word "boat."

The number one decision—to buy a new boat—doesn't come in a flash, anymore than buying a new house does. For a long time, maybe years, the idea has been brewing. A growing family, a growing income, or a growing dissatisfaction with the performance of the present boat sets a sailor up for a change. He begins to look at the ads in yachting magazines with more care, to visit more boat shows and boatyards, and to watch the boats that sail by to leeward with more than casual interest.

First mates are urged to detect the signs early and get in on this yeasty process. There is no point in letting the skipper fall blindly in love with the wrong boat—no point, that is, if she and the family plan to spend much time on it. Happy cruising is not the automatic result of choosing the best boat for the family for the best price available, because

wind and weather are also big factors; but fun with the family—and the "family" may be only the skipper and first mate—is more likely if the boat fits and suits most of the crew most of the time.

All small boats represent compromises. You have to give an inch of space here to get it there. A knot of speed may have to be sacrificed to obtain greater ease of handling or greater comfort for the crew. There are floating equivalents of split-level ranch houses as well as of three-story Victorian mansions, even in sailboats, and the first mate has as much stake in choosing which type of boat as does the captain. She should add up with him the pluses and minuses of the prospects. An alert first mate listens to the skipper from his first hint that he wants a new boat, goes shopping with him from the beginning, and has her say in the final choice.

She does, that is, if she doesn't marry a boat, as Mary and I did. We chose husbands and got boats too, but both boats were beautiful. We had made a wise choice of husbands.

Several years later Mary and I had our say when the Leonards chose our *Skylark* as their new boat and we made the big switch from a wooden boat to a fiber-glass boat, *Shag.* The Leonards had three small male reasons (ranging from five to ten) for wanting a bigger boat than their *Prelude,* a handsome, fast racing boat that they had converted for minimal, cramped cruising. Our reason for the "switch": too many cold winters in New York. After chartering a boat in the Virgin Islands for two winters, we had decided that we liked swimming on Christmas Day, and that we wanted to dive off our own boat.

The decision to give up *Skylark* was a hard one for us. For eighteen years (ten of them with me aboard) our well-loved yawl had handsomely performed everything asked of her, and sometimes a lot was asked. She is a comfortable, seaworthy boat, and we sailed her far and hard, but always in her kind of water. She loves the light winds of Long Island Sound and New England, but her sail area is large for the strong trade winds that prevail in the Virgin Islands. Worms and dry rot plague wooden boats in tropical waters and cause large maintenance problems. *Skylark* just isn't a tropical bird. We began, reluctantly, to look at what wooden boat owners call "bathtubs"—the fat, fiber-glass boats designed today to beat racing rules, big yard bills, and the high labor costs of building wooden boats.

Our first sortie into the market was dismal. After a 300-mile drive to one of the Northeastern seaboard's most thriving boatyards, we stepped into a huge shed that looked like an airplane hangar and smelled like nailpolish. The salesman, the factory owner's son, didn't stay with us long; he knew a losing proposition when he saw one. The entire upper half of a boat dangled on a crate over its nether part, looking like the top section of a monstrous fake Easter egg. Another boat, already mated, was stuck together with Scotch tape—I kid you not—while waiting for its permanent goo to stay stuck. These were *boats?* The skipper and I didn't have to say a word to each other; we got out of there—quick.

After another fine summer cruise in our old love and a winter cruise in tropical waters on an unsatisfactory charter boat, we were in the new-boat mood again—but this time all the way. We would go to Sparkman & Stephens and put our problem before their staff. This would be our "dream boat," probably our last boat. Why accept compromises?

We told the designer we wanted a wooden boat with a protective synthetic hull-covering. (Compromise?) We wanted a boat large enough to be seaworthy and autonomous for two to three weeks in terms of water, ice, and fuel supplies (which are sometimes hard to come by in tropical paradises). The boat should be big enough for two to live on comfortably for long stretches, and for four on short runs and in a squeeze. Finally, we wanted a boat that would be *easy* for a middle-aging couple to handle. And a boat, please. Not a bathtub.

Three months later we gave *that* plan up. The designer

was interested in our problem—even intrigued, we thought—
but, after study, he could not conscientiously recommend
any process or material then on the market for such a vessel.
Wood did not marry well with synthetic coatings. The two
materials had different expansion rates under certain
weather conditions, and trouble started between them. The
skipper and I had privately ruled out steel and aluminum
hulls already, perhaps for no good scientific reason, although
rumors of electrolysis are harrowing. (We do have friends
who have both types, and they can keep them. We want to
keep our friends, so we just ignore their hulls when we're
together.)

We were right back to fiber glass, and by this time we had
learned where to go. Henry Hinckley is an experienced
builder of fiber-glass boats. He builds boats that win ocean
races and have fewer breakdowns than their competitors.
As "bathtubs" go, he builds handsome ones, with mahogany,
teak, and holly cabinetry below deck that can be tailored
somewhat to individual tastes if you order in the yard's off-
season. We headed for Hinckley's in Southwest Harbor,
Maine, and stopped referring to fiber-glass boats as "bathtubs." (Compromise?)

Our Hinckley-built, Tripp-designed *Shag* is a love. We
picked her up in Miami, where she had been trucked from
Maine, and sailed her 3000 miles in her first year. She
crossed the Gulf Stream twice in her first few months of
sailing life, slogging her way at hull speed under jib and
mizzen through such confused seas that water coming from
all directions half-filled the cockpit at times, and she took
it with better grace than I did. (At about 3 A.M., wet, queasy,
and thoroughly fed up with the Gulf Stream, I said accus-
ingly to George, "Did you know it would be like this?"
Answer: "I've never been here before in my life.") In the
southern Bahamas, that giant wading pond studded with

reefs, *Shag* snaked her way past coral heads and over shallow bottoms only inches beneath her 4-foot keel, taking us into deserted anchorages where we could skinny-dip on pink coral-sand beaches. With her centerboard down and drawing a steadying 8 feet, she sailed a good course across the bottomless deeps to Eleuthera, Abaco, and Grand Bahama, farther north. Her sturdy diesel enabled us to claw off a lee shore—and, incidentally, a concrete wharf—when the wind hauled 180 degrees and blew for forty hours at 50 to 60 knots. The strain on the anchor rode (rope), in that blow, was great enough to flatten out the plaits on a brand new nylon line and to wear off the chrome coating of the anchor chock, but *Shag's* fittings and fastenings all stayed put. Hatches in each cabin, opening either to or away from the wind, keep her cool in the tropics, and her tiny, charcoal-burning Dutch fireplace warms us when the fog comes down in Maine. Big water tanks tide us over during weeks of sailing in water-scarce areas and allow us to take daily showers when we are nearer to "civilization." There's no pain or strain when the trade winds blow, because of her shortened mast and reduced sail area—compared to *Skylark's*—and her glass hull is the despair of worms.

I could go on and on about the merits of our boat, as most boat owners can, but it all boils down to this: *Shag* is a love-child, but she wasn't an accident; we planned for her a long time—both of us. *Shag* is a compromise; we miss lots about *Skylark*—her lovely sheer, her hand-hewn beauty above and below deck, her eager response to even a breath of wind—just as we miss our 170-pound Newfoundland dog who died last year. *Shag* will never take the place of *Skylark* in our affections, nor will our new poodle ever mean the same to us as the Newf, but we'll never get another wooden boat nor another huge long-haired dog. Neither one belongs in the tropics, and we do. What we have now suits us best—now.

As I have said, a small boat is a compromise. First mates can help the skipper fall in love with the right compromise for the family. If the skipper is a highly competitive type and would rather race than eat, some cruising comfort may have to be sacrificed. He will probably want a "rule-beater," one of the boats built today to get around the time handicaps, known as ratings, that are figured on a complicated base of sail area, weight, displacement, etc., and that penalize older boats, such as *Skylark*. These new boats are "racing machines" rather than cruising boats. Though from the outside they may look the same as a cruiser, below they have a skinned-down look that only a racer could love.

I went aboard one in our harbor recently, and I thought at first that the builder had forgotten to finish it. The cabin floor (the sole) was a 2-foot-wide catwalk made of wooden slats through which the bilge and water tanks were cozily visible. The naked, rough inner skin of the fiber-glass hull was visible everywhere, too, which wasn't very cozy. The rules for offshore racing require certain furnishings, such as bunks and heads, but they don't say you have to have mattresses, or a door closing off the head from the rest of the crew, or even a seat to sit on—and this boat had none of these. I didn't look into the shoe-box-size dish locker, but I'll bet it held one community paper plate. The purpose of this spartan layout was to keep the weight down and the rating low. It may win races for the skipper, but it would lose me as a first mate on a cruise. Fortunately, my skipper is not competitive, so I don't have to face the compromises that another first mate might. She may make them happily, but she should know she's making them.

Most boat builders today keep the racing rules in mind—they never know when a buyer will have an America's Cup-syndrome—but they spend hours at the drawing board trying to make the design attractive to a woman, too. Not all the comforts of home can be squeezed into a small boat, but enough of them, pint-sized, can. Many a 30-footer uses available space more ingeniously than the so-called efficiency apartments do. Some don't. Just so many changes can be rung on the living arrangements in small boats, but those changes are important to a first mate's happiness aboard. All the potential boats, for example, may have bunks, heads, and stoves, but are they bigger, better, or safer on one boat than on another? Every small boat has to give an inch here to get an inch there. Do you—the first mate—like one particular compromise better than another?

A quick check of the cabin in a boatyard won't tell you much. It takes a heap of living aboard a small boat to get to know the bugs intimately, and not everyone can, or cares to, exterminate them the Carleton Mitchell way. That eminent yachtsman-writer built a plywood mock-up of *Finisterre's* cabin in his living room and he and his wife lived in it "for size" before the keel of his Sparkman & Stephen's-designed yawl was ever laid.

Next best to the Mitchell Method is to charter the prospective boat for a pre-sale cruise, if the boat is secondhand and the owner is willing. (Some owners are willing to the extent of applying the charter fee toward the purchase price of the boat.) Second next best is to wheedle at least a weekend aboard a friend's sister boat, if possible. In a last ditch effort to get the word on the bugs—and beauties—of a new boat, track down and talk to a first mate who owns a similar one, whether you know her or not. The boat broker can usually help in this area, and if the sale of the boat depends on it, he will!

Failing all else, pay a lengthy visit to the boat, and while the skipper is inspecting the hull and rigging, take a long look below deck. Don't forget your tape measure, a pad and pencil, and, if you can't draw a straight line, a camera. Your

own snapshot of a boat's interior will be a lot closer to reality than the trick-angled picture in the builder's brochure and will help you make some sense out of the tape measurements you made.

WHAT TO LOOK FOR BELOW DECK

• *Headroom* (or Cabin Height): Can you stand up? In nautical terms, is there standing headroom? If so, is there enough? What is ample height for one may be head-denter height for another. My husband is 6 feet tall and our 6-foot-3-inch cabin overhead clears him nicely, but when towering Dr. Benjamin Spock came aboard *Shag* in the Virgin Islands, he hit it. There is no standard headroom, even among boats of the same length, but usually the shorter the boat, the lower the overhead. Nowadays some boat builders try to beat the system with standing *neckroom*. You can stand up all right, but only if you keep your eyes on your shoelaces. Beware. Cruising in a crouch on a boat with *sitting* headroom only is less painful than forgetting to keep your neck bent. Some small decked-over boats, with space for two berths and a toilet below, are neck-benders, even in a sitting position. On others you may be able to sit up straight, but there is no toilet (or "head," as it's called on boats). Which compromise is the happiest to make?

One couple from our harbor take their two small boys every fine weekend on Friday-to-Sunday cruises in a neck-bender, with a toilet. They cook in a hibachi, they take water in 5-gallon jugs, and they have a ball. An older couple might prefer the time-honored "bucket" toilet and sitting head-room. Every family to its own compromise, and the time to make it is before the boat is bought.

• *Grab-Rails* (or Hand-Grips): Full headroom is a mixed blessing if there is no place for a first mate to lay her hand when the going is rough. A lofty overhead usually comes only in larger boats with broad beams—too broad to span with steadying, outstretched arms—and a first mate can end up a black-and-blue pulp if there are no grab-rails. Wooden boats usually have their own built-in grab places, a carlin here, an overhead support there, but most fiber-glass boats, having no need for such structural imperatives, require extra help from the carpenter. A beveled strip of wood can be attached at an oblique angle and at a comfortable grip-ping height along the cabin walls, or one with hand-hold spaces can dissect the center of the overhead. After the third day of helplessly bucketing about the broad, grabless cabin of a fiber-glass boat we once chartered, I rigged a line at head height from the aft of the cabin to the forepeak. The owner has since added a grab-rail down the middle of the overhead, showing that he is a very intuitive fellow. (I left my line up when we returned the boat.)

So—throw yourselves around a bit, mates, if the cabin is

wide and high. If you fall on your face, ask for grab-rails, or a look at the next boat on the skipper's list.

•*Berths:* The trend in boat building today is to crowd as many sleeping spaces as possible into a boat, on the theory perhaps that the more prone bodies than can be accommodated, the merrier the cruise. I disagree with that thinking for two reasons: (1) when the bodies wake up and move around, the boat shrinks in size, and (2) valuable stowage or galley space must be sacrificed to squeeze in the bunks. However, since the skipper and I are middle-aged sailors who like our privacy, and our guests—much as we love having them aboard—in small doses, I am willing to admit we may be different from other people. Too, we cruise for months at a time and go thousands of miles without sleeping ashore a night, so we need more stowage space than weekend or vacation cruising people.

Still, a first mate would be well advised, for her own cruising happiness, to keep a taut watch on the skipper in the berth area. He may think: "Why settle for four berths in one boat when you can get six in another boat for the same money? Who knows when I might want to race with a full crew?" Or: "Wouldn't a cruise with four guests be a good way to entertain clients and/or friends?" If the skipper *does* race, if the first mate *likes* entertaining in close quarters, or, of course, if the family itself needs every bunk it can get, then the first mate can relax. The inches she loses in the galley and the hanging lockers are worth it, and she willingly makes one of the necessary compromises inherent in buying a small boat. If none of the above "ifs" is true, she will contribute to cruising fun if she suggests that they look for a less berth-y boat.

Once the number of berths is settled on, a first mate should lie down and roll over on all of them. Are they long

enough, wide enough, and soft enough? Can she sit up without cracking her head? Can they be made up without too
much pain and strain?

Again, compromises may have to be made in some of the
areas mentioned, but the last one a first mate should make
is in the length of the bunks. Anything less than the standard
length (6 feet, 4 inches), is dangerous to health and morale.
Width is only slightly less important, and varies from boat
to boat, according to the boat's beam. An average-sized person can make do comfortably with 22 to 24 inches, and be
blissful with a few inches more. A too-wide bunk will hit
the sitter's legs in the wrong place when the bunk becomes
a seat in the daytime, but that disadvantage can be overcome by stuffing cushions at one's back.

Our *Shag* is a stock boat, the fifty-second Bermuda 40
built by Henry Hinckley, but it's a maverick in the bunk
department. Instead of the standard six bunks, we have four
—two in the main cabin and two in the forward cabin. As it
was off-season when we contracted for *Shag* and the boatyard was relatively unrushed, we persuaded Mr. Hinckley
and the chief carpenter—after only slight protest and some
added cost—to remove the upper berths in the main cabin
and use the space for chart and storage lockers, but leave
the widened lower berths in their standard, pull-out arrangements. In the daytime the berths are regulation thigh-length
(width?), held flush to the wall with hooks, but at night we
release the hooks, pull out our "drawer-berths," and luxuriate in 33-inch-wide beds. The carpenter did a magnificent
job of tailoring tolerances so that our 6-inch foam-rubber
mattresses slide neatly under the lockers in the daytime,
and we aren't left too far from the centered table at mealtime. We love the setup; we gained enormous locker space
for me and inches for the skipper's broad shoulders.

No first mate can expect to sink out of sight on a luxuriously thick bunk mattress, but she can—and should—get 4 inches of reasonably comfortable give. A too-thin mattress on an otherwise satisfactory berth is no serious disadvantage, however; in order to avoid a whole new mattress and upholstery job, an extra layer of foam rubber can be sneaked under the old mattress, as Mary and John Leonard found we had done on *Skylark*. Mary said they found our "secret" the first night they made up the bunks, and their boys promptly made plans to invite two friends on the next cruise. They had two more beds now, didn't they?

• *Galley:* The galley has seen more changes in recent years than any other part of a boat's living arrangements, moving from its traditional stuffy hole in the forwardmost part of the boat to as far back, in some cases, as a couple of brackets for a charcoal broiler off the stern of the boat, because the first mate has replaced the paid hand at the stove and she wants to be where both the action and the ventilation are. Some boat builders have settled on a galley amidship, which is fine if there is an overhead hatch or a large opening porthole there, too. Seasickness breeds on cooking fumes.

I personally prefer the galley aft, right at the cockpit companionway, where I can cook with one eye on the stove and one on the passing scene. The skipper likes it that way, too, because if I am needed on deck in a hurry he doesn't have to lift his voice. Sometimes he doesn't even have to lift his eyebrows—I'm on deck in a flash, like the time when the spinnaker blew out in a 30-knot wind! All hands on deck —and the stew, in the sink!

Speaking of sinks, I miss *Skylark's* one sink even though there are two, side by side, on *Shag*. *Skylark's* sink is elbow-deep and widemouthed enough to hold a 6-quart casserole, thawing out from its home-frozen state, or a meal's worth of dirty dishes, hidden under a pop-on cover until the dinner guests leave. *Shag's* twin sinks, though handy from the wash-and-rinse point of view, are too shallow for such maneuvers, but their height is right. Beware of sinks that are too low or too high. I saw a sink on a "gold-plater" (the yachting term for a really expensive, custom-built boat) that was so low the first mate *knelt* to wash the dishes. Even then, she had to duck to keep clear of an overhead instrument panel that looked as if it belonged in the cockpit of a jet plane. Her skipper was a bug on electronics, so as the instrument panel grew longer, the sink sank.

A stove aboard a small boat can be anything from a portable, one-burner, canned-heat affair to a multiburner-plus-oven jewel, but whatever it is, it must be *safe* to use. According to a marine insurance broker, who is also a sailor and a friend, fuels in order of safety are:

1. *Coal, coke or wood (the safest)*
2. *Canned heat (Sterno, etc.)*
3. *Alcohol*
4. *Kerosene*
5. *Liquefied and compressed gas*
6. *Gasoline*

Few first mates will find either 1 or 6 aboard boats nowadays. Wood- and coal-burning stoves are disappearing from the small-boat scene, while tiny fireplaces and heaters are more and more ubiquitous. (*Skylark* has one—a lovely coal stove with a two-burner alcohol stove on top for warm-weather cooking—and I loved to cook on it.) Gasoline stoves are used only at the peril of one's life, and against Coast Guard regulations in some areas, and marine underwriters refuse to insure boats that have them.

Tiny boats are usually compelled, for reasons of space, to carry stoves that use fuel type 2, so a first mate doesn't have

much choice in the matter, even if she cares. She has one
distinct advantage over first mates with fancier stoves: she
isn't expected to turn out gourmet meals—though she well
may. I am not a great hibachi girl, though many of my
friends are, and these charcoal braziers are a godsend on a
tiny boat.

Alcohol stoves are the big-time favorite on medium-size
boats, both for safety and because the fuel is easy to stow,
and a first mate can be happy with one. Alcohol is a clean
fuel and it cooks fast. Kerosene—hmmm. Some of my best
friends are kerosene-users, but I think it's stinky and dirty.
Liquefied and compressed-gas stoves are low on the safety
list because they must be carefully, expertly installed (and
who is to know if they have been?) to avoid leaks, and the
tanks take more space than many a small boat can afford
to give them. Otherwise, they are great—as good as a gas
stove on land. Our stove on *Shag* burns propane gas, with
two tanks carried aft of the cockpit in their own compartment. We have never had trouble getting them filled, even
in the Out Islands of the Bahamas, though there we were
glad the stove had been Hinckley-installed (thus, properly!)
because, unlike gas available in the United States, Bahamian
gas has no tell-tale odor.

· *Iceboxes:* The more time the family plans to spend on
a boat, the more important the icebox, of course, but even
for weekend cruising a well-insulated, well-situated icebox is
a boon. Size is a less important factor than placement and
insulation (a block of ice can melt to an ice cube in one day
if the box is improperly placed and protected). One miracle
of bad planning was the box on a boat we chartered in the
West Indies. A space had been molded into the forward end
of one of the cockpit seats and there was a loosely fitting
cover to pop over it once the ice was stowed and a loosely

fitting cupboard door at another opening in the galley below deck. Drainage was via a needle-size hole into the bilge
—hopefully. By the end of our first day in the tropical sun,
not only the icebox but also the cabin was awash with water
and food, and we were on warm beer for the duration.

Today more and more boats of middling-to-big size come
equipped with electric iceboxes, and I say hooray—but
watch out. The power to run them has to come from somewhere, and on a sailboat it may take more than you're willing or able to generate. *Shag* has an electric element in her
ample box, but we mostly use shore-bought ice because we
don't think ice-making is worth the required two hours a day
of running the motor, especially on fine sailing days. Recent
innovations and improvements in electric marine iceboxes
have cut down the generating time, but still a first mate
would be wise to make sure there is plenty of space for
shore-bought ice alongside the electric element.

• *Decor:* We are back where we started at the beginning of
this chapter, in the green-or-blue-bunk-cushions department,
the area where a first mate is usually given her head and
where one might think she needs no advice. However, a
successful boat broker—a first mate herself—told me she
often points out possible pitfalls here, too. Women sometimes forget that colors that delight the eye on shore may
make the head swim at sea, especially if they come in swirly
patterns. It's best to stick to cool solid colors for curtains
and upholstery, or, at most, to a gentle stripe or plaid, if a
choice is offered (it is on many new boats). The time not to be
faced with a psychedelic print is when the sea is making up.

Bunk cushions take a beating from salt spray, wet bathing
suits, food drops, etc., so they should be of tough, washable
material. Ours, on *Shag*, are tough, but not washable, we
found to our dismay; in fact, they hate water. Our beautiful

teal-blue bunk cushions could not take even a drop of *fresh* water, let alone salt water, without freckling white. (Add a little spilled ketchup, a few drops of diesel oil, etc., and you get the whole slovenly picture.) Once they were dry-cleaned and pristine again we sprayed the cushions with one of the dirt-repellent preparations, and they have been reasonably spotless ever since. Spotting problems, of course, are avoided completely if a synthetic, leatherlike upholstery is used, but, as every car owner knows, the synthetics present their own problems on a hot, sticky day.

Curtains were never an item on boats of yesteryear, with their small portholes, but decency and a desire to sleep make them almost a necessity in today's "picture-windowed" cabins. *Shag's* curtains somehow were left behind in Maine when she was trucked, on her maiden voyage, to Florida and I well remember the overdose of holiday spirit we got from blinking Christmas tree lights atop the power boat moored next to us at Dinner Key Marina in Miami. We crossed the Gulf Stream, tied up at the Crown Colony Club in the Berry Islands (the Bahamas), and a half hour later, into the slip alongside us came the Blinking Tree. The next day we went to Nassau, Yachthaven Marina, and found the same Blinking Tree in the neighboring slip. At midnight my skipper stormed across the dock, knocked on a curtained window, and shouted, "O.K., we get the message. Merry Christmas, and turn off the damned lights." We all had an apologetic drink together the next day, and I got five yards of temporary blackout curtain material.

• *Stowage Space* and the *Head:* These are the final checkpoints below deck for first mates. The bigger the cupboard space, the better, of course, and the longer the hanging locker, or closet, the neater the contents. If there is a choice between several small drawers and one or two big ones, opt for the big ones. Tiny drawers are a wasteful nuisance. I prefer open niches, or bins, to a proliferation of dwarf drawers, but the opening should have a retaining, anti-spillage lip high enough to frustrate gear from escaping in a beat to windward. Drawers without special locking devices to keep them closed when the boat heels are worse than no drawers at all. Try the drawers, mates. Do you have to lift them a bit, and then pull? If not, they don't belong at sea.

An enclosed head is worth many a compromise if the boat is to do much cruising, and I doubt if skippers will have to be urged on this point. Given a head, enclosed or not, can the first mate pump it without undue strain and blasphemy? Buckets are better than back-breakers, which some heads are—especially those on older boats. A balky head is not an insurmountable shortcoming, however. We detached one on *Skylark*, closed the sea cocks, and threw it overboard on the last day of our last cruise one summer—an expensive gesture, but so satisfying.

Even if the first mate approves the situation below deck, that is, the compromises are acceptable, the skipper is still not home free. The size of the winches, the helm (wheel or tiller?), even the rig of the boat (sloop, yawl, ketch, cutter, etc.) are concerns of the first mate if she is to be an active crew member. If she is to do any sheet trimming, she should make certain the winches are big enough to ease her job. A tiller can pull a skipper's arm out—let alone a first mate's—on some boats. Does the boat have too much weather helm for a tiller? Would a wheel be better—or another boat? A crew limited to the skipper and his mate must be expert (and young!) to handle one rig, whereas another boat with a different sail distribution would be a breeze.

The first mate should be concerned about all the above considerations, but not unduly. Her skipper has already thought about them and probably has talked them over with her. They are the bones of a sailboat, while the living arrangements are the flesh. The only reason to bring them up is the possibility of the "blind love" bit mentioned earlier. He may be lusting after a sloop, with a tiller and winches the size of a spool of thread (how I love those two-geared Barients), and it may be the dream boat for the family. Again, it may not. A first mate is going to live with the lady for a long time, too. She should know her and like her—from the beginning.

JANE KIRSTEIN

Mostly in Praise of an Old Boat

If I were choosing a boat for myself, I know exactly what it would be—a nice fat cat! One mast, one sail (and no sails below!), no running backstays, a cockpit as comfortable as a bathtub, a cozy cabin with sink, stove, and head. She would have a little engine and she could be nosed right up on the beach. She might be fiber glass and she would be named *Molly Moon* for sentimental reasons. A really nice lady's boat. But I'm a minority of one in a family of five with one lean pocketbook. There's not much place or time for a lady's boat and the men favor the racy types anyway.

We have to maintain our boats ourselves (score one for fiber-glass cats!), but we can get a bigger, faster, and more commodious boat with fewer dollars if we stick to used wooden models (score one each for *Cantie, Prelude,* and *Skylark*). Nat Hereshoff, that grand old man of yacht design, followed the rule of 10 feet of boat per person. It's a good rule and one not to be ignored even in this day of the 22-footer that sleeps four. They do a good job of packing accommodations into the little fiber-glass jobs and the boats sail pretty well, but have you ever tried to live with kids on a boat that size? I hate to think of it! We recently went with friends to look at a new 30-footer. When we'd all climbed aboard and five of us were below, the wife said, "Well, that's that for this boat!" The boat had bunks for six, an enclosed head, a fancy galley, a forward cabin, a dearth of storage space, and nowhere for six people, sitting or standing. That was a comfortable boat, as Nat said, for three!

Cantie (the boat I married) was basically a day-sailer, built for class racing. When we were two, she was fine, even for weekend cruising, but she was too small for any more people.

Prelude (our second boat) was the most perfectly conceived boat ever built, next to *Ranger,* maybe, who was just a bigger model of the same sort of thing! She had been built to race and win against boats of the same class. Forty years later she was still winning under a completely different set of rules in a fleet of boats of every description. One of her former owners affectionately called her "Peter Rabbit." She outdid herself in light air. She was steady and strong in a heavy head wind and could not be outpointed by any boat we ever met. She had a balanced helm and she responded instantly. She was an aesthetic experience in the water and out and she had been built by Lawley—one of the best. But for cruising, *Prelude* hadn't much more to offer than as a weekender. She was sort of a giant Sailfish. We could get wherever we were going and beat most boats getting there, although everything and everyone might be soaked with nowhere to dry out! In miserable weather, we would be miserable. Do you want a racer or a cruiser? Well, all life is a compromise.

Skylark was our compromise. She isn't slow, but she doesn't clean up the racing fleet. She's long enough, deep enough, and comfortable enough for us to live happily together even under adverse weather conditions. She's strong and seaworthy and equipped with everything from sheets to cotter pins for safe and comfortable cruising. But she's wooden. She takes us a bit longer than her fiber-glass sisters would to ready for the water. And we would be sunk without a boatyard that lets us do our own work and is close enough to home for us to do it in. But we have a 40-foot wooden boat for the price of a 25-foot fiber-glass boat, which we couldn't live together on!

Only the most expensive fiber-glass sailboats have the warmth of a wooden sailboat in the interiors. Cabinetry and paneling are expensive items these days and little wood is used in the average fiber-glass boat. Counters, tables, and plywood are covered with formica, which is very utilitarian, but I haven't found *Skylark's* mahogany table and paneled locker doors any maintenance problem and they surely are pleasing to the eye. We find, too, that our friends with more modern boats like to gather in *Skylark's* cabin. Mildew can be just as much of a problem in a fiber-glass boat as in a wooden one if the fiber-glass hull and deck molding are not well insulated, something that is often omitted in less expensive fiber-glass boats. They can "sweat" as I have never seen a wooden boat sweat. Wood is a good insulator in it-

self, and we have found that we are warmer on cool evenings and cooler on hot summer days than many of our friends who have fiber-glass boats.

The very most practical sailboat for any family is surely the sailing dinghy, which can be carried anywhere and maintained at home. Sailors, though, have a way of always wanting to go farther in something bigger. There are any number of ways to rationalize the size and type of boat you want. It may be your camping equipment or vacation cottage. It may be your sports car or an excuse to travel. It can be an education for the children and a convenient way to entertain your friends. Sailing is good, healthy outdoor exercise; the more or racier boat, the more exercise. Our boats have been our amusement, our hobby, our sport, our vacation home, and our method of travel to new places, and they have been maintained with only a part of the funds we might have applied to those activities and their equipment otherwise—the cost is little enough for all the advantages!

MARY LEONARD

Woman's Role, or, What Every First Mate Should Know

3

~~~~~~

Any woman who desires or decides to go along on a sailboat will discover that she ought to know *something* about the boat. Few people completely enjoy a sport when they don't understand the rules and mechanics of it. Any woman might enjoy a football game for the beauty of the chrysanthemums and colorful costumes in the packed stadium, or the enthusiasm of the crowd and the music of the bands, but suppose she found herself *in* the game—for instance, before dinner with the Kennedys!

Sailing is not much of a spectator sport. It's much more fun to be on a sailboat than to watch one, but it can be miserable to be on one and feel useless and confused. Jane says that sailing never really gets to anyone until he has had the helm, kept the sails full, stayed on course, and then heard the captain say "Well done." It will get to you, too, when, sans captain, you can make a small dinghy move forward against the wind. It's not easy and it's all but impossible if you don't know *why* you're doing *what* you're doing. The whys and wherefores can be learned by trial and error, but there are shortcuts.

There are many excellent learning-to-sail books written by experts in the field, and a hopeful first mate should browse through her local bookstore for a well-diagrammed book that she can understand. No tomes on celestial navigation or the aerodynamics of sailing are necessary—just a book on the basic mechanics, for the time being! There are books written for every age and stage right up to the single-hand-around-the-world type of sailor, and you can advance through this library as your skill, interest, and experience dictate.

A first mate should have some understanding of herself, her skipper, and the teamwork that will be required for them to sail happily together. If you are not sure whether you are prone to seasickness (are you prone to motion sickness in cars or planes?), prepare for that possibility by taking Dramamine and trying out a few wind and sea combinations on short sails. Do you swim well and enjoy the water, or would swimming lessons and a life jacket add to your serenity? Are you a big, strapping girl, healthy and happy, perfectly willing to haul the garbage cans to the dump and bathe the Saint Bernard? If so, your skipper will undoubtedly consider you capable of hoisting sails and hauling anchors while he masterminds necessary maneuvers. Or are you just an average-size girl, maybe even small, who is capable of running a house, children, garden club, cocktails for sixty, and the local Cub pack? If you are, your skipper will feel confident that he can leave you at the helm to follow instructions while he hauls the anchor and hoists the sails. Is your skipper the "hard-driving executive" type who expects things to go like clockwork, on time every time? You'll have to bone up a bit harder and study the boat more conscientiously than the woman with a happy-go-lucky, ever patient, and philosophical skipper, but you'll be used to this since you've probably had the house running like a clock for years.

After appraising yourself and your skipper—mate rela-

tionship and boning up on the basics of sailing, learn the
working parts and pieces of your own boat and where all
the gear is stowed. (See the Glossary at the back of this
book for explanations of nautical terms.) It can be a bad
show if you drop the jib when the skipper says "Let the jib
sheet go!" You may really be out of luck if you can't find the
foghorn or the local chart, or the skipper can't find them
because you put them in the wrong place the last time you
used them. If you are supposed to "cleat it down on the
coaming," you'd better know what the coaming is, what a
cleat is, and how to cleat "it" down. As Jane says, a "well
done" is hard to come by if you don't know what you're
doing and don't understand the terms. Understanding of
what may sound like a foreign language and what may look
like a very complicated procedure will come quickly with
a little attention and practice. I knew a competent skipper
of six, and he couldn't even read! If your boat seems a bit
like a Marine Corps Boot Camp, with the skipper yelling
like a drill sergeant and the water up to your knees, be
joyful! It could be six kids fighting at the lunch table and
the washing machine overflowing instead. Just get that jib
(sail) down. The jib, not the mainsail!

Most skippers can single-hand their boats on special occasions, such as an evening sail or a single-handed race, but
most sailing, except for a few hardy souls, means teamwork.
When the sails are set for an all-day reach, the mate may
have little to do but enjoy the sun and fix lunch, but the sails
must be set and the anchor raised or the mooring dropped
before the sunbathing can begin. That means someone on
the bow and someone at the helm. The helmsman may hoist
the mainsail and retreat to the helm as the bowman hoists
anchor or drops the mooring, or the bowman may hoist sail
and anchor. The boat will "fall away" from the mooring or
anchor and the helmsman, handling mainsheet and tiller or

wheel, will aim to fill the sail ("fill away") and take off on port or starboard tack, whichever direction is free of obstruction. He may have to swing the boat around to reach or run out of the harbor; situations vary according to the wind, the channel, and so forth. The man on the bow will stow the anchor, coil down lines, and proceed to raise the jib; the helmsman, having cleated the mainsheet, will handle the jib sheets. Set the mizzen any old time now, if you have one, and there you go (for example).

If you must tack out of a harbor against the wind, there may be some sail-handling involved. *Skylark* has a self-tending working jib, but larger jibs must be let go on one side and sheeted down (or tied) on the other with each tack. She also has running backstays which must be set up on each tack—plenty of jobs for two people. Obviously, the jobs get spread around with a larger crew—maybe two on the bow and two in the cockpit (a nice arrangement).

The actual mechanics of hoisting anchor and sail vary with the boat and the anchor and are best learned on the spot. Some mainsails, with wire halliards, hoist entirely by winch. Others, usually on small boats or older gaff-rigged boats, have rope halliards and hoist entirely by hand, which means the one hoisting that sail must really "sway it up" as hard as possible. There will probably be a downhaul (line) from the boom to the deck along the mast to take out any slack along the luff of the mainsail. *Skylark* has a rope-to-wire halliard—the sail is hoisted by hand most of the way, three turns are taken on the winch, and the sail is winched up tight. The downhaul is set when the sail is hoisted but it may be adjusted whenever necessary. Each halliard is coiled as soon as the sail is up.

A mooring is easily cast away—starboard side for starboard tack, port side for port tack, the object being to clear all lines and buoys away from the path of the boat. Anchors are another story. An anchor will be rigged to port or starboard, and there's no tossing it over. It must first be "broken out" from the bottom, hauled up, then heaved aboard, unless you are lucky enough to have chocks to house it under the bowsprit. Breaking out an anchor is usually a tough job, often miserable. (Again, if you are lucky, you will have a winch to help with this, but that's not standard equipment.) Hauling the anchor up is a cinch, but heaving it aboard is tough and ticklish. You must wrestle the clumsy thing up the side and over the rail, hopefully without marring hull, paint, or varnish. If the anchor is caked with mud, you must try to get that off as you bring it up—either the anchorman dangles over the side with sponge or mop with anchor rode hitched to the capstan, or he splashes the anchor up and down the bow wave, hoping that the flow of water will be forceful enough to dislodge a portable clam flat. (At times like these, it helps a lot to have working children or guests aboard!)

Of course, all this may be done under power and the sails set in mid-harbor, but the skipper will seldom think that sporting, especially if there are other sailboats in the vicinity. Under power is the usual way to leave a dock (cast off the lines, stow lines and fenders), but there are sports who sail away from the dock. As long as the skipper knows what he's doing, cooperate fully—which will probably mean giving the dock a good shove or two!

When hoisting sail in mid-harbor (etc.), the boat is brought "head to wind," that is, bow into the wind, so that the wind will not be pushing against the sail as some poor soul pulls his heart out on the halliard. The boat is brought head to wind when dropping sail, too, since sails don't drop well when pulling (unless you let the main halliard go by mistake in some tight spot!). There are exceptions to this rule, of course. Sails are raised and dropped while under way when racing, in very light air, or when hauling into the wind would threaten the boat in any way. It can be a tough job. We've reefed (or shortened) the mainsail under way in a gale and raised and lowered jibs while under the bow wave, and it *is* possible—even with a crew of two—but it does take a team.

The whole process of getting under way is more or less repeated in reverse when entering a harbor or anchorage. Sails may be dropped in open water, with the boat then proceeding to dock, mooring, or anchorage under power, but most salty skippers, mine among them, would rather "bring her in under sail" when given an open or familiar

harbor. It *is* fun to enter a harbor full of fine yachts with all sails flying, to drop them all at once and come to a standstill right where you wanted to anchor. It can be done smashingly with, say, four able-bodied seamen. With two, you and the skipper, the procedure will have to be modified. The anchor will have to be set up and ready on the bow, the line clear (shrewd operators can rig the anchor to drop from the cockpit); the jib will have to come down and be secured before the bowman can let go the mainsail at the precise moment the boat is brought head to wind; when way is off (all forward motion stopped), the anchor is let go. And that's not quite all. Enough (but not too much) "scope" must be let out. Scope is the amount of anchor rode necessary to properly and safely keep your yacht from picking up and dragging anchor and/or conflicting with other boats, moorings, or obstructions. I give it some and let the skipper take over; necessary scope is judged by the angle of line from the boat to the water and I almost never judge it right. Your anchor will "fetch" when it catches hold and you must make sure it has set properly—the anchorman must give it a few hefty tugs to make sure, or the boat can "back down" under power to set it well. The sails must be bagged and furled, and then it's beer-and-cigar time.

Never let the mainsail drop without word or nod from the skipper. He may find when he reaches that spot he wanted that he hasn't room to swing as he would wish and must go around again. When you plan to pick up a mooring instead of dropping anchor, the anchor should be on standby, set up and ready to go. Moorings aren't always avialable (nor is dock space.) "Shooting a mooring" is the responsibility and art of the helmsman, but the bowman is expected to aid and aim him when the boat is so close to the mooring that the helmsman can't see it. ("A smitch to starboard, a hair to port, it's just ahead.") Or the bowman may point to the mooring buoy with his hand or, in great yachting style, the raised boat hook. *Prelude's* bow was so low to the water that a boat hook was a hazard when reaching for a mooring buoy, but on *Skylark* you *have* to "gaff it" and might as well point with the boat hook. *Never* make a last-gasp attempt to catch a mooring buoy when the boat is too far away or moving too fast—the skipper or helmsman would much rather make the approach and shoot again than drown a crew member or tear off his arm! The boat should be at or near a standstill when the buoy is picked up and the pennant quickly hitched to the capstan (down with the mainsail). Time enough when the sail is down to lead the mooring pennant through the chocks. If the sail doesn't come down as the mooring buoy is picked up, the wind may catch the sail and the boat will yaw wildly from one tack to the other around the mooring. This can cause conflict with other boats and makes a bad scene at best!

I would be scared immobile if John decided to dock *Sky-lark* under sail (that bowsprit could take down *any* dock and go right on up to the clubhouse), but it can be done with a favorable wind, plenty of room, and everything else going for you. Under sail or power, the fenders and docking lines must be rigged before approach to the dock is made. Snuggle up to the dock, drop sail immediately or cut engine, leap aboard the dock with docking lines or heave them to some hefty dockhand, rig the spring lines, and open the beer. Again, enough for a crew of two!

When sailing under difficult weather conditions (a squall, a heavy breeze, rough seas), unexpected things may happen. This is when teamwork really pays off. One lovely October afternoon we set sail for West Harbor, Fisher's Island, from Stonington—just a short hop across Fisher's Island Sound. The breeze was fresh, the sky was clear, and *Skylark* was creaming along with all sails set. We have a photograph taken that afternoon which shows everything—boat, breeze, sea, and sky—at perfection. We had crossed the Sound from Stonington to Eel Grass Grounds, off Noank, when a hot puff of air hit us. To the northwest the water was dark blue with small chop. "Drop the main!" was the order. Drop the main I did and we furled it together, quick and sloppy. The next puff to hit us was straight from the Arctic and the breeze continued stronger and stronger until we figured it was a fresh gale, force 8 on the Beaufort scale—which we didn't have time to check. *Skylark* stood up well under jib and jigger until the jib halliard block let go and the jib fell, flapping, onto the deck and into the frothing bow wave. With only the mizzen (jigger), *Skylark* started a swift circular swing. John leaped for the ignition keys and starter button as I dragged the jib aboard and tied it down. One of us dropped the mizzen and both of us secured the flapping thing *fast*. We proceeded to West Harbor under power, pitching and pounding. (You'll find that the average sailboat will do much less pitching and pounding, given the same weather conditions, than the average power boat— except when the sailboat's under power!) If we hadn't had power, we would have had to reef the mainsail and reset it—a miserable, spooky job when the boat is out of control. I still think, though, that sails and combinations of sails are more reliable than power. We had both power and sail and the power worked that time, but there have been times when the power didn't work and the sails *did* (in Edgartown's twisting and narrow channel where we had sludge in the carburetor). We made the mooring that time, as we have on other occasions, under sail. What do you do on a power boat with no power? (I know the answer

to that one, too. You yell for the Coast Guard over the marine radio, if you have one, or you set up distress signals and hope someone else will see you. I've never understood why power boats don't carry sails for emergency use!)

We've had to shorten sail under way, drop jibs, change jibs, and anchor, all of which is best done by a team. As to who does what and when, you'll learn this under ordinary sailing conditions. There has to be a helmsman at all times —if you can take over that job, you may get it, but you might prefer to wrestle sails with help, when possible, from the helmsman. Be assured that, with a bit of planning, even quite large sailboats can be handled easily by two people. Every boat has its warts, its whims, and its idiosyncracies, which you will have to learn aboard that boat with the skipper you know best.

None of this is meant to scare potential first mates, nor is it meant to be specific instruction. That you will have to get aboard your own boat, where all I've hinted at and described will become reasonable. I mean only to show that teamwork, while not always necessary, *is* always a big help and is sometimes *very* necessary. It is usually fun and satisfying as well.

There are other considerations bearing on the skipper-mate relationship and happy cruising. While you may be looking for fun and excitement, your skipper will very likely be looking for relaxation and a good measure of peace and quiet. To you, the boat may seem the ideal place to entertain and socialize, while to your skipper, social obligations on the boat extend only as far as a wave to the sloop across the channel and a discussion of good spots to find striped bass with the fisherman on the dock. Take care before you override his objections to inviting the Joneses on a trip to Block Island this weekend and the Smiths to Sag Harbor the next. Live-in guests are a responsibility for both skipper and mate and may even be a liability. Space on a small boat is always at a premium and crowded conditions make for bitter memories under certain conditions: bad weather, inexperience, conflicting personality traits, to name a few. At any rate, neither skipper nor mate should consider having guests away from the mooring or dock until they and their boat make a good working team. Then, have guests aboard for an afternoon sail or an all-day cruise (ascertain weather conditions carefully first when you're not sure of the experience of the guests) and drop anchor in an interesting spot for lunch or supper. After you've got the hang of being mate *and* hostess and the skipper is satisfied with the compatibility of the guests, their seaworthiness and cooperation, consider a weekend cruise. (And remember that your guests would like to be useful, too. Give them jobs they can handle, or make some up!) Never consider a lengthy cruise with anyone untried. You may love the Smiths dearly and know them well, they may mind your pets and feed your children and be the personification of generosity and loyalty. You still may find them unbearable for any length of time on a small boat. Mentally question those who "just love the sea" but haven't even a rowboat. There is an infinite number of Boat Bums, some experienced, some not. We spent a miserable weekend, feeling really put upon, with a friend who had credentials and sea stories not to be surpassed. To hear him tell it, he was the original sea dog. When it turned out that he didn't know where to find the mast, he said he was just out of practice. We should have found that out on an afternoon sail!

It is up to the mate, when inviting guests, to make sure they are fully briefed on the itinerary, the possible extent of the cruise, and what they are expected to bring, or, maybe even more important, not bring. Say whether bed linens will be provided or sleeping bags are in order. Extra sleeping bags are a storage problem—does the boat have enough or

should the guests bring their own? If a guest offers to bring food or drink, it is perfectly proper to accept his offer, but be sure to establish the limitations. For instance: "It would be wonderful if you could bring desserts—your cookies and brownies are so good—and a case of beer. I'll plan the meals and bring the bourbon." The arranging of things also extends to clothing. Explain to your guests what is most necessary, most practical, and most comfortable for the proposed trip, carefully mentioning that there will be very little extra space. If you have foul-weather gear for guests (and it's nice to have two extra suits aboard for nonsailors or out-of-town visitors, as *Shag* and *Skylark* have), say so. Otherwise, state clearly that your friends must bring foul-weather suits, but no ponchos or umbrellas! Perfectly wonderful people will arrive on the dock with mountains of strange gear just because they haven't been briefed on the situation and have never sailed on a small boat. There are others who will arrive with mountains of salty gear because they've told you so much about their prowess on the seas, and still others who will arrive with nothing but nylon windbreakers. Screen them and brief them!

Socializing between boats in a strange harbor is an impromptu and casual affair, meant, in most cases, to stay that way. We and the Kirsteins have made many a fast friend in a strange harbor, but sailors are people of the wind, for a time free and careless, and there is no future obligation attached to a spontaneous social gathering aboard a boat. If a deeper friendship follows naturally from a chance meeting, as it has between the Kirsteins and us and between the Kirsteins and the Murrays, as it has between *Skylark, Moulin,* and *Mahali,* it will be the pleasant exception. I find that it is best to let the skipper make the decision on visiting and visitors in strange waters. He is probably the best judge of a well-run ship, and a well-run ship is likely to mean a conscientious captain and a happy mate, a crew you will enjoy.

While talking of strangers in strange harbors, I would like to mention a few bits of protocol that may save an inexperienced mate and her skipper some embarrassment. Most sailors count on the courtesy and assistance of fellow sailors, and yacht clubs in almost every harbor will, in traditional manner, offer the use of their facilities to cruising guests— within reason. You would not think of demanding services or privileges in a strange home; no more should you in a strange yacht club, which is, after all, a private club supported by its regular members. If no moorings are available, accept that fact with grace and drop your anchor. If a charge is made for launch service, pay it cheerfully, or use your dinghy. (It is polite to tip the launch captain, just as it is proper to tip a porter or bell hop.) There may be a charge for the moorings, for showers, for tennis courts, and for the privilege of using the bar, or there may not be. Establish these facts by inquiring of the steward, the attendant, or the dockhand. Cruising guests are not, as a rule, welcomed into club parties except as guests of a member. You may be required, and it is always polite, to sign the guest log and identify your yacht club when using the facilities of another. Many yacht clubs expect you to be a member of another club with similar facilities, this being a sensible reciprocal trade agreement and certainly not to be resented.

There are many strange stories told of yacht clubs and I am inclined to lay any "fault" to the guests involved. We haven't visited all the yacht clubs on the East Coast, or even all those on Long Island Sound, but we've visited many of the oldest and finest. We know of only one club that is so exclusive that it does not tolerate visiting sailors on its premises (nor does it have guest moorings, but it's more of a country club than a yacht club, anyway.)

To show that some of the "oldest established" yacht clubs are the most hospitable rather than the most exclusive, I will recount an episode that occurred at one of two very fine island clubs whose facilities we have used. (In summer communities, the club provides a great part of the social activity—the more distant the island, the larger the club, is often the rule.) We were standing on the landing float of a club on an island whose population is several hundred in the winter and several thousand in the summer. A sailboat barreled up to the float, the mate calling to the dockhand, "Where are the moorings?" The dockhand politely replied that the club moorings were full but there were town moorings available off the town wharf. "That's too far away, we'll tie up here," said the mate, meaning the float, of course. The dockhand said he was sorry, but that wasn't permitted; the

club launch could ferry the sailors back from a town mooring. But that offer wasn't good enough. The boat sailed away
(to a town mooring, I'm sure, and club launch service, too,
no doubt) with much crude language and the query, "What
kind of place *is* this, anyway?" while those of us on the dock
blushed, for it was a most hospitable club. As we walked up
the dock, chatting with another visitor to the area, we mentioned that we'd never been to the island. A gentleman who
had just come in from the club's Thursday evening series
race turned around to shake our hands and exclaimed,
"Welcome aboard!" He didn't know whether we'd come from
a dory or a brigantine. We were asked to register at the
office and, for very small charge, were given keys to the
shower rooms (where we had our first showers in two weeks)
and a guest pass that entitled us to use the club facilities for
several days. The charge was for towels and soap. All weekend we used the facilities of the club to come and go, while
Skylark swung from a town mooring.

Yacht clubs come in all sizes, each with a different set of
rules. Don't expect anything from any club; politely inquire
what facilities are available and I doubt if you'll ever be
disappointed. One club has been a big disappointment to
me, just because I haven't been in it and it has a charming
history and I'm curious! The fault is all my skipper's. Year
after year we visit the harbor and swing from our anchor
in the cove off this club. Year after year my skipper refuses
to ask for launch service or landing courtesies from the club
and rows us over a mile of choppy and heavily trafficked
water to the town dock—simply because his uncle was
treasurer of the club for years and years and he wouldn't be
caught dead using family connections!

Children aboard, which will be discussed in more detail
later, present some of the same problems that guests do, but
with this definite advantage: the skipper and mate are their

regular superiors and know them very well. The mate will be doing most of their packing for them and can guard that precious space. As children get bigger, they take up more room but they become very useful as crew members. Buzz, now fourteen, can take over any of the jobs I can handle and a few more. Dana is right behind him, and even Nate can set the mizzen. A sailboat offers children discipline and adventure that they will appreciate forever, and children will add a new dimension to your own enjoyment of sailing (and if you sometimes wish to leave that dimension behind, that's justifiable!).

Pets are almost sure to go cruising if there are children aboard or if the skipper or mate is softhearted. Beloved though they may be on shore, they can be problems aboard a small boat. They take up space, they must be fed, and their general welfare must be seen to—additional responsibilities for the first mate. If she doesn't intend to tend the pet, or pets, she will have to see that they are taken care of by someone else, which may be even harder!

The cat, say several friends, is a good sailor, probably because of its fine sense of balance and its tidy habits. Cats don't like to get wet, but they can swim well and they seldom make the same mistake twice. However, a cat aboard a boat had better be *very* well trained, or you may want to throw the boat away. And cat hair is even worse than dog hair to get rid of.

Several of our friends have sailed with mice and gerbils with apparent success. These caged (I hope) creatures are closely related to that traditional seafarer, the rat, which might explain their cooperation. Of course, they can't complain very loudly, anyway. Still, I can't help but remember the smell of Nate's room the winter he kept a mouse. Dampness and mildew we're used to, but I know what *my* skipper would think of *eau du mouse!*

I am now mother to a parakeet at home but have had no experience with birds aboard. Sea captains and pirates of old had parrots, we know, and birds are used to swinging around in trees, so I suppose they could swing just as well in a cage on a boat. But birds are not supposed to be subjected to draughts and I don't know how draughts can be prevented on a sailboat! Besides, there's the birdseed-in-the-bilge problem.

The heart and meat of the discussion of pets on board is, undoubtedly, *dogs*. More dogs think they are people, and more people think dogs are people, than could ever be estimated. Naturally, the dog lovers think that their canine friends would rather come along than be left behind "in some old kennel," and the dogs will do all in their power to create that impression because they love their people and are, if nothing else, loyal. But dogs are not natural-born sailors. They are not used to feeling their ground pitch and heave beneath them with no possibility of escape. Your dog will probably get seasick, he may fall overboard, and he will absolutely *have* to have a walk at least twice a day. He will be clumsy, unhappy, and in the way most of the time. Think now, is a kennel so bad? Your dog would be safe, well fed, and clean, and don't you suppose it's interesting for him to meet others of his kind? (I don't know, but I hope so. For years we've mourned when leaving Moose at a kennel, but big, trusting, clumsy, gentle, shedding oaf that she is, she presents problems that we don't need on a boat—particularly with three boys and all our paraphernalia!)

Moose is polite, relatively content, and interested for the duration of a short dinghy ride along our beach. The Kirsteins, too, have enjoyed daysailing with their small, medium, and large-sized dogs, but they discovered too late that dogs, even the most noble, don't cruise well on small sailboats. They took their 90-pound Newfoundland pup (seafaring dog if there ever was one, companion of sailor, whaler, Humane

Society, and Coast Guard for a hundred years—start him young and he'll love it!) on a cruise to New Brunswick, Canada. They found that not only do Newfies get seasick, but that they are also susceptible to food poisoning from tidbits picked up along the shore during their necessary walks. Luckily the Kirsteins weren't out of range of a veterinarian. A few days of rest and medication restored the pup and the cruise was resumed—as gently as possible. Nevertheless, that big, black dog stayed green until they reached home. Sadder still, he developed rheumatism from sleeping in the damp cockpit, which he preferred to panting his heart out in the hot cabin. It was also discovered, at some point in his sailing career, that Skipper's hair had infiltrated the cylinder head of the engine. George and Jane did sail again with canine friends—day sails, weekends, and even short cruises, but no long-range affairs. They found that small dogs offered some advantages.

Small dogs, if they get seasick, do it in a neat, small-dog way. They shed less hair, take up less space, usually move more quickly, can leap from sailboat to dinghy without capsizing the dink, and may be able to manage the companionway ladder with little or no assistance.

Any well-trained dog is housebroken, something you have spent many long hours to accomplish. Your dog will recognize your boat as a temporary house and will do everything within his power to avoid embarrassing himself and you. A paper-trained dog would be an advantage aboard, but few dogs are paper-trained after the age of six months. What if you want to cross the Gulf Stream? The Gulf of Maine? Skipper, after twenty hours, apologetically used the anchor rode coiled on the bow. But imagine his anguish! Dog hair, sand, and mud accumulate on a doggy boat, and no one needs an extra case of seasickness, that most contagious disease. Shopping expeditions and meals ashore are com-

plicated by a pet's presence if he is apt to bark in a popu-
lated anchorage or leap overboard when left behind on the
boat. All those minuses should be weighed by a first mate
before she gives in to her own or the captain's impulse or the
children's pleas to add a pet to the crew.

To illustrate my contention that pets may get seasick,
sick of the sea, or cause complicated and unexpected problems, I'll tell you of Whiskey, the Norwich terrier who sailed
regularly with his master and mate. Dot, Ed, and Whiskey
sailed their yawl to Maine for the summer, where Ed had
business, and back to Philadelphia in the fall, when business
took him to that area. One fall the return journey was
charted via Delaware, where Dot and Ed's daughter Dotsie
and her friend were to be delivered to college. Ed radioed
his office when they were off Boston, two days out, but because of heavy weather and the rigors of sailing, he didn't
call the office after that. When the boat reached Long
Island Sound, the wind was from the west and the seas
were very choppy, making necessary a wet and rugged beat
up the Sound. When Dot and Dotsie climbed into the
cockpit with lunch, Whiskey failed to appear in his usual
eager fashion and a search of the boat did not produce him.
One can imagine the anguish of the crew, but they couldn't
figure a way to retrace their zigzag course to find the dog in
time to be of use to him. The boat was then off Execution
Rock, approaching the entrances to New York, and had
been more than half a day beating the length of Long Island. Since Whiskey often slept for hours under the dinghy
on the cabin top, no one could say when he might have
gone overboard. After an unsuccessful search of the immediate area, the boat proceeded down the coast.

Sometime later the mate on a Cris Craft off Port Washington thought she saw an animal in the water. Could it be
an otter, she thought. She asked the skipper to circle around

and they found one very small, wet dog swimming west, after his boat. The deck of the power boat was so high that the skipper had to hang onto his son's ankles while the boy swung overboard to retrieve Whiskey. After the dog was pumped out and dried off, it became apparent that he was a boat dog, perfectly at home in the cockpit. His benefactors assumed that he had fallen overboard from a local boat—a fleet was racing in the area—but before the boat reached shore, the boy discovered Whiskey's tag, which gave his owner's name and address. A call was placed to Ed's office in West Chester, Pennsylvania. Ed had not been heard from for nearly a week, so his brother in Maine was notified. If Whiskey had been found in the water, where was the boat and what had happen to the crew? It was known that the weather had been rough.

The Coast Guard was notified and a search was organized from Boston to Baltimore, the boat was called by all stations along the way at regular intervals, and a notice to mariners asking other vessels to report sightings was broadcast. It may seem strange that Ed never heard his yacht being called on marine channels, but I can attest to the fact that sailors may sail for weeks without turning on their radios. As for news of Whiskey, the family had logically, though sadly, concluded that the dog couldn't have stayed afloat for more than a few minutes in the steep chop of Long Island Sound. (But—never underestimate the aggressiveness and determination of a terrier!)

When finally the boat reached the Chesapeake and Delaware Canal, it was looked over by the Coast Guard, which is standard practice, but Dot and Ed felt that they were being given a bit more than the usual attention. Quite so. A short time later they were overtaken by a patrol boat and informed of the search for them and Whiskey's rescue. "All's well that ends well," but see what worry and suspense (also expense) one small pet can cause one's family and the U.S. Coast Guard!

There are some pleasures attendant to cruising with a dog. Dog walkers get leg-stretching exercise, discover hidden paths through lovely woods, become beachcombers, and make the acquaintance of other dog walkers and dog lovers. Nothing in the world can make friends faster than a dog—an idea that might appeal to teens and single members of the crew!

MARY LEONARD

Children
4   Aboard

~~~~~~

CRUISING WITH CHILDREN of any age can be a headache. Small ones can get restless after the first hour or two, and their parents exhausted. Teen-agers, after the first day or two, may be bored, and their parents exasperated. What was supposed to be fun with the family isn't. Why? What can be done about it?

One way is to start them young, as we did. Buzz first went to sea at the age of eight weeks in a gaff-rigged sloop—in a laundry basket. He was perfectly happy there for an afternoon sail and, on the strength of that, we soon tried him on an overnight "cruise." *Cantie* was seaworthy, as small craft go, and a nice little racer, but not much of a cruising boat. She was designed in 1909 and had beautiful long overhangs —the laundry basket could barely be jammed between the two small bunks (her total accommodations!)—but I was determined not to be left behind, so Buzz, and then Dana, went along. When the boys outgrew the laundry basket, they were leashed so that they could be in cabin or cockpit, on lap or seat, but not over the coaming. We put life jackets on them at that point, more for buffering purposes than for safety.

We purchased a larger boat when Nate was five months

old. She gave us more cruisability, although she was still very limited in accommodations. We pushed the limit and cruised—Long Island Sound, Block Island Sound, Narragansett Bay, and the Elizabeth Islands. We had four bunks (two were always filled with sailbags, sleeping bags, duffle bags, anchors, and the outboard motor), a head (exposed), an alcohol stove, and sitting headroom. *Prelude* was an R-Class sloop built in 1926, characteristically fast, characteristically incommodious. It was only after major alteration that we gained two bunks, making four, and a self-bailing cockpit, which we felt was only sane if we planned to cruise. During the season before alteration, the big boys (six and four years old) slept forward on sailbags and duffle bags. Other gear was moved to the cockpit for the night. Nate was secured on the cabin sole between the main bunks, head and companionway ladder at each end. I made him a wall-to-wall mattress, which we stowed on one of the main bunks during the day. Five people in such cramped quarters presented many challenging situations and I think we learned more about "togetherness" at that time than we ever did before or have since.

Gear had to be pared to the absolute minimum and waterproofed with diligence because *Prelude* didn't bounce over waves, she sailed through them. We never took "shore clothes" but we always found room for a small kit of toys, usually Matchbox vehicles (many will fit into a small ditty bag), small dolls, and plastic men and animals, and, always, the fishing lines and poles, which we stowed through the cockpit seats under the afterdeck.

We took a dinghy along—an absolute necessity with children, never mind the safety feature. Like dogs, children have to be walked. They also must be turned loose on the local populace, tied out to fish, or sent out in the dinghy— just to preserve everyone's sanity!

Fishing will keep small people busy for hours, and if you don't want to deal with the catch, make sure you have them use the wrong bait! A piece of bacon may not look good to a flounder, but it satisfies a young fisherman. The same is true of flour and water, molded into stiff little balls.

Dinghies are great time and energy consumers for small oarsmen, both while they are learning how to row and once

they are on their own. The lazy man's method of rowing instruction is to tie the oars loosely in the oarlocks, pop the young student into the dinghy, and push him off the stern of the boat (anchored, of course) at the end of a long line. If instructions shouted from the cockpit are enough to bring him paddling back to the boat, good. He is a happy child and can be untied and pushed off. If he can't make it back to the boat, and the shouts come from the dinghy instead of the cockpit, he can be pulled back in to try again, perhaps with Daddy aboard this time. Once he is a competent dinghy captain, he can be sent to find out what the name of the boat on the other side of the harbor is; it will take him quite a while, as the wind is almost bound to be against him, going or coming.

We always anchored out, and while the boys were small, even when traveling with friends, stayed independent. Rafting is very nice and social, but with small children often too much so. Tying alongside a dock presents many of the same problems and more—it is hard to keep the children under surveillance, and though you may have a slip to yourself, your neighbors are very close and privacy is at a minimum. An unhappy or unruly child will embarrass you and disturb others. Nor will you be happy when noisy parties along the dock keep the children awake late into the night. Docks are for power boats, which need that electric umbilical. Cruising is very like camping out, and who camps out on Times Square? We have always felt that a proper cruising sailboat should be self-sufficient, even if it is a joy to get ashore every once in a while.

It was during this stage of our family cruising that Jane first saw us—weathered in by rain and fog in Great Salt Pond, Block Island. How we envied Jane and George their big, comfortable yawl *Skylark!* Two years later Jane wrote to ask me how we had managed on such a small boat with three young boys. (In actual fact, *Prelude* was 6 inches longer than *Skylark,* but there the resemblance ended.) The main part of my answer, as I remember, was something about the three weighted burlap bags we carried in the bow!

That was not an entirely facetious answer—children must know from the start that the skipper is absolute boss. On a boat there can be no division of authority as there may be at home. Throughout history the navies of sea powers have operated under this principle. Mother, as hard as it may be, must cooperate—first, as a safety precaution, and second, because it is good business practice. Children chafe at rules, but they feel secure under sensible ones. They carry out responsibilities best when there is no question as to what their responsibilities are. If discussion and dissension are tolerated in the beginning, they will be hard to curb later, and there will be times when instant obedience will avert disaster. (I don't mean to say that discussion of situations, or possible situations, should not be tolerated—it should because this is part of the learning process—but when the chips are down and an immediate decision must be made, it's the skipper who must make it and he must be quickly obeyed in the harbor or on the high seas.) When disaster threatens, it is often only good training that keeps one operating rationally—sailors had better not be paralyzed by fear! A child must learn all the rules of safety on board, and since this is a progressive process, start in small doses early.

While weathered in at Block Island, we put on the foul-weather gear and explored widely, since it was no fun to sit in wet clothes on a wet boat. We had lunch at a hamburger stand once to warm up and dry out and make an occasion of the day. We examined the village and all the boats in Old Harbor. We walked out on the breakwater, climbed the cliffs, inspected the lighthouse, walked on the beach, and had ice cream cones several times. When we grew tired of prowling, we went back to the boat for naps. After naps, John took Buzz and Dana fishing in the dinghy while I amused Nate and tried to paint on ever wetter paper, or the boys were tied out behind to practice rowing. We had "high tea" one afternoon when Jane brought the boys a box of fancy cookies. Supper was early and by the light of the alcohol stove. The boys were bedded down at sunset and we followed soon after. We had no lights on *Prelude,* the cabin was crowded with children, and the cockpit was soaked—there wasn't anyplace to be but in the bunk, and why not? We were well worn out, too.

Had the weather been fair, our explorations would have been less thorough. We would have spent time on the beach and in the water. There would have been little need for thoughtful tour planning and we would have been sorry to leave so soon. At the end of the third day, though, we were ready to sail in any weather! George had related every weather report he received over marine channels on *Skylark* —they predicted clearing by noon, but by noon there was very little clearing. The fog was drifting, but it was always there. The clouds broke and rolled back in. We spent the afternoon (boys tied out behind in the dinghy, fishing) waiting for the predicted cold front to pass.

And it did. A gusty wind blew, the sun started to shine, and suddenly rain poured down in torrents. The cloudburst must have done it—both boats set sail in a brisk northwesterly the next morning, *Skylark* headed for Sakonnet, and *Prelude* for Cuttyhunk.

People, basically, don't like to be wet, but being wet on a sailboat is nothing compared to being closeted in a house for three days with small children. We had a whole unfamiliar island to explore, new boats to see, plenty of fresh air and exercise (how often do you take children for a half-day walk in the rain at home?), and a good excuse to take long naps. Simple meals were received with great appreciation, and we were all very eager to sail on when the time came. It's a pretty good way to fill an empty rainy spell!

By the end of that day on our way to Cuttyhunk, everyone except the skipper was laid low by sun and ground swell. We ran out of wind and drifted and roasted. When songs and games failed to disperse the symptoms of seasickness, we went below to sleep it off. This was before we discovered Dramamine—a ration of Dramamine to everyone in heavy or rolling weather does help, although it may not be an absolute preventive and it does make you very sleepy. It is best to stay on deck when feeling queasy. Plain crackers may help to settle a child's stomach, but if he has been actively seasick, he will probably be happiest in a bunk. Our boys often slept much of the way between harbors, but they were always ready to howl when the anchor dropped. (If accidents happen where they can't be washed down with buckets of salt water, scrub or sponge with a solution of baking soda and water. This solution is excellent for cleaning the cooler or ice chest, too.)

Be careful of too much sun. Children should wear hats (sailor hats turned down are great because they pack flat and are washable) and be basted regularly with burn-preventing sun lotion. Long-sleeved shirts and long pants should be kept handy. People burn more readily on the water because of the reflected light, and children's skins are more sensitive than adults—a little sun goes a long way.

Cruising with small children is happiest in short hops with layover days in attractive harbors and plenty of time to explore and run off energy. Long hauls make children restless, tired, and cranky, which certainly won't make cruising any more enjoyable for the rest of the crew.

Children should wear life jackets at all times when on deck, whether in harbor or sailing, until they are competent swimmers; after that they, as well as you, should wear life jackets in heavy weather, which will make you all feel more relaxed and secure. Don't treat slight mishaps with unnecessary alarm—the scratched finger, the tumble from the pony, and the spill from the dinghy are all the same. Sailing is no more dangerous than any serious sport and much less dangerous than many as long as the coaches have good sense. Give a child freedom and encourage him to develop sailing skills, and he will become very interested and capable. A child overprotected or prejudiced by a fearful adult will find it much harder to become a natural or happy sailor. Swimming is one of the biggest steps toward love and trust of the water and boats. Small children are naturally attracted to water and, often to Mother's chagrin, can't be kept out of it, be it the sea, a stream, a pond, or a mud puddle. Capitalize on this attraction and teach them, or have them taught, to swim as soon as possible. We swung Buzz

out over Little Narragansett Bay on the end of the boom
one day—he was not a swimmer, but he had his life jacket
on and we could all laugh at the situation as we headed
into the wind to get him back. But life jackets, even the
best, are bulky and uncomfortable and they don't give a
nonswimmer the confidance that swimming ability would.

We had many fine trips on *Prelude* and everywhere we
went there was something to explore, but in the course of
several years we felt her growing smaller around us. To
John, vacation is synonymous with sailing. The boys were
getting bigger and more adventurous and we all wanted to
extend our cruising territory but we were definitely uncomfortable under adverse conditions on *Prelude*. So, when in
1966 we met *Skylark* again in Block Island, we were all
thinking of a roomier boat. All things (and people) con-
spired to make her ours, and in late August we sailed her
from Mamaroneck to Stonington, feeling as if we had stolen
the Maharaja's fortune.

Most sailing families progress, as we did, from small
children and small boat to larger (and/or more) children and
larger or roomier boat. The basics of provisioning and planning remain the same, for the most part, and the first rule
is: Never take more than you need. If you find extra space,
treat it with great respect or it will vanish, never to return.

Provisioning for babies these days is easier than stocking
for adults! Canned, boxed, and plastic packaged formulas
that do not have to be sterilized or heated, prepared food in
jars, instant cereals, disposable diapers, and moistened towel-
ettes for faces, hands, and fannies make babies on boats
really feasible, even fun. All these supplies can be restocked
in most harbors along the way. Take big plastic garbage
bags along for diaper disposal, to be placed in a shoreside
trash can upon next landfall. (Disposable diapers have a
plastic layer that never disintegrates, so don't dump them

overboard! They are an added pollutant and litter that our cruising areas don't need.) Take a good supply of paper towels for general mop-ups and family use.

While we carried our baby aboard in a laundry basket wedged securely on the cabin sole, our friend Angie Robinson swung hers in a net hammock from the cabin beams. She later rigged one bunk with fish netting hooked from bunk board to cabin trunk, where the baby or toddler could nap or play in perfect safety. The main aim is to keep a child from being thrown about—if he can sleep in security, you will all be happier.

Clothing for a baby should be the wash-and-wear, quick-dryable type that can be rinsed out along the way and dried on the rigging. There are Laundromats in many harbors and marinas, but you shouldn't have to count on them. I liked the stretchy nylon suits and fuzzy, footed sleeping bags for cool weather and night wear. We took a small quilt instead of blankets for whoever was too small for a sleeping bag.

The toddling stage is a restless one. A toddler has awakened to the excitement of various situations and should enjoy sailing for itself. We leashed our toddlers because we had very little safe area for them to roam. Angie never leashed hers but put life jackets on them and turned them loose to get their sea legs. This may sound daring and I guess every one of the children has gone overboard several times, but those boys got their sea legs quickly and are now excellent crew. (It's a matter of how many rescues you can stand!)

Skippers are terribly proud of offspring who show an aptitude for their favorite sport. To nurture such a situation you must have the child under control, but at the same time you must allow enough latitude so that he will try, and be able, to help. As soon as he has mastered small skills, give him small tasks: putting winch handles away, coiling lines, finding the fenders, putting out the ensign, pulling in the dinghy, bailing the dinghy, swabbing the decks, wiping the varnish, etc. The most coveted job on the whole boat is hoisting the mainsail—let him do that (or help) as soon as he is able to. That's the crest of the wave—he is then a sailor.

Small children need warm clothes, dry clothes, a change of clothes, and foul-weather gear just as adults do, but don't worry about having immaculate outfits each morning. When planning clothing, be practical and casual. Children seldom need fancy "shore clothes" (and neither do you). If you should want to eat out, go ahead in your sailing clothes. You will be recognized as yachtsmen; what more could you ask?

I will list our regular clothing supply for weekend cruises. For each person, a pair and a spare of dungarees or slacks, one pair of shorts, one bathing suit, three shirts (one long-sleeved), three pairs of socks, three underpants, one heavy wool sweater and/or a jacket. (A heavy sweater under foul-weather gear is almost as good as a parka.) Two pairs of sneakers or boat shoes are desirable, but we get along with one each as often as not. We have foul-weather suits for all, but the smallest size is about eight; until they reached that stage, the boys had slickers and Sou'westers. For fall cruising, they each have a hooded nylon parka.

When they are old enough, children should be made responsible for packing their own clothes (other equipment, such as toys, should be reviewed by the skipper with regard to space available) so that stocking the boat won't become a one-woman job. (The successful yachtswoman should become an administrator as soon as a "group" can be formed. Otherwise, she will have the whole job of provisioning to herself and that would certainly be anti-family fun!)

Games that pack flat, playing cards, and books may be taken as space permits. A book on knot tying and a ball of marlin will keep someone busy for hours. With luck, the boat may get whipping and serving repairs or turksheads and block pads! Nature books of the field-guide type are wonderful to have along. Of course, if you encourage an interest in fish, wildlife, and conservation, you may then find that you must make room for collections. We have carried many funny things in funny places—there was once a great black-backed gull (dead) in the galley; rocks are usually to be found in any corner; the pieces of an antique chair discovered in the brush were carried from Cuttyhunk to Edgartown and around the loop to Stonington in the dinghy. We have sailed with four styrofoam logs salvaged from Race Point on deck.

We recently met two men on a motor sailer who had a sport particularly applicable to children on boats. During their cruise they built 6-inch sailboats of wood and scraps of paper and each evening in harbor they would race their small fleet.

A sailing dinghy is a wonderful training device and vehicle for exploration. Informal races can be organized on the spot. Many cruising boats tow sailing dinghies and several are sure to be found in any harbor. This is a versatile toy—adults love it, too!

MARY LEONARD

Cruising with Teen-agers

Even teen-agers can have fun cruising—despite the general tendency of that restless age group to resist any activity including parents—if certain concessions are made to their developing glands when the cruise is planned. It is not enough for the captain and his mate to bilaterally plan short sails, with a romp on a beach at the end, and let it go at that. *Which* beach must now be considered. Is it where the girls (or the boys) are? Is it near a friend's summer camp, a movie, or a bicycle shop? Picking up shells on a deserted beach is seldom a teen-ager's idea of a whole lot of fun.

The captain and I found that out on the first cruise after our marriage that included my fourteen-year-old daughter. Linda wasn't a "captive" crew. She had gone day-sailing with us, took to it easily and happily, and thought that a two-week cruise to Maine was a "cool" idea. Cool it was, and foggy. We had felt our way through the clammy stuff for days and spirits were visibly drooping, mine as well as Linda's.

Taking note of my recent cruising status, the captain took over temporarily as Cruise Director and Morale Officer aboard—rightfully, I now know, the first mate's roles.

"Cheer up," he told me, privately and properly.

Then he headed us on a whole new course—away from

deserted coves, which were delightful in the sunshine but dismal in the fog, and toward marinas, movies, and "men" of sixteen.

We ate ashore that night, not in the quiet, excellent seafood restaurant at the water's edge that we would have chosen, but in the crowded, brightly lit diner smack in the middle of Main Street, where the movie house and all the "action" was.

Linda had two cheeseburgers, a chocolate malt, and apple pie, all the while exchanging the accepted number of studiedly indifferent glances with the teen-agers swirling about us and smiling fleetingly at the endless succession of youths who (oh so accidentally) brushed against her where she was seated at the edge of the booth. Later on, the movie was good—I guess. At least, it *looked* good. Only an occasional word came through to us above the din of adolescent voices. On the dinghy ride back to the boat Linda chattered like a magpie herself. It was the first time we had heard her voice in days. Morale, it was obvious, was improving.

The captain proclaimed the next day to be a "layover day" —a day of rocking at her mooring in the harbor for our boat, and a day of fun and games ashore for the crew. Linda, he was absolutely sure, *needed* one of the imported English sweaters from the little shop on Main Street if she were going bicycle riding with me—which, of course, he had no doubt, she was. (Of course. I hadn't been on a bicycle in fifteen years, but never mind. I could tell by the look in the captain's eye that I was going to take it up again.) It just so happened, he said, that the oil in our auxiliary engine needed changing, and it would take just about the same amount of time for the captain to see to that as for us to take a brisk cycle tour of the village's hinterland. He would meet us back at the dinghy dock at noon and (bright sunlight was beginning to burn off the fog) we would have a nice afternoon sail to a cove down the line where an old schoolmate of his had a summer home, the captain had just remembered. His friend's children must be about Linda's age—maybe a little older, he thought. Two boys, as he recalled.

Well, it was like that for the next ten days, and a happier young crew member you never saw. After a while I had shamefacedly caught up with the captain's ploy and had taken over my duties as Cruise Director and Morale Officer, leaving the captain free to loll in the cockpit, a beer in his hand, basking in the warmth of the smiles on his crew's faces. Before the cruise was over, Linda had learned a lot about sailing and, in the captain's words, was turning into a damned good crew. At least once, I remember, she opted for a long day's sail with a deserted cove at the end rather than a two-hour run to a sizable harbor, certain to be full of "action."

"Gosh," she said. "You can't let this nice wind go to waste."

A sure-fire method of forestalling teen-age gloom aboard a small boat is to bring along a teen-age best friend, if the boat is large enough. A couple of sleeping bags in the cockpit, with an awning or a tarpaulin slung across the boom for protection on rainy nights, can expand the sleeping quarters of most small boats admirably. Adding a best friend to the teen-age crew doesn't allow the first mate to shuck her responsibilities as Cruise Director completely, but it does lighten them. For instance, in the area of bicycle jaunts ashore, she no longer has to pedal—and pant—along. She can just point the way, from the cockpit. An evening at the movies for two teen-agers can mean a quiet evening of reading for the old folks, with the captain picking up the young ones at the dinghy dock at a specified hour. Whereas one lone teen-ager might be too shy to "case" the other boats in an anchorage, via the dinghy, two of them may happily spend an entire afternoon at it. In essence, it is usually easier to live with two teen-agers aboard a small boat than with one.

If the second teen-ager is a best beau (or girl) instead of just a best friend, offspring need no further attention. Sailing parents may find young romance aboard a small boat a bit nerve-wracking at times, such as at midnight when a guitar is still twanging away in the cockpit, but it has certain definite advantages. Number one is obvious: no faraway expressions on the face of their own teen-ager. But the great hidden plus is that not only do the captain and his mate have their first real look at the young beast—or beauty—but so does the offspring. There is nothing like a small boat to bring out the worst in someone. (The best, too, but it's usually the worst that parents want to find out about.) The confines of a small boat have a much more abrasive effect than the family car at home, and personality defects, if any, are glaringly exposed by the third day out. It can work both ways, of course. The he or she in question may turn out to be a charming and helpful sailing companion, in which case the cause of young romance may be furthered. Loving parents will find comfort in that, surely, for apparently they can trust their offspring's judgment in choosing beaus or girls. Perhaps when it comes time for their child to choose a mate, they will gain a crew member instead of losing one!

A first mate who values her captain's good disposition will see to it that word is passed along to all teen-age guests on what gear to bring aboard and in what container. There is nothing less conducive to peace and tranquility on a cruise with guests of any age than having one of them approach the dock with a large regulation suitcase. The family teen-ager should be urged to give his or her friend a skeleton list of things to bring, and if the guest wouldn't be caught dead bringing them aboard in a disposable paper carton, to at least settle for a collapsible suitcase that can be folded under a berth. First mates can expand stowage space immeasurably by hanging Pullman-type net hammocks over the bunks of the young.

Teen-age guests should be further warned that privacy is a sometime thing on a small boat, and that the "skeleton" list of gear *should* include a pair of pajamas. On our boat we observe the major proprieties by bedding down teen-agers of the same sex in the forward cabin, but when it's a beau instead of a best friend, the captain gets him and "the girls" sleep in the main cabin. There is still the problem of dressing and undressing and using the head with any kind of privacy; we usually cope with that by taking turns in the morning, with everyone else on deck for the duration. For the rest of the day, or if the deck is weathered out, we turn our backs and turn up the radio, according to the privacy need. After a day or two, the shyest guest will usually have shed his land-made inhibitions. If he hasn't, don't take him cruising again! A small boat is no place for a Nice Nelly.

A variation on the two-teen-agers-together theme is to include a teen-age rendezvous in the pre-cruise plans. Many a captain and first mate I know have formed sailing friendships with other sailing couples largely because they have counterpart teen-agers and, therefore, counterpart problems. If vacation and cruising schedules permit, the two boats either sail in company, anchoring near each other at night, or set target dates to meet in certain harbors. Though both versions tend to cut down on the mobility of a cruising schedule by eliminating the possibility of a sudden change of plans in mid-sail, there are more pro-parents than con.

Once at the anchorage, the Children's Hour is neatly

taken care of, and with less disruption to comfort than having an extra young body aboard a small boat. It's like having the next-door neighbor's child over to play for the afternoon, with the blessed possibility of being able to send her home if she is bratty.

A by-product and a bonus of the "sailing-in-company" method is the excitement of an informal race between the boats from anchorage to anchorage—a source of titillation to young and old alike. Sometimes the two boats exchange young crew members, or double them up on one boat. All sorts of changes can be rung on the combination. The teen-agers can sometimes be "conned" into preparing a dinner or two for the combined crews of the boats, particularly if it's to be a clambake on the beach.

The rendezvous method offers less continuous diversion than the "sailing-in-company" plan, but it has the advantage of being a cliffhanger. *Will* we make it to Clam Cove by Wednesday? *Will* Susie's boat be there? Parents can by-pass a few ports where "the action" is if a rendezvous with Susie dangles like a carrot from the bowsprit.

Then there is the off-again-on-again method of cruising with teen-agers. The young crew comes aboard at the outset of the cruise, sails for a while, and then leaves via bus, train, or plane. Or he joins the boat at a convenient place, in the same way. Some parents object to this method for reasons having to do with the family car, girls or beaus, etc., back home, in the non-sailing period. If willing relatives or friends help out as interim parents during that time, the off-again-on-again method works well when a few days of cruising with teen-agers would be feasible and fun for everyone, and two weeks wouldn't.

The summer Linda was sixteen she interrupted her duties as a volunteer nurses' aide to join us in New Brunswick, Canada, for a week's cruise. Fog had delayed us en route to the scheduled meeting place, St. John, so plans were rearranged, via telephone, for me to meet her plane at the inland town of Fredricton, seventy-five miles from our anchorage at the Canadian resort, St. Andrew-by-the-Sea. A local taxi driver got me there, and the two of us back, and a very knowledgeable and interesting man he was about his country and countryside. The harbor of St. Andrew was almost unrecognizable as we waited on the wharf for the captain to pick us up in the dinghy. When I had left a few hours before, it was a sizable curve of water lapping almost at the foundations of stores and hotels on the shore. Now it was a vast mud-flat dotted here and there with pools of

water, with our boat in one of them. After the initial shock, it was clear to me what had happened; the famous huge tides of the Bay of Fundy had been at work and had drawn off 30 (?) feet of the water level of St. Andrew Harbor in one of their diurnal whooshes.

We saw we had a problem when the captain hollered up to us from the dinghy—way down at one of the dock's pilings. That day's tide was apparently a whopper, even for the Bay of Fundy. Six feet of unbroken air separated the bottom rung of the dock's ladder and the dinghy (named *Judas*, incidentally, for its treacherous, unstable ways). Getting Linda's gear, and then Linda, into the dinghy without upsetting the beast was bad enough, but the captain hung onto the piling and coped. When my turn came, the captain wasn't hanging, he was *clinging*. I leaped, we all prayed, and somehow in the process I sprained my ankle.

On shore it may be good therapy for a sprained ankle to keep on painfully walking around on it, but it isn't good sailing sense to do so on a small boat when it is under way. A first mate has to move fast when the captain needs her, and she can't when her ankle won't.

So I was confined to the cockpit for the rest of the cruise. Linda took over most of my duties as captain's helper— furling sails, letting off and pulling in running backstays, winching in the jib sheet, etc. She spelled me at the helm. She helped me in the galley. She fetched the captain's foul-weather gear from the cabin when the fog turned into rain. She just generally became an indispensable member of the crew. When we put her on a plane in Maine a week later, she said it had been her best cruise.

Teen-agers need to feel needed aboard a small boat as much as their younger brothers and sisters do. They may not seem as eager to spring to their posts as the little ones, but, given specific duties and the conviction that they can do them better than anyone else, inertia and boredom are routed, at least for a time; it varies with the teen-ager.

All in all, children of any age are no different aboard a small boat than they are on land; they are just underfoot more. If they tend to brattiness on dry land, sea air is not going to make little angels out of them. However, sailing parents who do not expect miracles and who are willing to put thought into planning a cruise with their young are more than likely to have as much fun as they had hoped for when they bought the boat. The others will just have to live through it!

JANE KIRSTEIN

Housekeeping
5 Aboard

~~~~~~

A WELL-FOUNDED COMPLAINT of too many first mates is that going to sea in a small boat is no vacation from keeping house. Not only do they have to shop and cook, but they also have to perform these chores without the aid of a telephone or a proper stove. Sometimes the nearest store lies at the end of a three-mile hike through the rain, and many a meal is prepared while standing on one's ear.

This is fun?

Nor can a first mate just "let things go" on a small boat. If she fudges on housekeeping, grease from the galley floor will soon end up on the cushions and blanket fuzz in the soup.

However, there is no need to be a "cruising Cinderella." Far from making a slavey out of the first mate, housekeeping at sea (I say this at the risk of sounding like a TV commercial) can be fun! There are ways and means of making a shopping expedition a breeze instead of a burden—rain or shine. A minimum daily routine with a modicum of well-chosen cleaning equipment can get the first mate out of the cabin and into the early morning sun on deck well before her captain finishes wiping the salt off the brightwork. The proportions of the space below deck to be cleaned are lilliputian, and so can be the properly expended effort.

Don't misunderstand my "happy talk." An apron is not my favorite piece of wearing apparel on shore. I find no challenge in a dirty kitchen floor. To me, greasy restaurant food is ambrosia and nectar on our occasional nights out on the village. I freely admit that I can think of more interesting things to do than keep house—on shore. But on a boat I feel I am not *keeping* house, but *playing* house.

Any first mate can play, if she has the right toys. Some she has brought aboard early in the season; certain components of happy living on a small boat can be considered as permanent boat-gear, coming aboard at commissioning time in the spring and never going ashore again until fall (as suggested in Chapter 10).

Among those components already on board are the basic clean-up items, such as swab, broom, dustpan, etc., having been in demand on spring-cleaning day. Some will be used every day on a cruise, but others can go along, just for the ride, until a foggy, layover day comes along, which seems just the right time to poke into the corners of the shelf behind the stove with a toothbrush or shine up the copper bottoms of the pots and pans. The rest of the time a daily once-over-lightly is enough to keep the blanket fuzz and grease under control. Why be a "compulsive cleaner" on a cruise when there are more important things to do, like sitting in the sun on deck?

Orderliness, however, cannot be a sometime thing on a small boat. Keeping each thing in its place is not only the best method, it is nigh compulsory. If every piece of gear, from tools to clothing, does not have a proper place to which it is returned each time it is used, the resulting confusion below deck will not only be irritating, it can also be dangerous. A pair of pliers needed in a hurry is not easily found if it has been "temporarily stowed" under a pile of clothing on a bunk.

"Proper place" does not necessarily mean "out of sight." That would be impossible on a small boat. When I first started sailing, I tried. I set about tidying things up—stowing the captain's visored caps in his sweater locker instead of on the open shelf over his bunk, stuffing each book into the bookshelf whether it was the one being read or not, moving the box of tissues from the open shelf to the bin in the head, and just generally making a nuisance of myself. Of course, you know what happened: the caps' visors bent and broke, the book was no longer just an arm's reach away when the captain climbed into his bunk, and we found ourselves using paper towels instead of tissues when we sneezed because the towels were at hand. Our noses found it rough going.

I soon stopped all that nonsense. Now *Shag* below deck has the raffish air of an aging French actress, and—we think —the same accumulated charm.

The cabins bulge, here and there, with unconcealed equipment for living and sailing, but the bulges stay put, in the same place, until their components are used and then returned home. Each first mate will learn the easy-reach stowage spaces on her own boat, and if she doesn't know already, she will also learn, as I did, that unexpected visitors from a neighboring boat won't be inspecting her boat-keeping with a critical eye; they have a small boat of their own. (My only concession to my "housekeeper's conscience" is to pop the sink cover over any unwashed lunch dishes as I hear the captain call "Why don't you come aboard?") However, if caps, jackets, charts, and what-not cover every available place to sit, a first mate's guests, if not critical, will be uncomfortable. There is a difference between organized disorderliness and downright messiness.

A bit of pre-cruise planning of easy menus and provisioning of the nonperishable components can take much of the curse out of cooking. Twenty minutes over a hot galley stove are worth two hours in a kitchen on shore; sea air breeds gourmands rather than gourmets, and a hungry crew is an easily pleased one. And, with very little friendly persuasion, the captain may trade places occasionally with the first mate at meal-preparation time. Some of the most delicious dinners aboard *Shag* are the work of the captain. He claims to be stumped by our push-button electric stove on shore, but put him in front of a coal or alcohol stove at sea and he turns out a banquet. Whoever is doing the cooking, it is not a lonely chore. A galley is not a ghetto, segregated from the family fun, as most kitchens are on shore. The cook is usually no farther away from any activity on deck than a head-up stretch through the hatch. Some good and quick recipes will be found at the end of this chapter— tried and true, boat style!

Pre-cruise planning of menus, I have found, breaks naturally into two main categories: hot food and cold food. Naturally! It is not quite as simple as it sounds, though. Subcategories to be taken into account are: the duration of the ice supply, weather changes, and the probable itinerary. Whenever possible, we eat fresh rather than canned foods on *Shag*, and that practice, together with the other considerations I just mentioned, governs what food I plan to give the captain or have him give me.

The refrigerating systems on small boats range from none to deep freezers, so the supply of fresh or frozen foods will vary accordingly. (So, of course, will the menus planned.) *Skylark* had an icebox and except in unusually hot weather we could count on our store-bought ice lasting three days. *Shag's* refrigerator may use block ice or be run on the boat's electrical system, so it is possible to keep food fresh for longer periods.

I used to be very proud when the non-ice side of the icebox emptied in direct ratio to the dwindling amount of ice in the next-door compartment; I had planned well and shopped wisely! Now, on *Shag*, I am limited only by the size of the refrigeration compartment. The captain, well aware of the food cycle, does his own planning and heads us into a good shopping harbor rather than a picturesque, people-less cove when the fresh foods give out.

Weather makes menu planning a necessarily elastic exercise. A first mate has to be ready for anything. Who is to know when the wind will blow hot instead of cold, or a rough sea will make the galley the last place a girl should be at mealtime? Fried chicken may be the family favorite at home, but neither a heaving pan of hot grease nor a heaving stomach are good shipmates when the sea is making up. A thermos of hot consommé made in the morning and lunch meat or cheese sandwiches made on deck are indicated that day.

I should know. One stubborn spell of mine, early in my cruising career, caused more unpleasantness below deck than I like to remember. Any intelligent person, I contended one cold, rough day, could make a simple pot of coffee and scramble eggs under any conditions, if she (meaning me) just went about it right. There was nothing wrong with my line of attack; I broke the eggs into a double boiler in the sink and mixed them. No problem. I filled the coffee pot in the sink. Not a drop spilled. I lit the stove with magnificent ease, barely having to steady myself. It was all a matter of leaning in to the rhythm of the boat, like posting on a horse. The stove was on gimbals, so it swung level, and adjustable bars, fore and aft, secured the pots from shifting back and forth. With my bare hands I would keep them from jumping *up*. The trouble was I had only two bare hands. During the split second that I let go of the double boiler to slow down the coffee, the eggs took off. And as I tried to catch them in mid-flight, the coffee went. The only reason the galley wasn't completely swimming in the mess was that much of it was on me. And it was hot. As I say, sandwiches made on deck are great. Take a loaf of sliced party rye and a hunk of cheese and pass out small sandwiches as fast as they disappear.

Weather can also play havoc with itineraries, further complicating menu planning. A storm or a series of foggy days may throw the captain's sailing schedule out of whack

by stalling the boat in a protected harbor for several days instead of just overnight, as was planned. Then, in order to make up for lost time, a nonstop day-and-night passage may be necessary. Menus planned for the original leisurely, harbor-hopping course are out the porthole for the time being, with coffee, consommé, and beef stew substituting for more complicated dishes.

So, all things considered, a first mate should take a philosophical approach toward menu planning, but she should take an approach. If she has, say, three basic menus with their components in mind, and a standby supply of canned goods, she will have a fair idea of what edibles she should bring aboard from home port, and what she will be looking for in supermarkets along the cruise-way. And she won't have to row over to the neighboring boat for the loan of a cup of sugar because she didn't plan ahead. She will, of course, interchange specific dishes on the menus so as to vary the routine, but because of limited stowage space, ice, etc., she is best advised to stick with a few basic combinations.

Some first mates spend a few relatively cook-free days at the beginning of a cruise by bringing prepared dishes from home, but sometime, somewhere, someone has to spend time over a hot stove, and whether it's on shore or at sea is the cook's choice.

We are "on-boat" cookers on *Shag* from the first day of a cruise, and self-admitted gourmet cooks, at that. Though our two-burner, ovenless alcohol stove does not permit a wide range of cooking methods or cuts of meat, what we do with wine, herbs, and a little of this and a dab of that is a subject for long, narcissistic comment when we sit down to eat. Our canned food locker is filled, chockablock, at the beginning of the season, but the bulk of it goes back, into winter storage, at decommissioning time. Except for canned soups and, occasionally, beef stew or hash, we prefer fresh food and nearly always have it.

To be sure, some of the exceptions to that rule have had a banquet quality about them. Christmas dinner off Peter's Island in the Virgin Islands group was one. Tinned beef-and-kidney stew (it was a British product) and a wassail bowl of canned grapefruit juice and Puerto Rican rum was the menu. We ate in bathing suits still wet from a Yuletide swim, and we never enjoyed a party so much. Perhaps it was due to our guests: two pelicans sitting solemnly in the

dinghy, digesting their Christmas fish. Admittedly, beef-
and-kidney stew was not on our shopping list the day before
when we stopped at Road Town, Tortola (British West
Indies), but there wasn't much evidence of available food
of *any kind*—let alone fresh—on the afternoon of Christmas
eve. Spirits, yes—natural and bottled. The entire island's
population, it seemed, was gathered on the town dock to
decorate the Christmas tree—a baby palm tree. Business was
definitely not as usual, if at all, but really, did it matter? We
had been out of ice for days, but the last bit of fresh food
from St. Thomas was long gone, too. So? Tortola was reputed to be the only possibility for replenishment of both
in that part of the Virgins. Possibly. We had had wonderful
sails before Tortola's Christmas winds, had snorkeled among
its technicolored fish and coral reefs, and had sunbathed on
its deserted white-sand beaches backed by palm groves.
Ice and fresh food seemed highly unimportant. When one of
the less spirited citizens, actually named William Jennings
Bryan, genially broke way for us through the pirouetting
celebrants and led us to a warehouse store stocked to the
ceiling with canned goods from everywhere, we, gourmets
that we were, chose beef-and-kidney stew. Ice? It only
melts, anyway.

But under most conditions we opt for fresh food, even
though fresh food creates more maintenance and stowage
problems than compact, self-armored canned goods. Many
of the iceboxes aboard small boats are bin-shaped and receive food through a top opening. Bottomless they are not,
but sometimes a first mate thinks they are when she is digging about for an elusive bar of butter. Systematic stowing,
from the bottom up (orderliness in the food locker), cuts
down on bruises and blasphemy while icebox fishing.

First to go into *Shag's* non-ice compartment of the icebox
are the bottles or cartons of milk and cream, well tucked into
one corner. I drink skim milk and the captain, whole, so to

expedite the reach-and-feel, or Braille, system, the captain's bottle is stowed always to the right of mine. (According to marine protocol, the captain rates the right-hand position of everything on the boat: the bunk, the locker, even the green running lights, if he wants them for his very own. I find this procedure a handy way of remembering which is "his" and "hers" at times, especially drink-mixing times when one of us has cold germs we don't want to pass on.)

Side by side with the milk at the bottom of the bin go heavy, sturdy items, such as grapefruit, melon, and a round cheese. Then, snugged in around them go butter, bacon, and sliced meats, and finally, in ascending layers according to their resistance to crush, go salad components, berries, and so forth. Everything, including the milk, has been twisted into a plastic bag before stowing, because not only is messy spillage isolated that way and freshness prolonged, but also it's easier to get a good grip on the chosen item. Uncooked meats—again, in plastic bags, and clearly labeled on their butcher-paper wrapping—go on the ice side, as do such essentials as frozen squid and sandworms for fish bait.

Spillage and breakage, irritating mess-makers on a boat, are inevitable if a first mate doesn't take a few preventive measures before stowing food, both on the ice and off. Products that come in paper cartons, such as salt, flour, and sugar, travel better if transferred to glass jars with snug-fitting tops to which distinguishing labels have been affixed. Once opened, a loaf of bread can spread itself over an entire cupboard if it hasn't been imprisoned in a plastic bag. Eggs, of course, need the armor of a protective carrier, be it the carton they came in or one of the plastic or metal containers on the market. Whatever the item the first mate is stowing, she is wise to consider if it will spill, break, dry out, or attract moisture if left as it is, and to do something now, before it does spill, break, etc. A jar labeled in time saves you-know-what.

No matter how wisely a first mate has planned and prepared before leaving home port for a longish cruise, there
will come that day when fresh food, cooked or uncooked,
runs out. Shopping day has come, and rain or shine the
first mate must get herself to a grocery. Or rather, the captain must get her there. Shopping day is a family affair on
a small boat. Meals cannot appear, magically, on the table
at sea without the active cooperation of the captain, as they
may on shore. An experienced and thoughtful captain will
have taken that fact into consideration well before shopping
day is upon him, and planned, if possible, to be in a good
supply port rather than in some delightful but deserted
cove. More often than not, ice, water, or gas need to be
replenished, too, so the ideal stop would be at a marina
near a shopping center. A marina with shower facilities is,
of course, a little heaven on earth after several days at sea.

Shopping will take only a small part of the day, under the
above conditions. The captain and the first mate may coor-
dinate their shore activities so that their separate missions
are accomplished simultaneously and they are both back on
the boat in a trice, ready to shove off for a good sail and
an isolated harbor.

For instance, my captain and I have made it in and out
of a certain convenient but otherwise unattractive port on
our way to Maine in less than an hour many times. As soon
as *Shag* is tied to the gas dock, I go ashore, my shopping list
in hand, while the captain takes on water, ice, and gasoline.
I go directly to the nearby supermarket, wheedle the
butcher, who is lurking in a secret room behind the frozen
meat section, into cutting me fresh steaks and chops, fill my
cart with necessaries and goodies, and, if possible, arrange
with a clerk to deliver the lot to the boat. As I stand in the
telephone cubicle at the head of the dock calling home, I
wave to the captain who, his dockside duties accomplished,

has picked up the morning newspapers or replenished the liquor supply and is on his way back to the boat for his towel and soap and first whack at the marina's shower facilities. Then, a beer in his hand and his face bright and shining, he reads the morning papers in the boat's cockpit while I have *my* shower, wash my hair, and, shining pretty brightly myself, return to *Shag.* While the captain threads his way, under power, past fishing boats and lobster pots out of the harbor, I stow our purchases, and presto! we are ready again for three days of uninterrupted "coving," of looking for seals instead of supermarkets.

Not every shopping day goes so smoothly, particularly in

ports new to us. There may be a plethora of likely looking
stores lining Main Street, but which one to choose? Only
one of them may be willing and able to get the yachtsman
and his purchases out of the store and back to his boat in a
hurry, and by just turning into the first store she comes to,
the first mate may miss it. Or she may, unwittingly, bypass
a first-rate butcher or fruiterer.

We have developed a system for shopping in virgin territory, and only once did it break down, and then only
because we had forgotten it was Sunday. (Losing track of
time, incidentally, is one of the joys of cruising.)

Our system goes like this:

1. Before coming into port, we read the information given
   in the cruising guide, if we have one for that area. If not,
   we start from scratch.
2. If we tie up at a dock to take on ice, water, or gas, we
   ask the attendant for his advice on the best store—one
   that will deliver to the dock. If there is no attendant
   above the age of twelve, or if we anchor in the harbor to
   pick up a mooring, we start from scratch.
3. Once ashore we "case" the shopping district, on foot if it
   is nearby, or by taxi if the cruising guide or the dock
   attendant or our senses have told us the shopping district
   lies thataway—five miles thataway. Local taxis are usually
   not hard to come by, once we find a telephone. (Many a
   dockside telephone booth has a "Joe's Taxi" card stuck to
   its wall; if not, the local telephone directory shows the
   way.) If we are in Joe's taxi, one problem is eliminated:
   delivery to the boat of our purchases. He parks in a cen-
   tral spot and we converge on him from time to time
   with our bundles, until, shopped out, we say "Home,
   Joe" and he takes us back to the boat. Using Joe also
   eliminates much of the "casing" of available stores be-

cause of his local knowledge. I have found, however, that Joes sometimes let loyalties to their cronies color their judgment as to the best store in town and now double-check their advice with certain "casing" aids of my own.

4. The best store in town, to my mind, is one that concentrates in one building fresh, top-quality meat, fruit, and vegetables, and fancy canned goods—such as S.S. Pierce, on the Eastern seaboard—and, if necessary, will deliver to the boat. To determine if a store meets those qualifications, a quick walk through and a word with a clerk about delivery is enough. If the store is in a harbor frequented by yachtsmen, the clerk already knows what is up and is eager to be of service; yachtsmen are usually good customers—hungry people with long shopping lists. Part of the store's service is to allow itself to be used as the focal point, if there is no waiting Joe, for all the day's purchases—newspapers, magazines, spirits, a new anchor —and to deliver them to the boat. Many a time the store delivers the crew, too—especially if it is raining.

Good supply ports are, of course, not always spaced at proper intervals along a cruise itinerary, nor would we want them to be. Many of the adventures, the illuminating chance encounters with "friendly natives" long on local lore, the stumbling on a fine old house or a dusty, delicate ship model in a lobsterman's shed—the unexpected joys that are as much a part of cruising as fine, fair winds—come to one more often while tracking down a general store than on the way to a supermarket at the end of a dock.

In a way, we were "living off the land" in a place like Letite (see Chapter 1), but the phrase is more frequently applied, on *Shag*, to describe a less precarious way of acquiring food.

In between the opulence of the "everything-available"

shopping harbor and Letite, there is the cove that hasn't any stores but does have a fleet of lobster boats, or a nearby beach imbedded with waiting, toothsome clams, or a farm with a ripe corn field reaching down to the water. A word with a lobsterman, or a half hour on the beach with a bucket and a shovel, or a dinghy ride to the farm can yield the *pièce de résistance* of a delicious supper. After a few cruises in the same general area, the itinerary seems to just naturally take the boat back to those special lobster, clam, or corn coves, and their whereabouts are secrets as carefully guarded from other yachtsmen as the location of that happened-upon swimming hole in a spring-fed deserted granite quarry on that certain island. "Living off the land" means different things in different places to different yachtsmen, but to all it means a sense of discovery and of self-sufficiency: "I don't need a supermarket. I can live off the land." It's a delightful way to shop—and the food is good.

Cleaning, cooking, and shopping—the three major housekeeping duties aboard a small boat—have to be done, to be sure, just as they do on shore. But against a background of wheeling seagulls and blue water, the drudgery is somehow lessened. Cooking supper in a bathing suit gives a certain fillip to the task. Sweeping the cabin with a child's broom cuts the whole cleaning bit down to size—child-size. Shopping in a new port each time is not like going back to the same old shelf for the same old loaf of bread at home.

Housekeeping aboard not only *can* be fun. It *is!*

JANE KIRSTEIN

Laundry the Navy Way

Any boat with a head, be it ever so humble, should have a plunger aboard. Even on *Prelude,* where space just wasn't, we had a plunger (I can see it now—it had a chipping yellow handle), and the skipper had to use it in its usual vocation quite frequently. On *Skylark* I have discovered that a plunger is a multipurpose tool. In combination with a bucket, it becomes a washing machine.

Laundromats are not always within walking distance of the anchorage, and sometimes there are no Laundromats. Also, there are times when a first mate would rather not spend half an afternoon waiting for the clothes to wash and dry in a stuffy building. An ordinary bucket will hold enough water and detergent to wash several shirts, shorts, and blouses, or the week's underwear. Drain-water from the ice chest or water from the hose on the dock are also good for this washing machine. Sheets and dungarees are unwieldy, but smaller items can be quickly plunged clean and hung on the rigging or lifelines to dry while the skipper and mate explore the countryside or picnic on the beach. Do the wash on deck or in the cockpit if it is self-bailing. Your feet may get a good washing, too!

MARY LEONARD

Recipes

These recipes are all tried and true in the Leonard style, i.e., the whole family likes them and they don't take long to prepare. Canned meats may be substituted for fresh in any of them, but be careful not to overcook canned seafood and chicken. Amounts may be varied according to what you have or can get. None of the dishes are "touchy."

Crab Curry
Generous pile of dehydrated onion flakes, or fresh onions, chopped
1 can condensed mushroom soup, undiluted

½ *pint sour cream*
Curry (to taste)
*Canned or frozen peas (optional; their addition makes this a
    one-dish dinner)*
*1 large can king crab or fresh cooked crabmeat (the more the
    better)*
Rice (enough for 4—Minute Rice preferred here)

Put dehydrated onion flakes or chopped onions, mushroom soup, sour cream, and curry in sauce or frying pan and heat just to boiling point. If frozen peas are being used, simmer in sauce until tender. Add crabmeat and heat until mixture is hot. Serve on rice. Serves 4.

This is not an exact dish and can be expanded with more sour cream, soup, crabmeat, and rice. Good with a tossed salad and French bread if you want a fine big meal.

Shrimp Creole (?)

1 large jar or 2 cans spaghetti sauce
*Pile of dehydrated onion flakes, or fresh onions, chopped (to
    taste)*
Green peppers, celery, peas (optional, but good)
*2 cans shrimp, or cooked frozen shrimp (deveined), or fresh
    shrimp aplenty*
Rice (enough for 4)

Heat spaghetti sauce to boiling point, add onion flakes or chopped onions and vegetables and simmer until vegetables are tender. If fresh shrimp are being used, simmer with vegetables until cooked. If canned shrimp are being used, add shrimp, heat, and serve immediately on rice. Serves 4.

This is a good one-dish dinner for the family, which may be extended with more sauce, vegetables, and shrimp. Serve with salad and bread or rolls if desired.

Hamburger Stroganoff

1 lb. hamburger meat or 2 cans hamburger patties
Dehydrated onion flakes (to taste)

Canned mushrooms or condensed mushroom soup, undiluted
½ pint sour cream
Dash nutmeg
Salt (to taste)
Rice or instant mashed potatoes (enough for 4)

Fry hamburger and onion flakes together until lightly browned. Add mushrooms or mushroom soup, sour cream, and nutmeg until you really get that interplay of onion-nutmeg. Heat until hot but don't boil. Serve immediately over rice or instant mashed potatoes. Serves 4.

I serve Stroganoff on baked potatoes or noodles at home, but substitute rice or instant mashed potatoes on the boat. If you really want to make it the right way, use stew beef and simmer it all afternoon before adding sour cream. Serve with tossed salad, rolls, or bread if it's a spread. This is another expandable recipe.

Chinese Chicken
Chicken breasts, legs, thighs, or canned chicken (enough for 4 or 5)
Dehydrated onion flakes or fresh onions, chopped (to taste)
2 cans plain chop suey, or 1 can chop suey and 1 can fancy Chinese vegetables
2 cans fried rice

Season and brown chicken and onions. Simmer until tender. Add chop suey and vegetables and bring to a boil. (Or place canned chicken on top of vegetables and heat to boiling point.) Prepare fried rice as directed on can. Serves 4–5.

Breakfast Hash
2 cans corned beef hash
2 eggs per person

Warm hash in large frying pan, stirring now and again. When hash is hot, drop eggs on top, cover pan, and poach until whites are set.

Portuguese Hot Sausage Soup

This dish can be prepared ahead and taken along in freezer boxes or jars, or cooked aboard on a miserable layover day. It's very, very good when the weather is wet and cold.

Dehydrated onion flakes, or fresh onions, chopped
1 lb. hot sausage, or 1 lb. sweet sausage, or ½ lb. hot and
*   ½ lb. sweet sausage (hot sausage is very hot)*
4 large potatoes, cut into pieces, or canned potatoes, cut up
2 cans whole-kernel corn, drained
2 cans red kidney beans, rinsed and drained
1 large can tomato or V-8 juice
1 small head cabbage, chopped

Break up and brown sausage with onion in bottom of soup kettle. Add potatoes and enough water in which to cook them until tender. Add corn, beans, tomato or V-8 juice, and cabbage. Heat and simmer until cabbage is tender. Serves 10 or more.

With crackers, this is a whole meal. It may be reheated for several days. Children may like it thinned with more tomato juice or made with only sweet sausage, in which case you can season adult portions with plenty of pepper.

MARY LEONARD

Clothing
for Fair Weather
6   and Foul

~~~~~~

FIRST MATES HAVE a double-edged dressing problem. To be comfortable and contented aboard they must be equipped for heat or sleet—both on board and ashore—and still keep their wardrobes within the available stowage space on a small boat. The problem is complicated by the ever-lurking presence of mildew, lack of a washing machine and ironing board, and such contingencies as an unexpected invitation to a yacht club dance.

A good way to tackle the problem is to do some on-shore planning before the cruise, with pad and pencil in hand. Where are you going? What are the weather prospects? Going ashore much? What is the locker and drawer situation on your boat, and what space is allotted to you?

No matter how small the boat, the first mate should have her own, segregated, compartments. They, or it, may be no more than the left or right half of an open shelf above one of the bunks, but the space should be hers alone.

I am allowed one hanging-locker, four drawers in the forward cabin, a two-shelf cupboard backing one of the bunks in the main cabin, and a lazarette beneath it. The captain has the equivalent except for one less drawer, which is the tool chest. That is our agreed-upon space, to have and to hold against all encroachment. Admittedly, we do a fair amount of cross-encroaching before the end of a two-week cruise, but it is always negotiated.

So, with the private stowage space firmly in the captain's mind as well as hers, the first mate should consider what she will put there, starting with absolute necessities and tapering off into favorite fripperies, if there is still room. (Incidentally, if there's a nonnecessity she really wants to have aboard, she should take it. She will find room for it, if she wants it enough.)

Clothes for wet and cold weather should be given highest priority on a cruise of any duration, even in the middle of the summer. From Maine to Miami or from San Diego to Seattle, there is always a possibility that some part of the cruising day or night will be chilly or damp. Cloud masses can obscure the sun, a sudden wind shift presage a storm, or a damp fog settle over the summer sea, and the first mate who wishes to stay happy and healthy reaches for her woolies and her foulweather gear. (Most of the time that we were cruising in the heavenly-blue Caribbean waters

of the Virgin Islands my "foul-weather" gear was a bathing suit and a yellow oilskin fisherman's hat, but one day even the trade winds blew cold on my wet suit, and I reached for my waterproof jacket.)

"Water-repellent" does not mean "waterproof"; first mates, beware. A whole new clothing category known as "boating wear" has entered the market now that yachting has become big business, and sailors can get into trouble if they don't read the small print on the labels. The manufacturers are not out to deceive; they just have their own terminology for what will keep you dry, semi-dry, or miserable. Stay away from "water-repellent" labels for your foulest weather gear. For that, the label should say "waterproof," loud and clear.

Avoid, if possible, foul-weather gear with stitched seams. Some stitched-seam manufacturers claim that their thread swells when wet and effectively stops up leaky needle holes. Maybe. I'm a vulcanized-seam girl, myself, or have been ever since one wet day off the New Jersey coast; my captain also favors vulcanized seams—he was close to having to look for a new crew the minute we got into port.

It was early spring, and cold. The boatyard had been fifteen days behind schedule in getting our boat into the water, and every day we had visited her in the dank shed where she spent the winter, we wistfully watched the tortoise-like progress of the workmen. (We knew it was useless to prod them; all hands, including us, agreed that this was no weather for painting or varnishing. The paint would lift and the varnish would blister if applied in that dampness.) Finally, more drying stoves were moved into the shed, the sun came out, and in due time our boat was in the water, her masts stepped, her motor tested, and ready for commissioning. A busy weekend took care of that, and with creaky backs and complaining, winter-softened muscles, we set off from Mamaroneck the following Monday for Chesapeake Bay.

That was our *first* mistake: no spring shakedown cruise. In other years the normal procedure for us in the spring had been to make one or two weekend sails to harbors near home before officially opening the long cruising season. Missing gear—from shackles to toothbrushes—would then have been duly noted and subsequently supplied, sails and motor given a real workout inspection, and bodies eased back into sailing shape.

Not this time. We were off and running down the East River for the Chesapeake the minute we had commissioned and provisioned, shaking down as we went. After two days and two nights on board, there wasn't a lazy muscle in our bodies; neither was there one that didn't ache. But memories of another early spring cruise on the Chesapeake, when we sunbathed while New Yorkers froze, made Pollyannas out of us. I was still on rather surly footing with certain protruding parts of the boat, such as the support bulkhead over the icebox (as I am every spring until the instinct to duck returns), and had just cracked my head for the nth time as I dug out luncheon ingredients, when the captain called for his foul-weather gear—in a hurry.

He was right. This was no spring shower; rain was coming down in that steady, determined way that says "I've got a lot more where this is coming from. Cope."

I handed up his waterproof pants, jacket, and rubber boots, and pulled the hatch cover over to protect me and my luncheon preparations. Ignoring the captain's kindly advice to stay below, I wrapped the sandwiches in waxed paper, put the bouillon in a thermos, donned my own foul-weather gear, and climbed to the cockpit. Not only was I playing Pollyanna; my handsome rain gear was new and this was as good a time as any to try it out.

There was water everywhere. The wind had freshened right on our nose and we were heading into an increasingly choppy sea. A contest between the sea and the rain seemed to be in progress to see which could dump the most water on us. So far, we were undaunted. It was cold, but we had layers of woolies under our rain gear. The bouillon, liberally laced with sherry, tasted and felt good, and we were only a day or two away from the Chesapeake and sunshine, weren't we? Then a clammy hand seemed to settle around my neck, my head felt dank and awfully cold. I looked at the captain. He was smiling at me, encouragingly, questioningly, anxiously. Obviously from my expression, Pollyanna had gone with the wind and the rain. Indeed she had. Subsequent inspection below deck showed that I was soaked from my head to my shoulders and there was no doubt as to the culprit: from the stitched seam traversing the hood of my new jacket, water was dripping in shamelessly. The inner side of the jacket was soaking wet, and very, very cold. No tragedy, of course, except that there was no other rain gear on board and, seasick-proof as I am under most conditions, I have never found it wise to stay in a stuffy cabin when the sea is as rough as it was that day. I made it into port with my lunch intact—but just.

So watch your seams. As boating-wear manufacturers learn there is more to selling their products than meets the eye, they will undoubtedly effectively plug up the holes in their stitched seams. There is no reason to doubt the word of some manufacturers that they already have. But to be absolutely safe, purchase your truly *foul*-weather gear in a tried and true sporting goods store for male sailors, hunters, and fishermen, buy a small man's size, and leave fashion for drier days. A smaller version of the captain's choice is the best bet.

Whether to zip, snap, or slip on your jacket is a multiple-choice question. I have tried all three methods, and have settled on snap closings. True, a snap front closing offers several gaping opportunities for water to enter if the double flap is not snugly fitted over its mate. But the ease with which a snapped jacket can be donned over thick undergarments in a hurry, and shed when the rain stops, is a great convenience. Slip-ons are hair-mussers and cap-removers as well as offering greater resistance to quick changes. Zippers, if unavoidable, *must* be of a synthetic material rather than metal, or sea air and salt water will have corroded them hopelessly by the third wearing. A dab of Vaseline and much patient tugging and hauling will usually repair the damage temporarily, but a metal zipper in foul-weather gear will always be a nuisance.

Boots are bulky things to stow, but when the time comes to use them you won't begrudge them their stowage room. You can be dry topside, but if your feet are wet, they are cold, and so are you—everywhere. Best bets—and buys—are men's boots in small sizes, if a reasonably snug fit can be achieved, because men's boots are longer in the leg than boots made expressly for women. The pantslegs of the foul-weather suits are best worn *over* the boot for greater protection from wetness, and the short boots made for women have a way of sneaking out from under the pants; down the leg and into the boot goes a chilling rivulet of water. It's buyer's choice between boots that pull on over sneakers and those that go over socks; both have their advantages. The over-sneakers variety are heavier to lug around and the fit is usually less perfect than the fit of the over-socks boots. But socks have less clinging power than sneakers, and it is not considered good sailing practice to lose a boot just as you are rushing to let down the main halliard in a rainsquall. Any boot you wear on a boat should have a squeegee, deck-gripping sole, the same kind of sole that you find on the only sneaker allowed on any self-respecting boat, the Top-sider or its make-alikes.

Stowage space permitting, more than one version of foul-and semi-foul-weather gear is recommended. In addition to the standard set of rubber-coated jacket and pants, a pull-over waterproof poncho or a full-length raincoat can be a boon. On days when the weather can't make up its mind whether to be just threatening or downright miserable, a raincoat over a sweater and slacks, or shorts, more quickly adjusts to the weather's caprices than full-dress foul-weather gear; it is easier to put on or off and it keeps the first mate's bottom dry, which I find a boon, indeed. Moreover, such a raincoat is excellent for shore-going expeditions, for the same reasons. Show me a dinghy with bone-dry seats, rain or shine, and I will turn in my raincoat. On even the fairest day *some* water splashes over the bow on either the trip to shore or the boatward-bound one, and a raincoat either over you or under you on the seat does the trick. It can be left in the dinghy during the shore expedition or carried to the supermarket—according to the weather.

There's no reason to be so all-fired practical in choosing every piece of clothing, fair weather or foul. Have a fling at the boating fashions that appear in magazines and news-papers in the early spring. Some will look as pretty on you as they did in the pictures and may even fulfill their prom-ises to keep you warm and dry as well. What if you *can't* bend over in that madras one-piece jump suit that you saw advertised and ordered, or wear anything more than a bikini under it? There are layover days when your only duty, to yourself as well as to the captain, is to loll about and look pretty. Cruising is not all toil and trouble, or I wouldn't be writing this book. Take along a pair of hot-pink raw silk slacks and a wild-print blouse. You will probably wear them, and enjoy them. My nonsense items are a pleated white skirt and a navy Italian silk knit sweater. The one time I have worn them in the two seasons that I have taken them along was memorable for being a delightful evening at an unscheduled party ashore. It wouldn't have been memorable—at least, delightfully so—if I had been the only woman there in blue jeans.

Admittedly, though, basic items should have first priority at the available space, because it is they—not the hot-pink slacks—that keep the first mate healthy, warm, and happily aboard. What are "basic items"? How many should you take? Those are questions each first mate must answer for herself. But first mates, collectively, have the same two factors to consider: where and how long the cruise will be. Maine? Baja California? For one week? Two? Now is the time for thinking ahead, mates. It is list-making time.

For instance, my basic list for a two-week cruise off the coast of Maine in August is:

3 Woolen slacks
6 Cotton slacks
6 Cotton shorts
4 T-shirts
4 Cotton blouses
4 Woolen sweaters
6 Woolen knee socks
3 pairs Sneakers for boat wear
Sufficient changes of underwear, plus 1 set woolen underwear
Pajamas (flannel and cotton)
Shore-going clothes (shoes, dress, skirt, etc.)

The above list is, of course, only a "for instance" and, I realize, it is lengthier than many first mates will have space for. We are just two people—the captain and I—on a roomy, 40-foot yawl, and I can afford to be generous in my quantity calculations. We use only two of the four bunks for sleeping or sitting and pile the other two, in the forward cabin, with gear if we need to. Occasionally my grown daughter joins us for a weekend or we take guests along for a few days. Then I either cut down on my clothing supply or pack it more snugly in order to free space for the others. Many a happy cruising boat has less space than ours, and many delightfully more, with a more numerous crew. So my "for instance" is given only as a rough guide. First mates can carry on from here.

Three pairs of woolen slacks consists of one mighty heavy pair and one light-weight pair for boat wear, and one in-between pair for going ashore.

Four pairs of cotton slacks are for warmish days on the boat; two clean pairs are in reserve for going ashore. Ditto the cotton shorts, just in case.

I am a T-shirt girl. They are warmer than blouses, but cooler than sweaters, and stow easily, neatly folded, at the bottom of my sweater cupboard.

Cotton blouses take up hanging room, but are more comfortable on hot days and twin up better than most jerseys with shore-going skirts.

My estimate of woolen sweaters is actually low—the minimum for me. Two favorite turtlenecks stay on the boat all summer. The same is true of two cardigans. A discarded pullover of my daughter's usually sneaks in too.

Woolen knee socks: well, I just prefer woolen to cotton socks—if I wear any at all—with my sneakers. Wool feels less dank than cotton.

Three pairs of sneakers are par for the course. One pair is inevitably damp, and another pair dirty. One of the three is the handy, slip-on variety (but with a nonslip sole) rather than the orthodox tie-on. I can take a shoeless sunbath with them at my side and still be ready to spring into action at a moment's notice to help the captain on deck. This may be the place to say that never is anyone allowed to move about barefoot while the boat is under way. Even on the driest day sea water may lurk in some spot on deck, and the easiest way to go overboard is to slip over. At the least, bare feet on a slippery deck add greatly—and unnecessarily—to the number of bruises, sprained ankles, etc., acquired on a cruise. And, to repeat a statement made above, sneaker soles must always be the nonslip type that are designed to act as suction cups on a slippery deck. These sneakers don't always perform flawlessly, but they are better than the others.

Sufficient changes of underwear means, for me, more than enough. These are easily stowed items, and when baths are not easily obtainable, I like my underwear supply to be even longer than usual. I have found one set of woolen un-

derwear—vest and pants—to be ample. Rare is the day cold
enough, even for me, to wear woolies under my heavy
woolen slacks, but on that day—what a comfort to have
them. There are many varieties on the market made especially for sportsmen. Some look like Chinese coolie quilted
or padded pajamas and have an inner core of synthetic
fiber insulation between outer skins of nylon or cotton jersey. I have seen some sailors wear them on brisk days with
nothing over them. (One such set is advertised for women
as "figure flattering, in pastel blue.") Usually, however, they
are worn under foul-weather gear, and some first mates I
know swear by them. I prefer a soft, skinlike set with an
outer layer of viyella and an inner layer of cotton jersey.
Because it is less bulky than the insulated set, it goes easily
under slacks on a really cold day and generates less moist
body heat than those of synthetic material.

Pajamas cruise better than nightgowns, I find, as they
are a more practical cover-up when the captain needs sudden help on deck with a dragging anchor at night, or when
there are guests aboard. Flannel pajamas are snug comfort
on cool nights.

The quality of boat clothes is as important as the quantity. An old pair of soft, pure wool slacks, too frayed at the
edges for shore wear, is preferable to a brand new pair of
scratchy cheap ones bought just for the boat. Cotton slacks
and shorts may all look more or less alike on the store rack,
but some are made of hardier material than others and will
fade less in bright, sea-reflected sun. There is no need to
eschew all the boating-wear fashions that have burst on
the scene in recent years, but it would be well to view them
with somewhat the same skepticism that a mother views
children's wear with: will they shrink, fade, split at the
seams, etc.?

There is little need to include a "for instance" list of boat clothes for a cruise in a hot climate. A bathing suit, or shorts and a sleeveless top, is usually my costume for the day while at sea. However, at least one pair of cotton slacks and one long-sleeved blouse or light jacket should be included in every hot-weather cruising wardrobe, as protective cover against sunburn. I learned this the hard way one day at the beginning of a Caribbean cruise, when I underestimated the power of the tropical sun and had to spend the following two days either inside the sweltering cabin or inside an equally sweltering suit of foul-weather gear for lack of any other protection against further burn. A brimmed hat, preferably straw, is also a must. Not only does it keep you from looking like Rudolph the Red-Nosed Reindeer, but it also wards off sunstroke. The pith helmet was not invented just to distinguish the Bwanas from the Boys; it served a protective purpose.

Shore-going clothes are the biggest headache both to choose and to stow. They vary, of course, in shape and form with each first mate just as on-shore clothes do. I felt great in my white pleated skirt and navy silk sweater at a party in Boothbay Harbor, Maine, whereas a sleeveless cotton or silk shift would have better pleased another first mate. Some sailing wives I know *never* take along shore-going clothes; they feel that what's good enough for the boat is good enough for the folks on shore. However, they are in the minority. Most first mates, I have found, take at least one skirt with them, even on the smallest of boats and most in-formal of itineraries. Not only may they unexpectedly dine ashore in a restaurant that frowns on ladies in pants, but they will also find it more comfortable to wear a skirt rather than shorts or slacks while shopping for food in some of the more isolated, often conservative villages. The sidelong glances at your shorts in a Maine fishing village can make you feel as uncomfortable as if you were entering a cathedral bareheaded.

Non-creasability is a big factor in making the choice of what shore-going clothes to take on a cruise. The ease with which they can emerge from cramped quarters and still look more or less pristine should be the criterion. Noncrushable material is obviously the answer, but again, to each first mate, her own. Many a fabric, I have found, makes overly optimistic claims for itself in the wrinkle-proof department. A good test is to ask yourself if the fabric in question would pack well in a suitcase, if it would withstand the rigors of a trip on land. There are methods for comparatively wrinkle-free stowing given in the next paragraph, but the basic, cooperative material must be already there.

Where and how to stow clothing begins on shore with a mental survey of the available space on the boat, and that space doesn't necessarily have to be marked "for clothing only." My sea boots go in a lazarette beneath my bunk, along with a wooden salad bowl and my own private flashlight. (The sea boots are always carefully wiped clean and dry before being re-stowed after use, and the salad bowl *before* use.) The important thing to keep in mind is choosing a *permanent* spot for each type of clothing; nothing is less conducive to clothing neatness than having to riffle through a cache of jerseys in order to find an elusive pair of pajamas. There are some items, such as shore-going shoes or sweaters, that we store in plastic bags and move about the boat from niche to cranny at times, but the basic wear stays put.

Stowing begins on shore with the packing and the method of transporting the clothing from home to boat. It's easier, for instance, to pop things into plastic bags in the relative spaciousness of one's own bedroom than in a confined cabin on a boat.

Standard, hard suitcases are taboo on our boat as they should be on most small boats. I have heard of some sailors who tolerate small ones aboard, for use as extra stowage space. But since there is usually no other place to put them but on the bunks during the day and on the cabin sole at night, they clutter up precious space needlessly. Collapsible suitcases are handy, both because they can be stowed under bunk mattresses, if necessary, and are respectable-looking receptacles for clothes for a possible overnight stay ashore.

Canvas carryalls, available in Army-Navy stores, sporting goods stores, and at sailmakers, and large cardboard cartons do most of the transport work on our boat. The captain and I have two canvas bags apiece, and we also pack our cartons separately. The canvas carryalls double as ice-carrying bag and all, for a while, free and swinging in the forward cabin are packed together, and the same holds true for main cabin items. Much edging back and forth between cabins is eliminated this way. Once emptied, the cartons stay on the fantail until they can be disposed of—either far out at sea, or loaded with garbage and taken ashore in the dinghy in a harbor.

I am a fortunate first mate in that I have a full-length hanging locker, or closet, all to myself. It is deep enough to have a double row of hanging poles, though they are so close together that things do overlap. I was only mildly successful in getting around that contingency by using child-size hangers; most grown-up clothes slip off the baby hangers unless they can be buttoned or pinned tight at the neck, but turtleneck jerseys hang well. Clothes to be hung in the locker are brought aboard on hangers, with—most importantly—plastic, protective covers already in place on shoregoing items. The covers keep the garments clean in transit from shore to boat, and dry and quite free from wrinkles on the boat. Water in some form is irresistibly attracted to clothes at some time on a cruise, and plastic covers frustrate this attraction admirably. Too, as all travelers know, plastic covers are wrinkle-fighters in close-packed quarters. The best commercial plastic covers for boat use are those with foldover openings, rather than zippers, because they neither snag nor rust. I hoard the plastic bags our cleaner thoughtfully provides, finding them nonbulky and the best wrinkle-fighters of all. When a shore-going expedition is in prospect, I liberate the bagged apparel from the locker and hang it, bag and all, for a while, free and swinging in the forward cabin, to let it freshen in appearance.

Except for woolen slacks, jackets, foul-weather gear, and blouses, all our boat clothes are stowed in cupboards and drawers, folded as neatly as possible. Sweaters coexist with jerseys on the top shelf of my bunkside lazarette, and cotton shorts and slacks go on the bottom shelf. They are given no care other than an occasional refolding, or airing if the weather has been damp.

Sneakers go in the bottom of my hanging locker, unless they are wet. If they have been caught—on me—in a salt-free rain shower or have been soaked with harmless dew on a walk ashore, they are simply left on deck or in a warm corner to dry. If salt water has been the dampening agent, they get another bath—in fresh water. Salt residue left in sneakers will draw moisture from the air, and before long little creeping patches of mildew will form beneath the sneakers and spread to other articles near them.

First mates sailing on fresh-water lakes and rivers will not have as grave a problem with mildew as their saltier comrades at sea have, but they will have it to some degree. An overabundance of moisture and an undersupply of circulating air, on salt or fresh water, breed mildew if they are allowed to mate for any length of time. Moisture cannot always be wiped off, or out, so the best method of combating the nuisance of mildew stains and musty odor is to let in as much circulating air as possible.

If there are no air vents in lockers and cupboards and permission to bore holes in the woodwork is not granted by the captain, the first mate should leave the compartments open as much as possible while the boat is at anchor during the cruise, and the whole time she is rocking at the mooring at home. Occasional airing of all your clothes, especially woolen apparel, along the boom on a sunny day is a good anti-mildew medicine and, messy as it may look to the land-lubber, is standard practice on a small boat. Various commercial products that combat mildew can be handily spread around the boat, even, as one first mate I know does, in the pots-and-pans cupboard, where accumulated dampness can cause rust.

The joy of living aboard a small boat would be immeasurably diminished for me if it weren't for the constant presence of a few favorite items of clothing.

For instance, Lilly. Lilly is the captain's name (after Lilly Daché, the famous milliner) for a straw hat I bought for a dollar one day in a gardening store. She is my friend. She goes on my head on a sunny day and never flies off in a wind; she goes over my face to keep out the light during siesta hour on deck; she covers up dripping, freshly shampooed hair on the way back to the boat from a shower on shore; she hides my shame of bobby pins while my hair is drying underneath. She has been sat on, crushed behind pillows on deck and below, drenched in a sudden downpour, and even slightly burned while drying out too near a stove, and she has come through it all in great, original shape. Even the captain, who hates hats on women, says she is becoming. I look for her replacement in every hat-selling store I enter, but never have I found a hat with all her qualities. One hat-seller stood by, openmouthed, as I tried one of his offerings

on over my *face*. The crown sloped at too abrupt an angle into the brim, instead of gently sloping, as Lilly does, over the nose area. "No good for sleeping," I told the man. He was still holding it in his trembling hand as I left the store.

Another favorite hat, for cold days, is a bobble cap I got on the Isle of Wight. Bobble cap, I was interested to learn, is the name in that salty English yachting center for a knitted woolen cap with, of course, a bobble on the top! I wouldn't have to go back to England to find a reasonable fascimile— unlike Lilly, knitted caps are not hard to come by anywhere —but I am sentimentally attached to this one. The day I bought it we had an excellent lunch at the sixteenth-century inn where we were staying. After wandering about the delightful village of Yarmouth in the crisp April air, we stopped in to look at the jumble of fishermen's equipment in an ancient, gabled building on the square. It was a day ashore to remember, and I always do at sea when I don my bobble cap.

Waterproof gloves for a cold, rainy day, a warm, soft muffler to go with them, and a particularly beloved sweater are other pleasure-giving bits of clothing that I always take along on our boat. Every first mate will have her own favorites, for reasons of comfort or sentimental attachment, and she shouldn't move without them.

Every first mate who reads this will know by her second cruise, if not her first, the kind, quantity, and quality of clothing that will contribute most to her aid and comfort on a small-boat cruise. Noncrushable shore-going clothes and weather-wise boat clothes will vary in size and shape, as do first mates themselves, but one common denominator is the advisability of thinking ahead a bit, for all hands, if the most fun is to be had from a cruise. Of course, few cruises take first mates out of the range of stores, so that purchases along the way can fill in any clothing gaps that may appear. To have the right jacket or jersey, in wearable condition, at the moment it is wanted, however, is handier than having to buy a reasonable facsimile thereof in Clam Cove the day after tomorrow.

JANE KIRSTEIN

The Duffle-Stuffables

Until we bought Jane's *Skylark*, we sailed on boats without lazarette, locker, drawer, or shelf. We found that we could carry our necessary clothing only in duffle bags, because they are stuffable and have drawstrings to tie them shut and keep them shut when they roll off the bunks. They are also "water-resistant" when moved to the cockpit for the night. We were limited in amount of clothing not by the number of duffle or sail bags we had, but by the number of bunks we had on which to stow them. Usually we sailed on weekends only, and the duffle bags didn't always get unpacked between trips—it helps to have strictly ship's stores to be left aboard at all times!

If you must pack and stow your clothes in duffle bags,

concentrate on knitted materials—cotton, nylon, Orlon, and *wool*. Don't bother with synthetic sweaters—wool is warm even when wet and synthetic sweaters aren't worth their weight or space in the bag as warm clothes. If you can manage a small bag for everyone's underwear and another for everything else, you will prevent a great deal of frustration. A separate bag for foul-weather gear is a must—the gear is almost never dry on a small boat, and it's either the bunk, the deck, or the bag until you can dry it out!

We prefer the parka, or slipover, foul-weather jackets. When you're under water on the bow, the type with snap flaps have a way of becoming leaky. Neither John nor I has a hairdo to get mussed by then, anyway, and the boys haven't enough hair to make any difference. Straight hair, short or long, is an advantage in this case.

For shore wear I found a dress that would pack well in a duffle bag. It was a wild tropical print, second-hand and nylon sheer knit, from Nassau or Miami, I think. Sandals pack flat and make do as dress shoes, and a bangle bracelet or two can pack anywhere. An Irish cardigan can serve as all-purpose woolie and complete the costume.

MARY LEONARD

7 Racing

~~~~~~

A WOMAN WHO IS MARRIED to a sailing enthusiast may very well find herself racing. She may realize that she won't see her man or her boat from May to November (or longer) if she doesn't race, she may have a bloodthirsty streak herself, or she may recognize racing as a good excuse to get away from house and kids.

I had had some racing experience and had concluded that sailboats were for exploring and sunbathing. Having won a race or two, I knew the feeling of Glory, but it was a lot of fuss and bother just to go around in a circle. I had decided that I was a cruising catboat fancier (and I've never wholly given up that idea).

When John bought *Cantie* with the express purpose of racing her, there was only one tack to take. We weren't yet engaged and I knew that if I was going to land that man, I'd better become a racing enthusiast. I've been scraping paint ever since. I've learned a little bit about sailing and "local waters" and a lot about skippers. (My skipper called the boats I used to race "tubs." He rescinded that statement after he sailed one. When he discovered that they'd been designed by Sterling Burgess, he actually apologized! I didn't know that they'd been designed by Burgess, but I'd never *think* of name-dropping like that, anyway!)

Our wedding was planned for the first weekend of June, but it was discovered that the Off Soundings Races were scheduled for that weekend. The wedding was moved to Friday, June 13th. *Cantie* was still in the boatyard when Off Soundings came and went. The wedding, a honeymoon with the black flies on Kennebago Lake, a new apartment,

and a fifty-four-hour work week held up progress further.
The boat was finally launched in August.

Our first race was our second sail on *Cantie*. On Friday
afternoon we set out to sail her from the boatyard in Niantic
to her mooring off the Thames Yacht Club in New London.
There were gale warnings flying as we put out through the
bridges into Niantic Bay, but we'd followed the storm reports closely on the radio and the gale was off Maryland,
not due to hit the New England coast before midnight. The
Ram Island Race might or might not be sailed on Sunday,
but, according to a skipper already frustrated by delays, we
were going to be there!

We drifted through Niantic Bay and didn't get any wind
until we were off Millstone Point, heading east. The breeze
came then, in moderate force, from the northeast. *Cantie*
took off like a bird for Fisher's Island, and we were loving
every minute of it. When the rain hit and the breeze
changed from moderate to strong, Fisher's Island disappeared and the skipper decided we had to reef down—
double. The waves coming aboard had the impact of baseball bats. John gave me the tiller, the last thing I wanted,
and, pointing to the compass, put a knife between his teeth,
found a lashing line, and dropped the mainsail. We roared
along under jib alone. John was bellowing bawdy ballads
(with the knife between his teeth!), no doubt for my benefit,
but I wasn't appreciating them—I was trying to work out my
course of action should he go overboard, and it wasn't coming along very well. Skippers thrive under such conditions,
but mine wasn't so joyful when he started to hoist the mainsail and it caught on a cleat. What the cleat didn't do, the
wind did, so he furled the mainsail, determined that we
would get it patched up before the race. We beat back and
forth, now pumping, now bailing, for what seemed like
hours until I saw a light.

"A boat, a boat!" I cried (hopefully).

"That's New London Ledge," said John.

I kept remarking on it until I got a lecture.

"We're doing fine. *Cantie* can't go any faster. We'll make New London before dark." (It was dark already.) "That's the light on New London Ledge. Isn't she a great boat!"

I didn't contradict him. (Never, never show lack of faith in your skipper's judgment or his boat!) But then there were *two* lights. John didn't see two lights.

"That's the light of New London Ledge," he repeated.

Well, New London Ledge or not, one of the lights was getting closer, and with and above the gale we heard a deep roar very like that of twin diesels. I can't do justice to the next scene. John became aware of the noise and saw a second light. Soon we could see a bow, a beautiful high bow, bow waves flying above crosstrees on a cabin, a big swinging spotlight, and big black numbers: 40516. Considering the visibility and wind velocity, and regardless of the fact that we were the only boat out there, I can't understand how the Coast Guard converged so perfectly on us. You could almost hear the bugles as the hero and heroine were plucked from disaster! (John still says, "She was a sweet boat. We were doing fine.")

But that wasn't the end of it. We couldn't drop sail and lose all control—we would broach. Nor could we come into the wind to meet the patrol boat—we would drift downwind too fast. Boat 40516 didn't seem to understand this; perhaps she thought we were refusing assistance. She wasn't having any of that, and she proceeded to run us down as we sailed on. It was a good chase! With our bowline finally secured, 40516 headed for home with both diesels full speed ahead, nearly ripping our stem out and swamping us. I bailed frantically and clung to the tiller while John gesticulated wildly from the bow. After a bit more misunderstanding,

40516 finally slowed down. *Cantie* was a very wet boat when she was deposited at Burr's Dock. It's no wonder that the New London *Day* described her as "a sailboat found drifting around in Long Island Sound." That they also named the skipper and listed me as "passenger" was inexcusable!

We got the missing clue to the mystery of how the Coast Guard knew of our predicament as soon as our lines were over the pilings. A man on the dock told us that he had been looking out the window from his home on Goshen Point when he sighted a boat in distress. Obviously it was in distress because it was sailing in a northeast gale under jib alone. I smiled, John grimaced. The man had, he explained, immediately called the Coast Guard. I thanked him, John growled. That's another thing about skippers—they don't like Coast Guard rescues, even successful ones.

But all this for a race?

We spent Saturday drying out and mending sails. Sunday was a crisp, clear day with a heavy northwesterly breeze. We made the start of the race, off Groton Long Point, in plenty of time and crossed the line in good position. That was the last I saw of the race. I spent the day in the forepeak as ballast. The seas were rough and ballast forward was supposed to minimize pounding. We had John's former roommate along and he would shout progress reports periodically, always ending with, "You're doing a good job, stay right there." (I was too sore to mutiny anyway.) My miserable deployment must have paid—we won our class. The skipper had trouble looking modest, and the silver bowl convinced me that racing might have its good points.

I continued to race whenever possible, soon making frantic searches for baby-sitters, relatives, or friends to take care of the children every weekend. I hate to remember how unscrupulous I was when securing these people. No one ever knows when a race will end or when the boat will get back to its mooring. When the crew will break away from the yacht club is even more indefinite. I always promised to be back "before suppertime," after leaving instructions about supper in "case of emergency." It fooled people for a little while.

Few small children are found on large boats when racing, but we once took Buzz in a race around Fisher's Island when our expected crew of two backed out at the last minute. About eight, he was big enough to tail a line off the winch and might as well be put to use! The skipper had to set his own spinnaker that day, while I took the helm and Buzz and I handled spinnaker sheets in the cockpit. In spite of heavy going on the windward legs, we did all right with our short crew—we took third place. The skipper was a bit overworked, but he hadn't missed the race!

The Shennecossett Yacht Club in Groton sponsors a Block

Island Weekend that includes a race out, a layover day, and a race back—and kids. We seldom make the Friday race out, but rendezvous with the fleet on Saturday. I was awfully glad to be watching the fleet from shore one Friday evening as it sailed through Watch Hill Passage in a thundersquall— those who didn't get their spinnakers down in time, and some who did, took knockdowns. A good place not to be with three small boys!

I remember a race back that had its ups and downs, too. We were bouncing around the entrance bell off Great Salt Pond, waiting for our starting signal, when two of our three boys lost their breakfast in the cockpit. The third went below to do the same on the cabin sole. I held the two in the cockpit while counting off seconds, and the skipper managed mainsheet, tiller, jib sheets, and running backstays single-handed. *Lola, Valiant,* and *Vega* were well out ahead at the start. After I'd gotten the boys all mopped up and stuffed into bunks and had sloshed the decks down, the wind veered easterly and the spinnakers went up. *Prelude* (designed by Burgess!) didn't do as well downwind as she did on the wind, and we were pretty sure this was going to be just another sail home.

Halfway through the Sound, fog settled in. *Lola, Valiant,* and *Vega* were still out ahead. When we heard the sea buoy off Fisher's Island and the horn on Watch Hill shortly after, we decided to take the spinnaker down and go in under mainsail alone. Watch Hill Passage is seldom a snap under the best of conditions, and Fisher's Island Sound is crowded on a summer Sunday, fog or no fog. The rental rowboats carry neither foghorn nor bell, and the runabouts run about anyway. But at that moment the fog drifted just enough for us to see the top of *Lola's* light-green spinnaker to the east. If she was behind us, we were still in the race—the Genoa jib went up!

Buzz, now recovered, joined me on the bow, and we peered into white fluff, listening for motors, voices, bells, or horns, knowing we were moving too fast. We nearly ran down a rowboat tied to Napatree Bell. But we found the mark off Stonington and a gray shape that turned out to be the Committee boat. They hadn't seen another sailboat; in fact, they never did see many of the others until they turned up at their moorings. A Cap Horn, one of those small, light displacement jobs used to winning 75 per cent of the races she entered, didn't find the finish line and couldn't get back to look for it—she was flushed by the tide into Noank. (We deep-keel sailors like to repeat that story!) John is a very good navigator. The weather, if not his crew, may very well have been to his advantage.

Incidentally, our races with the children have probably been as successful as those without, on the average, but, except in dinghies and small boats, racing is a very rough sport for children and they are apt to make racing life pretty complicated for the first mate, too.

Standing rivalries between boats are common and tend to make crews very bloodthirsty (but sharp). Everyone on our end of the Sound was out to beat Ed, a sailing master who knows every pebble and back eddy from New York to Boston. For fourteen years we traded places and races with him and watched him like a hawk, trying to learn every secret he knew. It was even more personal with a boat called *Valiant* because our boats were very similar and her skipper was a card. Paul did everything he could think of to shake us up, bluff us out, or distract us. He would quote imaginary rules every time he got within hailing distance; he would point out ripped seams (which weren't there) in the mainsail; he would tell us how mossy the bottom was every time we rolled it out. I remember John leaping into the cockpit from the deck one time when Paul called, "The helmsman must be in the cockpit at all times. Number 18a, page 12." It sounded good. We haven't lived that one down, but we haven't trusted the man since. We could *sink* before we'd dodge any rocks Paul pointed out!

A pair of 6-meters from New London had an even fiercer rivalry. Buckets were tied to rudders, personal duels would beat off to sea while the rest of the fleet ran by, spinnakers would stay on until the spreaders were in the water. There was a case of beer traded back and forth between those boats for five years. Not the same case, of course.

Our interest in racing has involved us in a small sailing club founded by a young engineer from Maine who wanted to race dinghies with his friends without a lot of folderol. He found a fleet of International 12-foot dinghies for sale and bought the lot. Maynard is a salesman and a Yankee traditionalist—he sold all the boats to his neighbors and registered the neighborly association with *Lloyd's Register of American Yachts* as the Noank Sailing Club.

At the first meeting dues were determined by dividing the cost of *Lloyd's Register,* with flag plates, among the members. Wives could be full voting members and could hold office (at least secretary and treasurer), and new members were to be invited with the unanimous approval of the club; membership was not to exceed the number of people an average living room could hold. The crew of each dinghy was limited to two—presumably man and wife. Since the crews didn't match in weight, compensatory sandbags were discussed, but that smacked too much of formality and technicality and at the last meeting it was voted that "anyone's wife is preferable to a sandbag."

Interest is keen in the spring and races often end with family cookouts. Most of the members have "big" boats that are likely to be cruising or racing on summer weekends, when dinghy racing becomes sporadic. There is another big push in the fall. The club was once described by a local newspaper as a "frostbite fleet," but that epithet was flattering. Corinthians we may be, but not Spartans! As soon as skim ice forms on the edges of West Cove (in Mouse Island Sound), we become a purely social club. (Frostbite racing, by the way, is best survived in a wet suit!)

Winter activities range from dancing lessons to birthday parties, and meetings may be called by any member for any reason at any time. These are often covered-dish suppers at which there may or may not be any official business discussed. One social gathering turned into an official meeting when the men decided that any respectable yacht club should sponsor an annual invitation race and that the most interesting race would be a single-handed one for boats rated over 18 feet. Although we were skeptical of the outcome, we women readily agreed to such a race—we were curious to see how many Slocums and Chichesters would turn up. If we had thought our husbands would be the only salts, we were mistaken: almost every skipper we knew was a Slocum at heart, and the races have been a surprising success. (It's fascinating to see your husband horse a 40-foot yawl around when you can still hear "Sheet it in, sheet it in!" ringing in your ears.)

We take a provincial pleasure in challenging Fisher's Island with a fleet of boats from the Continent and they love to lick us. We're out to beat *Diogenes* and take the half model of *Gesture* from Watch Hill, and *Skylark* should have her name on the Commodore's Trophy, but, truth be told, your chief racing rivals will likely become your best cruising companions. Just mention to Joe that you hope to be in Hamburg Cove on Friday night and you'll probably find half the racing boats in the area there with you.

We cruise often with *Volunteer*. The boats are about equal in size (please forget our rating, which we do, of course, when cruising) and *Volunteer's* crew outnumbers ours by one two-year-old boy. The rest of the crew matches in ages and stages. We race from port to port, naturally. When we arrive at our destination, we politely anchor away from the rest of the fleet, which is already assembled or about to arrive, and put all kids on one boat and all adults on the other. (We raft with *Volunteer*—we can't do each other much damage!) The next day there are dinghy races of some sort for children and men, and the children end up all over the rest of the boats in the fleet, being fed on each one. (I always hope this means that I won't have to get lunch—but it never does.) We race back home, too—unofficially. (When *Volunteer's* spinnaker goes up, so does *Skylark's!*)

You may be interested in the anatomy of a handicap fleet, which is made up of boats of different sizes and speeds. The boast are "rated," or given time allowances, based on size, displacement, and sail area, figured by a complicated formula I've never understood. What it amounts to is that the big, fast guy has to allow the little, slow (maybe) guy plenty of time. You race the clock, not the boats. Thus the boats supposedly begin evenly and the results of the race are determined by weather, skill, and luck—they say. I'm skeptical. *Skylark* is big, fat, heavy, and tall, and is penalized. We haven't come close to beating our rating once. We keep hoping for a big dose of luck!

A handicap fleet may sail as one class or group, or may be divided according to size into several classes. *Skylark*, being basically a cruising boat and large, is a Class A boat, but she is close to scratch boat in the fleet when we sail as one class, worse luck! (The scratch boat is given no handicap or time allowance—it's much better to be bottom dog on the pile.) *Prelude* was a Class C boat because she was a pure racer. Class B is a cruising-racing combination (midget ocean racers, for example). There may be more classes or subdivisions of classes.

A racing start is a wild business with milling boats jockeying for favored positions, guns going off, and flags running up and down the mast of the Committee boat. Each class is given a warning, preparatory, and starting signal at five-minute intervals. At the shot, a flag signifying which signal has been fired is raised on the Committee boat. The starting gun for one class may be the warning gun for the next class. At the warning signal, boats in the class affected must stop engines so that no one will be able to breeze across the line on momentum from a recently stopped engine. (That's a protestable offense and few skippers would dare accuse another skipper of such a thing, but we've seen it done.) Stopwatches are set at the warning, reset at the preparatory signal, and clutched tightly until the start—the last minute is counted off by seconds, usually in a loud panicky voice. Any boat that crosses the starting line before the gun goes off must return, keeping clear of all other boats, to cross the line again, or take a thirty-minute penalty. We have theorized that it would be possible to stop engine at 5:50, cross the line at 6:00 for a 9:00 A.M. start, take a thirty-minute penalty, and make out like a bandit. Unfortunately, the line isn't set that early and all boats must identify themselves to the Committee boat prior to the start of the race. Starts are confusing and that's where first mates can be of real assistance.

A sailboat race is, as my skipper defines it, an exercise in decision making. A skipper must weigh and calculate weather, position, navigation, current, and time information. Even the best skipper can use another set of eyes and ears. Watch the flags and watch the clock for him. Watch buoys, boats, and tide. When action isn't necessary somewhere else, check your position and time allowance against the threats in the fleet. Put the stopwatch on them at the marks—the skipper might decide to put up a bigger jib!

You will have to psych your skipper to know exactly what he expects of you (if you dare to find out). He may be very serious and "run a tight ship," or he may be relaxed about who does what (but not when!). Remember the old game

where you categorized your friends as Bird, Horse, or
Muffin? (My skipper considers that the best psychology test
ever invented.) Your skipper will psych you, too, and put
you into one of these categories, at least to start. If you are
to be trusted as eyes and ears, you are Bird (sense-perceptive
extrovert). If you are to haul anchors and sheet Genoas, you
are Horse (intuitive extrovert—John says I am a pure type).
If you are to "keep the hell out of the way," you are Muffin
(intuitive introvert) and should, temporarily, open beer cans.
Very soon, if you show any aptitude for your first assign-
ment, you will become the Compleat Bird-Horse-Muffin.

All of Jane's advice to first mates applies as well to racing
mates. Take those jobs you can handle. Any skills you can
develop will add speed to the boat. Do learn the parts of the
boat—if you drop the mainsail when asked to sheet the jib,
you're likely to hear some pretty salty expressions!

Here's one rule: Equipment should be stowed in its
proper place and returned to that place immediately after
use. And another: Sails should be bagged, stopped, or rolled
from foot to peak and stowed as soon as they come down,
ready to be reset the minute they are needed again. These
are jobs a woman can do very well and a man hardly at all!
Putting things away neatly folded just isn't in his nature.

Women are good at sorting and coiling lines, sheeting
small jibs and walking big ones around the bow, and standing bow watch. They are good at finding things below and
passing out lunch or beer. They can hoist sails, drop sails,
furl sails, and find sails. They can take the helm happily,
after a bit of practice, less happily at a critical point when
things are tight. There are a lot of jobs I approach willingly,
if with trepidation, but the one I try hard to avoid is setting
up the spinnaker—even with expert help. (But I can *pack* a
mean spinnaker!) I admit to a mental block in the spinnaker
department. I've never seen a more temperamental sail, nor

have I heard as rough language used in connection with any other object on the boat. When it comes time to set up the spinnaker, it's a good idea to be busy sorting lines or finding charts. You needn't carry this subterfuge to the point of insubordintion—if you foul up a spinnaker once, you can be sure the skipper will there after have an expert aboard or will set it himself!

The start of the fall Off Soundings, off New London, in 1966, was—oh, horrible thought and beautiful sight—a spinnaker start. The wind was going to be right behind us as we crossed the line. (A start in a fleet of 150 milling boats is tense enough without mad scrambles on the foredeck and temperamental sails!) We were a crew of five on *Skylark*. Marcia and I had painstakingly packed the spinnaker en route to New London. Just to make sure it was perfect, we'd packed it twice. Ray and Dave, the spinnaker expert, set up the sheet, guy, pole, halliard, topping lift, and downhaul under the eagle eye of the skipper. Marcia and I took stations by the sheet and the guy in the cockpit. As the gun went off, the spinnaker broke out and filled (shudder) in two sections—it was hourglassed! The men on the bow tried frantically to twist or shake it open, but the wind was too strong and down it had to come. There was a horrible noise from the direction of the helm (where John was). Marcia and I tried to get the sail into the cockpit and failed—we were fighting a wild thing and before we subdued it, it was in the water. The skipper was fighting the helm, trying to stay clear of other boats, and growling like a tiger. The flapping sail, now a sea anchor, made *Skylark* almost unmanageable. Dave and Ray at one end, Marcia and I on the other, finally got the thing aboard, losing skin on knees and knuckles in the process. The spinnaker was set flying the second time and, for some happy reason, it went up beautifully. But we'd lost at least ten minutes and Marcia and I had lost any repu-

tation we might have had (or earned a new one!). I say to this day, though, that the men crossed the sheet and the guy!

Bow watch is a particularly good job for a woman. As she may not have the brawn needed to winch in the Number-One Genny (Genoa), she's the perfect one to watch out below it. The sail is big and powerful, cut close to the deck, and reaches far aft, blinding the helmsman to vessels and hazards off his lee bow. We were not quite run down by *Tomadrus* one day because we had a bow watch who yelled.

In the first of the Block Island Week races last summer, in a heavy southerly wind, we watched the boats beating up the shore with big Genoas set. There were several collisions, two of which we watched with horror. A Columbia 50 on starboard tack was rammed amidship by a boat on port tack. Five minutes later the identical accident happened to two different boats, and a Cal 40, rammed at the chain plates, lost her mast. Any skipper will relinquish right of way if he knows a collision is imminent. Make sure he knows or frightening things can happen!

In the Fisher's Island Race when Buzz was our crew, *Valhalla*, a fiber-glass sloop, was rammed by a Challenger yawl clawing off the shore. The collision was so tremendous, and the cracks in the deck and hull so gaping, that the skipper and crew of *Valhalla* leaped aboard the other boat, thinking that their ship was about to sink. But *Valhalla* didn't sink, the crew went back aboard, and she continued on to win the race. (It raised an interesting question: Can a boat that has been abandoned win a race? She did.) The damage, though, was so extensive that the boat was declared

a total loss by her insurance company. So, Birds, arise and use your eyes and ears for your skipper!

A crew is skipper's choice, but if a racing mate is consulted, she might consider a few things. First, too many skippers are worse than too many cooks. We took two other skippers along on *Cantie* during one race, and there was a three-way split at every mark and on every tack. We made the same mistake on *Prelude* when we took a crackerjack skipper and his wife along on a race they were used to winning. That time it was two against two, but they were our guests; we dropped out of the race when they repeatedly assured us that it was more sensible to go on home than to sail on toward a time limit we couldn't make. We had never before dropped out of a race—nor have we since.

Skippers *should* make excellent crew, but they tend to have trouble keeping their opinions to themselves in situations in which they are used to taking charge! A sailing enthusiast who doesn't own his own boat is usually a good bet. One always looks for the experienced sailor, but one of our best crew members was totally inexperienced—(he'd never been on a sailboat and didn't even know whether he was prone to seasickness. He was slight and he wore thick glasses, but he was congenial and eager. This boy turned out to be a natural. Tell him something once, he had it. He loved games and worked with a will throughout the day. He had told us that he'd never sailed before, but he hadn't been a bit hesitant about expressing his desire to go. Novices who are willing and eager are far superior to the experienced with braggadocio! The braggarts we've taken along have all been disappointing. Would you believe it, they're lazy! They almost never know anything about spinnakers either, which *I* resent.

It's very important to keep up the morale of the crew.

Don't distract them by wearing a bikini early in the day.
The very best thing for morale is to win the race. Second
best is to beat your biggest rival. If you can't do either, at
least overtake a few boats. If none of these things seem to
be going for you, put on the bikini. It might be good for
your morale and will very likely brighten up the crew, unless
it's predominantly female. And even then it may. I have a
bikini that the skipper kindly picked out in Nantucket. I
wouldn't wear it within ten miles of anyone but that skipper,
but if I did, it would certainly cheer up most women in the
fleet! If you can wear a bikini to advantage, it will distract
other crews and, hopefully, skippers. A racing skipper can't
be distracted from his business by anything less than a
bikini. (I mean more than a bikini. Less would work, too.)
You might overtake boats, beat rivals, and win the race if
the boats out in front aren't already out of binnocular range!

Treat your crew like children; it makes them happy or at
least keeps the status quo. Open their beer cans for them.
Give them homemade cookies (baked before the race, probably at midnight). Offer them food off and on all day. Find
their sweaters for them. Offer them your foul-weather gear
if they forgot theirs and hope they'll refuse it. (The odds are
generally in your favor.) Never say "Yes, sir" to your own
skipper—he'll call it insubordination!

Lack of wind often breaks down morale, but there's a
nine out of ten chance of beating that situation. When
caught in a dead calm, take off your sweater. A cold wind
will spring up immediately. Don't put your sweater back
on until the boat is overpowered—the wind will drop when
you do.

It's also demoralizing to have a mechanical breakdown
in the galley. In the Halifax Race several years ago the only
can opener on board *Ondine* fell apart. It's a tedious business to open ten cans each meal with a marlin spike; it can

be done, but variety and size of portions tend to diminish. On *Skylark* we carry four different types of can opener with a preponderance of the beer-can type, a suitable substitute for the marlin spike in many cases.

Clothing for racing is no problem at all. You can almost always go from your front door, through the day, and on to the after-race party in foul-weather gear and boat shoes. (Rest assured that those gals in the silk shifts and heels haven't been closer to a boat than the yacht club dock.) Dry pants and a sweater are nice, but they don't have to be your best—you'll have to get back to the boat or get the boat back to its moorings, and in the process someone is bound to fall out of the dinghy. If it isn't you, you'll get wet anyway.

Whistles, Bugles, and Daisys, those great cocktail snacks, and cheese are of prime importance when provisioning for a day or weekend race. I understand, too, that you can get to Bermuda on not much else. You might add apples to balance out the cheese and candy bars for dessert. You cannot overlook these items. If there are any left over at the end of the race, it must have been a close one all the way! Since I'm not happy in a bouncing galley for more than the time necessary to find the Whistles or five cans of beer, and the skipper insists on lunch whether we have time to eat it or not, I pack sandwiches late the night before, while burning the cookies.

We often don't get to the sandwiches until halfway through the party at the club—just so we can get through the other half of the party. We've saved more than one skipper from disgrace by sharing our sandwiches.

Skylark is seldom stocked with hard liquor, and few skippers tolerate its use while under way, but we stock a lot of beer and a few cans of soda. I conveniently forget the number of cases of beer carried aboard for the '66 Off Soundings Races, but if it hadn't been in cans, I would have thought we had a leak in the barrel. Beer "evaporates" most quickly in calm weather. In calm weather you will need lunch, Whistles, Bugles, Daisys, cheese, and apples, too. Don't forget cigars for the skipper.

My skipper advises that the subject of ocean racing be left out of this book completely, for the simple reason that no novice should consider it. Dinghy racing, frostbiting and day-racing, which are exciting but seldom dangerous, and overnight or weekend races when you have a bit of experience, are fine, but few women brave the ocean race and those who do are competent sailors of great cruising and racing experience, generally having been born with a mainsheet in their teeth. Many skippers feel that even these women shouldn't be encouraged! Much better to fly BOAC and meet the boat at the Royal Yacht Club.

You may, however, find yourself provisioning for an ocean race. Everything comes in cans, but cans add weight. Consider the instant and concentrated dry foods—the ice will run out in a few days anyway. Stuff every nook and cranny with instant orange juice, coffee, tea, bouillon, soup, rice, potatoes, noodles, oatmeal, powdered milk, powdered cream, freeze-dried meats and dinners, and dried casseroles. (Provide the cook with a general index, too!) The only problem with these foods is that they require water, so make sure the skipper fills the water tanks to capacity. So that the crew won't complain about instant everything, stock meats and vegetables enough to last as long as the ice does, but make them quick to prepare. Apples and eggs are hardy and will keep in any cool place. Bread may or may not remain fresh, depending mostly on the temperature. Hardtack is the traditional substitute, but crackers will do, to go with cheese, peanut butter, and jelly. Then if the cook turns out to be allergic to heaving galleys, the skipper can djin up something.

Since the crew will be standing watches and "hot bunk-ing," forget the ship's linens and fill that space with more stores, the crew's clothing, the third and fourth spinnakers, or the emergency life raft. Replace the old flare kit with a new one and make sure the first-aid kit is well stocked. Then make your plane reservations.

Just to show that racing can be very funny, and often ridiculous, I've a volley of parting tales. In the Yale-Harvard 100th Anniversary Regatta Handicap Race, sponsored by the New London Chamber of Commerce, Classes A and B, which had started twenty and ten minutes ahead of us, piled up together in a lack of wind on the fairway buoy. They found themselves entangled in a technical and tacti-cal problem of the first order. They tangled with each other and fouled the mark. Booms were caught in neighbors' rig-gings. People pushed at boats and dodged spinnaker poles. There weren't enough arms and legs in the fleet to get spin-nakers down. *Galatea,* the scratch boat, had been hit on all quarters and was jammed against the buoy. The aces of Class C, who had carried the wind a little longer, piled right into the middle of the heap. To us, it was a beautiful sight. Those of us who arrived at the convention late and rounded the fleet instead of the mark made out like minks! It took some time to untangle that mess even after the wind came up. If the Race Committee had seen that tangle, they would have resigned on the spot!

Then there was the time when the wind died just as we crossed the finish line and we beat the scratch boat, a few yards behind us, by thirty-seven minutes.

Two of the better flukes of nature, as far as we were concerned—but they don't always go our way!

The Ram Island Race in '65 was sailed on a perfect day. The breeze was just right; not too strong, not too light, and steady. It looked like a good tight race with no time for lunch. *Prelude* creamed along not far behind Class A. We were pleased with ourselves. When the boats ahead got to Race Rock, they started milling around, slipping sideways, going backwards, and turning full circle. We'd never seen a tide rip yet that *Prelude* couldn't work her way through. We'd show those guys a boat! It was at the same spot a year or two before that we had passed *Barlovento* while three hands searched for her Genoa sheet. We hit The Race "like it was a stone wall!" There was a mad scramble for the anchor, the Yachtsman, not the Danforth, while we slipped at 4 knots from Race Point buoy toward Niantic under full sail. Our buddies (rivals in any other circumstance) came along one by one and we made loud noises as anchors dragged by and boats disappeared over the horizon. *Valiant* ended up right alongside and there was a contest to see who could hold out the longest. We won. When we last saw *Valiant*, she was headed for Millstone Point stern first. *Audax* was the only boat to sail through and she never made Wilderness Point. *Limbo* went through, too, but on a counter current with a plastic garbage can tied to her bow. She never made Wilderness Point, either. And there were nine engraved trophies . . . and no winners.

The Off Soundings fleet traditionally rendezvous at Burr's Dock in New London before the weekend races. On Thursday night before the start, some 200 boats gather along the pier to sniff around, pick up crew, stock ice and water, and plot the next day's strategy. A few boats never make the start. Some crews turn in early, while others spend the night stocking ice and alcohol. What, exactly, were the duties of the crew of *Blackguard* (I'll call her) on the eve of Off Soundings several years ago I don't know, but her skipper was busy surveying competitors and stocking up. Friday morning dawned late, wet and hazy, and the fleet put out to make a 9:00 A.M. start, *Blackguard* with them. Her skipper's last thought the night before had been to set two alarm clocks and leave a call with the mate. *Blackguard* started on schedule but soon found herself in great banks of fog. One minute you could see a boat next to you, the next minute you couldn't. When yardarms and square topsails loomed above him, no hull visible, the skipper took evasive action and wondered about the Flying Dutchman. When a gray shape glided by, the skipper took evasive action again and wondered about Moby Dick and whether whales were common in Long Island Sound. When black snakes descended from the clouds above her, *Blackguard* came about and headed for home. It was decided by those who heard the story that *Blackguard* was a victim of Burr-sitis; too much time alongside Burr's Dock. One expects to see the Coast Guard cutter *Eagle* setting out through The Race, submarines coming down the Thames River, and the Goodyear blimp hanging low over the fleet in the fog—ordinarily.

Your husband's company, other companionship and resulting activities, and competition all make racing exciting and attractive. Add to these just plain good outdoor exercise. There are few times on a racing boat when the skipper won't keep you moving, even in a dead calm. ("Check that jib." "How's the tide running there?" "What's *Valiant* doing?" "Sheet in the jib." "Break out the ballooner." "Pack the spinnaker." "Where's lunch?")

Racing also serves the purpose of being a useful winter topic of conversation. When the boat is snowbound in the yard, skippers and mates love to rehash the past season. Trading wild racing stories (and racing stories are always wild) is almost as absorbing as racing itself. Just the other night we were arguing with the men about . . .

MARY LEONARD

8

Dangers, Emergencies, and the First Mate

~~~~~~

W**HAT SAILOR HASN'T BEEN ASKED**, at one time or another, "Aren't you afraid to go to sea in a small boat like that?" And what sailor hasn't made vague dates with landlubber friends to take them sailing "someday"? When the person who asked the above question is the same one who got the vague invitation, and the "someday" is today, a sailor prays for light winds.

Small-craft warnings flew from the flagstaff of our neighboring yacht club when our "today" arrived. Our anemometer clocked the wind at 20 knots, gusting to 30, out of the northwest. We weren't worried about Bill. Neither he nor Ellie had ever been on anything smaller than an ocean liner before, but Bill was just naturally a salty type. Not Ellie. She had asked the aren't-you-afraid question. But, intrepid sailor or not, we loved her and wanted her to enjoy her sailing day.

We broke them in easy, with as much even-keel running before the wind as possible. But, inevitably, it came time to beat back to windward, and the relaxed smiles on Ellie and Bill's faces fled as *Shag* heeled sharply to the wind. Bill rallied quickly and soon took the helm for a quick lesson in working to windward, but Ellie clearly was not happy.

Despite urgings to brace herself on the companionway or the mainsheet traveler, she clung with both hands to the windward coaming and never took her eyes off the water rushing over the lee rail. Suddenly I remembered *my* first beat to windward, and my only half-joking demand that the skipper give me a scientific explanation for his statement that sailboats with a keel would heel (or lean with the wind) but could not tip over completely. This seemed a good time to reminisce a bit, out loud.

Sailboats are designed, George had said, to lie over on their sides when sailed close to the wind, wetting the maximum amount of their waterline length in order to attain maximum speed. He had said that the simplest parallel example in the average person's experience is the way in which the child's toy with a rounded, weighted base, such as a toy soldier or Donald Duck, will refuse to stay down, no matter how hard it is pushed. These, too, were designed to snap back to "an even keel" when the pressure is off their superstructures. Sometimes a sailboat just can't take all the pressure it's getting, which is more than it was designed to take, so something has to give. A deck fitting pulls out, a sail rips, or even a mast will snap, but the boat stays right side up—not over. All this was true of keelboats only, of course, I said, and a keel boat was what we were on.

Ellie's fear of capsizing is one of the "imagined" dangers of going to sea in a small boat, and it is shared by more women new to sailing than old salts might think. There are also deeper-seated, "real" fears that gnaw at women, most of which come under the heading of "fear of the unknown."

"Man overboard," for instance, or child, or even dog overboard is a frightening phrase. What if it's "captain overboard"? What should a first mate do? What if someone aboard breaks a leg or an arm, or is in any way disabled? What if it is the captain himself? Storms and fog pose problems for the first mate, as well as for the captain. And fire—perhaps the biggest frightener of all since it is the greatest cause of loss of life at sea—how do you cope with a blazing cabin?

These may be unspoken fears, and some first mates may have completely different ones, but whatever her fears are, they are best brought out in the open. The more she knows

of potential dangers, and what her role can most helpfully be should they arise, the less likely she is to worry. Women like to be surprised on birthdays and anniversaries, but not in emergencies at sea. Family-type cruises seldom come anywhere near an emergency situation, but what a first mate doesn't know can hurt not only her, but the captain—especially if he's the "man overboard."

One day on Buzzard's Bay, Massachusetts, we watched with interest, and then growing concern, a boat under full sail. It had been abeam of us for some time, some 500 yards off, when it began to behave erratically—jibing, then shooting into the wind, then jibing again, and all in a rather sloppy fashion. The wind was piping close to 20 knots, in

true Buzzard's Bay tradition on hot summer afternoons, and
we decided that no one would be playing around with it as
that captain was unless he was in trouble. Changing course,
we headed for the "distressed vessel," but within a few
minutes, called off our rescue mission; through the binoculars George had identified the boat and knew it to be one
of the best-sailed craft on the Eastern seaboard. We could
see clearly, now, that a woman was at the helm, a man
standing beside her in the cockpit, and a small person was
leaning over the side with a boathook in his hand, trying to
retrieve a floating cushion. Obviously, a "man overboard"
drill was in session, and the first mate was at the black-
board. The incident was a good reminder to us. We hadn't
had a "man overboard" drill in several years. What, my
captain asked me as we went back on course, should be the
first concern of the man in the water?

1. Don't panic.
2. Grab the life preservers and floating cushions that have
   been thrown over.
3. Shed heavy gear, such as boots and jacket, if possible.
4. Beware of the propeller when the boat comes back to
   pick you up, and when within plucking-out distance,
   hold up an arm.

Procedure for the man, or first mate, left on board is much
less instinctive than the above. True, his or her first reaction
—get the man back on the boat—is pretty instinctive, but
how best to turn the boat in its tracks, come up to the person in the water without running him down, and stop near
enough and in time to rescue him before he panics, tires, or
becomes numb takes planning and practice. There are dif-
ferences of opinion among sailors as to the best way to
handle a man-overboard situation, just as there are varia-

tions among boats as to ease of handling, so each captain will know best how to drill his mate. I have been taught as follows:

1. Throw over the life preservers (two are always attached to the after lifelines), as well as the buoyant cushions from the cockpit.
2. Jibe, and then shoot into the wind next to the man overboard.
3. Turn on the motor if it is needed to maneuver further.

The captain thinks I can take it from there, if I have to, and because we have practiced, I think he's right. I might add that the greatest number of man-overboard incidents happen right at the mooring, either because of overreaching for the buoy or overcelebration at the end of a fine sailing day. A helping hand is all that is needed in these cases.

The fear of a medical emergency at sea nags at many first mates, especially if there are children aboard. Minimum precautions against unforeseeable ills are a well-supplied medicine chest and a book on first aid. With those, a first mate who has done her homework need not worry. "Homework" means that the first mate should not only have a first-aid textbook on board—preferably a recent one put out by the Red Cross—but that she should have read it several times. A well-supplied medicine chest includes both a standard first aid kit and an additional supply of drugs, recommended and prescribed by the family doctor. Our doctor, who is a sailor too, recommended the following "bare essentials" for *Shag:*

> *Demerol tablets, for severe pain*
> *Achromycin, for serious infections*
> *Opium drops, for diarrhea*
> *Anti-nausea pills, for seasickness*

We add our own favorite remedies, such as aspirin, Sloane's liniment, mineral oil, and calamine lotion, as will every skipper and first mate. Boats with special medical problems, such as crew members with diabetes, heart ailments, or some other chronic disease, will, of course, have an adequate supply of the proper medication aboard.

There is no "proper medication" for seasickness—if Bonamine or the like doesn't work—except getting the patient to dry land. Prevention is the best policy when the sea is rough. Give him the pills early. Keep him on deck, away from stuffy cabins, and urge him to nibble at a dry biscuit. If everything fails, wherever he is most comfortable is the place for him to be. If it's necessary to clean up after him, a water and baking soda solution is the best cleanser of all.

Most medical emergencies aboard a small boat are minor, and many of them are on someone else's boat. As marine tradition makes everyone's emergency within hailing distance one's own, however, some first mates may have to bind up "strange" wounds, as I did one day in Chesapeake Bay.

We were anchored in the yacht harbor at Gibson Island, trying, against odds, to hear the broadcast of a baseball game. Two boys were playing a noisy game of "bother-the-grownups-on-the-neighboring-boat" (us) by throwing dry bread at the seagulls and hitting us, shooting off leftover fireworks, and just generally acting up. We had protectively turned our backs to them and were pleased that our indifference had seemed to work after a while; quiet had settled in. Then we heard a high-voiced, tentative "Hey!" Expecting more impishness, we turned to see one white-faced boy standing in the cockpit beside the other, who had both hands clamped over his face, with blood dripping copiously between his fingers. We hesitated only a minute—thinking it might be some gruesome joke—and then sprang for the first-aid kit and jumped into the dinghy. The injury was less serious than it appeared; the child had cut his lip deeply, but a gauze pad smeared with an anesthetizing disinfectant cream from the first aid kit soon diminished the flow of blood. Nevertheless, a few stitches might be in order, we felt, so we bundled the two subdued children into the dinghy and headed for shore.

"We'll call your mother," I said. "She may want to take you to a doctor."

"We don't have a mother," the uninjured lad said. "We haven't had one since we were little."

Sobered ourselves now, we turned the boys over to the yacht club steward, who knew them very well. He would find their dad, he said. He was just over there, making a phone call.

Few cruises have to deal with even a cut lip, but storms and fog are bound to engulf a boat sometime, somewhere, and fear of them is not unreasonable. The sea is a worthy antagonist at all times, and wise captains have a proper respect for it. But with a seaworthy boat under her, and a competent skipper at the helm, a first mate need not worry.

Storms of impressive size have little chance of sneaking up on sailors nowadays. Hurricanes rate headlines and the weather bureau keeps every erratic move they make under a taut watch. The sailor who hasn't battened down everything he is supposed to batten down as the eye of a hurricane nears his anchorage is either deaf or blind.

Less imposing storms also get their due share of attention. We have our little joke about the Coast Guard's small-craft warnings on summer weekends in Long Island Sound; let anything over a 10-knot wind be forecast, and up goes the red warning pennant in a vain attempt to cut down on traffic on the water. We recognize that our joke is a poor little one, however, because the hard-working Coast Guard

is bedeviled with more yelps for help on a lovely sunny
Sunday from powerboats that have run out of gas than they
can handle, or should be expected to.

But, try as it will, the weather bureau cannot predict
every local thundersquall, particularly on hot and humid
summer days when anything can happen. Sailors who learn
to be their own weathermen, who know how to read the
portents in low-lying cumulous clouds with dark, hard-
edged bottoms and get the storm message of a sudden,
marked wind shift don't need the Coast Guard to tell them
it is time to bring in the spinnaker and reach for the foul-
weather gear. A first mate who bones up on weather lore
not only lends aid and comfort to her captain, she also has
fun. Clouds will no longer be just "fleecy" or "puffy," but
fairweather clouds or thunderheads. She will be able to
match her weather hunches with the captain, and he will
welcome that.

The least a first mate can do in weather forecasting, and
the most immediately conclusive, is to turn on the radio.
If there is a great deal of static, she knows she has tuned in
on an approaching thunderstorm. She may then discuss
with the captain the possibility of heading into a protected
harbor, or she may "prepare for the worst."

Preparing for the worst, on our boat, begins with handing
up foul-weather gear to the captain and putting on my own.
Then I close all the portholes, batten down the cabin by
snugging bunk cushions around loose objects on the shelves
above the bunks and trying to make sure that everything
that might spill or break is secured. The teakettle goes into
the sink, the captain's pipes into his top drawer, and I go on
deck, closing the hatch cover after me. There I usually take
the helm while the captain works with the sails. Once the
jib is down, I leave the helm briefly and go forward to help
him furl the whipping piece of cloth, if he needs me. His

foredeck work done, the captain takes the helm and I move to a spot in the cockpit where I can keep my back to the wind and the rain. Though I am still ready for anything, my duties from then on are mostly limited to lighting dry cigarettes for the captain, staying calm, and staying put.

Staying calm in a storm is no longer the conscious effort that it was for me at the beginning of my sailing career. I now believe the captain when he says that, for all its sound and fury, a thunderstorm is little or no threat to a seaworthy boat. I know that when we set sail the boat is in the best possible shape. I can't expect him to have X-ray eyes and to detect every hidden weak spot in the rigging, but like any sailor who knows and cares for his boat, he has checked and repaired all the potential troublemakers he knows about. He is like a doctor who practices preventive medicine.

Staying cheerful in a storm may not be a first mate's duty, but it is certainly a comfort to her captain. He is miserable enough himself, sitting there with rain pelting into his face and leaking from time to time under his foul-weather gear. The captain didn't go out looking for a storm just to make you unhappy. Have a cigarette, and light him a dry one. You may even find you are enjoying yourself, once you realize there is little to fear in a storm. A storm can be beautiful, and it's always memorable. You and your captain will be talking about it on many a long winter's evening to come.

I find it difficult to be a Pollyanna about fog. Give me tall seas, high winds, and a downpour any day, rather than a peasouper. I have listened, unsympathetically, to sailors who find fog no problem—who rather like it, in fact. "Mysterious, lovely, a challenge," etc. I differ. Fog, to me, is the enemy.

There are not many fog-loving sailors. A layover day in a

fog-bound harbor may seem to be a waste of time on a short, summer cruise, but wise sailors reluctantly prefer it to running blindly in fog. Noise-making aids to navigation are generously scattered about traditionally foggy areas, such as the New England coast, but they still have to be found to be heard, and sometimes they hide.

Certain standard combinations of weather conditions in each sailing area are fog-makers. On the Northeastern seaboard of the United States, a few days of a heat wave on land combined with a southerly or southwesterly wind is a sure-fog situation. In the normal summer weather cycle the wind shifts before long into the northwest and the world comes into sharp focus again, and in the normal summer cruising schedule on our boat we wait for this change, as most cruising boats do. Sometimes, however, fog is as un-

predictable and localized as a summer storm, and with the best will in the world a captain cannot avoid it. Sometimes, fog or no, a plane must be met the day after tomorrow, a job resumed, or a baby-sitter relieved, and the boat must go on. There are times, too, when a captain who knows his local weather picture is rightly convinced that there is a better than even chance that the fog will soon burn off, or that he is sitting squarely in the middle of his own private fog bank.

A first mate might as well face it. She will be shipmates with fog from time to time, whatever the reason. She can learn to live comfortably with fog, if not to like it, if her captain is a responsible man, a man who has respect for fog and its hazards, and acts accordingly. A first mate can also learn to be of great help to him.

On our boat stopwatches, protractors, pencils, dividers, charts, foghorns, and patent logs come pouring out of the cabin when a fog descends. If we are lucky enough to have a buoy still in sight, the captain takes off a compass course from it to the next buoy—hopefully a whistler or a bell buoy—taking into consideration the probable drift caused by the current. He then trails the patent log from the stern of the boat, hands me the stopwatch and the foghorn, takes the helm, and smiles at me.

"In one hour and three minutes," he says, "we should hear old Hen and Chickens," or Great Wass, as the case may be. We sail at such a time, if there is any favorable wind at all, because it is easier to hear a horn or a bell when the motor isn't running. If we are under power, we turn off the motor just before we should hear the buoy, and drift until we do. Fog is sly, and not only blocks out the sight of buoys sometimes until they are a boat-length away, but can also muffle the sound. (Once, groping our way into Northeast Harbor, Maine, we had decided that, despite all possible careful calculations, we had failed to run down the huge horn on Bear Island and were lost, when its blast, about 50 yards away, nearly knocked us out of the cockpit.) The captain takes the helm in fog and keeps me so busy working the foghorn, checking the stopwatch, and keeping a taut watch for buoys or other boats that I have little time to brood. His carefully thought out system for desensitizing me to fog has broken down only once—the very first time we tried it—and even then, only momentarily.

We were on the third day of our first summer cruise after our marriage, and so far the weather had been unpleasant but not dreadful. Rain and wispy fog had followed us up the coast from Mamaroneck, New York, to our anchorage at Sachem's Head, Connecticut, but the winds were good and visibility had been no real problem. Then came the dawn on the third morning, and the fog—oh so thick. We dillydallied about our morning tasks, wondering if we should take our Newfoundland dog ashore for a second walk, when out of the soup at the harbor entrance ghosted an incoming sailboat. As any skipper would, George asked about "conditions out there," and to our vast surprise learned that they were great. It was only Sachem's Head that was "socked in." Just past the entrance buoy there was no fog. Well, very little.

That was good enough for us. We were on our way to New England, and Sachem's Head, though lovely, was still too close to home. We would up anchor and be off and running. Being of a mildly distrustful nature, however, the captain plotted a compass course to nearby Duck Island, just in case. Even if we didn't need it, and it was as clear as a bell out there, as the man said, today would be a good time to show me how to run the buoys on the time-and-distance system. We would pretend we couldn't see the buoys, and we wouldn't fudge; the captain would keep his eyes on the compass, not the horizon, and I would keep mine on the stopwatch. I would see, that way, that locating buoys in a fog is little different from finding street signs on a dark night. It would be good practice.

Within an hour's run from the harbor entrance it wasn't practice—it was the real thing. Local fog-making conditions were working solidly together to lay a blanket over the sea, the buoys, and us. Strangely, I found, I wasn't afraid. As my husband had predicted, we found each succeeding buoy with little difficulty. And the foghorn I blew, perhaps more than was necessary, warned men on other boats that we were there. We were doing our part, and they would do theirs.

Then we heard another foghorn, and the more I blew, the closer it sounded. George changed course 90 degrees, and it followed us. We went back on course, and in a few seconds the horn was with us again, very close. Then I panicked and fled, sobbing, to the cabin.

"Hey there," I heard a strange voice say. "I've been trying to catch up with you. Do you know where you are? Where the heck is Duck Island?"

We were one and a half miles from Clinton Bell, on course 105 magnetic, George said, and the course from the bell to Duck Island was 058. His voice was grim. I saw through the porthole that there were small children on the other boat, pinch-faced and frightened. That captain had shirked his responsibility.

The story is not over. We saw that boat again—dimly, through the fog—at anchor in Duck Island, and we didn't return its wave. For they must have heard, as we had, distinct cries for help coming from somewhere in the fog off the island's breakwater, and they had done nothing. But, to be fair, perhaps the cries hadn't reached them; we were ashore when we heard them, walking our dog. We listened,

unbelieving at first. When the cries came again, we hurried our poor, bewildered beast into the dinghy and then onto our yawl, upped anchor, and groped slowly through the fog toward the voices. They were only one mile or so off the breakwater and belonged to two boys in an outboard motor boat tied to a buoy. They were two very lost and frightened young men, mighty relieved to hitch their boat behind ours and clamber aboard, where they were promptly licked from head to shivering toe by our foor-footed crew, the Newf. Back again at our anchorage, we opened two cans of beef stew, after (I admit to contributing to child delinquency) administering a large dollop of sherry to each boy, and waited for a parent, whom he had called on the ship-to-shore radio telephone, to come pick them up in a Harbor Police boat.

A Radio Direction Finder (RDF) or a depth finder—or both—is often used on small boats as a supplement to the time-and-distance method of running in fog. The RDF, an electronic device for receiving signals from aids to navigation such as lightships and beacons, is better understood by the captain than by me. Only once—on a foggy night run —have we used the RDF, but some captains are RDF devotees, tuning in on it frequently to check course and location, even on a clear day. The depth finder is a simple mechanism to operate and interpret, straightforwardly telling anyone who turns it on how much water is under the boat. By reading the successively recorded depths as the boat moves forward, and checking them with the depths marked on the chart, a first mate can help a captain find himself—sometimes. If, for instance, the depth finder says there is 30 feet of water under the boat, and the captain has been going on the theory that the boat is in an area marked 50 feet on the chart, he knows, at least, that he is wrong. With that piece of negative information, he can more easily zero in on the nearby 50-foot spots marked on the chart. It's rather like a game of hide-the-thimble, if anyone remembers that venerable child's game; the depth finder signals "cold, warm, hot," and the captain finds the "thimble," the 50-foot depth.

Handy though they are, both the RDF and the depth finder are expendable in a fog, but a radar reflector is not—at least, on our boat. We carry a collapsible aluminum radar reflector that we hoist from the signal halliards, both in fog and while running at night if there are apt to be any of the Big Boys around, and I am comforted to know that I am a blip on their radar screens. More than once we have heard the thump-thump of a ship's engine ahead of us fade off abeam, and then thump loudly back astern. They had seen us on their radar screen and had changed course to avoid us. With a radar reflector, any first mate can be a blip, and should be.

In sum, a first mate equipped with good eyes and ears, helpful hands, a cool head, and a responsible captain need not fear either storms or fog—though both demand respect.

Fire, the biggest hazard of all to life and boat, is rightfully feared by first mates, and more than an ounce of prevention is needed to set their minds at ease on this score. Marine underwriters lend a helping hand by refusing to insure boats with certain hazardous types of galleys and heating stoves, as well as by insisting on inspection of the auxiliary motor installation and whatever electric wiring is aboard. The Coast Guard requires that each boat carry the proper number and type of fire extinguishers, according to the size of the boat, and reputable boat builders take care that safeguards against fire are built into their craft. Nevertheless, fire and explosion are statistically the greatest causes of serious injury and loss of life and boat today. Some skippers—though very few—foolishly bypass both marine insurance inspectors and the Coast Guard, and more grow careless after receiving the initial stamp of approval: leaks develop in the fuel lines and are not attended to, fire extinguishers that have lost their "zilch" are not replaced, an extra stove of the banned variety is brought aboard, or a highly explosive amount of gasoline fumes is allowed to accumulate in the bilge. (The power equivalent of a half-pint of gasoline in the bilge is 5 pounds of dynamite.) A stray spark from an improperly sheathed motor or a live ash from a cigarette can shorten a cruise, and sometimes a life, in a flash of fire.

Prevention begins, for the first mate, when the boat and its equipment are chosen. The galley stove should be of the "safe" variety, to begin with, and the first mate, as the one most likely to spend time over it, should keep the captain alerted as to any leaks that may develop. (The safeness of the various fuels used in galley stoves is discussed in Chapter 2.) Too, any self-respecting first mate does not have to be told to keep the stove and the drip pan clean.

On *Skylark* we had a two-burner alcohol stove, set on top of a cast-iron Shipmate coal stove. (The latter was used for both cooking and cabin warmth in cold weather.) I became firm friends with the alcohol stove, but readily admit that it was some time before I lit it happily. The small tank of alcohol in front of and just below the burners had to be pumped to the proper pressure (registered on the gauge) before alcohol was let into the preheating pans beneath the burners, and once or twice in my early cruising days I didn't pump enough, or let in too much alcohol, and lit myself a fine, frightening fire. The captain finally convinced me it wasn't as bad as it looked by simply upending a bucketful of water over the flaming stove. It took me quite a while to clean up the messy result, but I was comforted to see that the fire had been extinguished immediately. I also learned how to light the stove properly after that.

Alcohol is the only liquid fuel that is extinguishable by water, so first mates with other types of stoves will do well to check the fire extinguishers aboard to see that they are working properly and, above all, to have one permanently affixed near the galley.

The National Fire Protection Association, a society formed in 1896 to "promote the science and improve the methods of fire protection and prevention," recommends, in their booklet on the prevention of marine fires, that all woodwork above the stove top and within a radius of 18 inches be protected with noncombustible material, such as a ⅛-inch asbestos board covered with sheet metal. On *Skylark* Monel metal did the job, as it does on *Shag*. Coal, charcoal, and wood-burning stoves should preferably be mounted on a hollow tile base. If not, they should be on legs at least 5 inches from the deck and set on a metal-covered asbestos board.

The Association divides fires aboard small boats into classes A and B. Any first mate who is confronted with a class A fire (bedding, cushions, clothing, wood) *can* reach for the fire extinguisher, but drenching with water is better.

"The material should be opened up to expose burning embers and drenched again until extinguished, or smoldering material should be thrown overboard." Class B fires (inflammable liquids such as gasoline, diesel fuel, or kerosene) will succumb only to fire extinguishers.

What if an emergency arises that is beyond the "do-it-yourself" scope? Suppose help from outside is needed, and fast, and the first mate is the only able-bodied member of the crew aboard? What if land is far away, or she is unable to take the boat in alone? What should she do?

She should keep cool—and consider. *Is* the situation really serious? Has she done everything she could, according to the first-aid book, to cope with the problem? The reason for asking herself these questions is that a distress call at sea is indeed a serious thing. With the growth in boating, too many calls go into the Coast Guard nowadays for help in minor or avoidable emergencies. Skippers who take their boats to sea on a Sunday with no charts, or who haven't learned the "language" of the red and black buoys, and get lost, deserve little pity or help from the Coast Guard. Captains who fail to carry an adequate anchor and line with sufficient scope, and have a motor breakdown with no sails or no wind and find themselves drifting onto a rocky shore, have no business calling on the Coast Guard to get them out of their self-imposed mess. They will get help—if no pity —nevertheless, if they ask for it, and a boat in real distress may suffer. Hardworking and cooperative though it may be, the Coast Guard cannot be in several places at once, nor should it be asked to unnecessarily.

The above harsh words for irresponsible yachtsmen presuppose that the craft carries a radio-telephone. Safety regulations do not require that there be one aboard, but first mates with an ounce of apprehension about going to sea for more than a day-sail will be happier with one around if it can possibly be fitted into the family boat and budget. Some sailing seasons go by without our radio-telephone being used except as a receiving set for the daily weather reports. Nevertheless, it is always, comfortingly, there.

Given the presence of a radio-telephone and the first mate's considered opinion that she needs help, she may use the International Calling and Distress Frequency, 2182 K.C.

"MAYDAY, MAYDAY, MAYDAY, this is *Shag*"—meaning "I am in great distress," that is, the vessel is in danger or a person aboard is seriously injured. Just to reassure first mates that someone "out there" loves them if they are in trouble, they should know that a MAYDAY call cancels out all other traffic on the channel, that radiomen in the nearest Coast Guard station, say Boston, are copying the information while another radioman presses a button that alerts every other Coast Guard radio station along the coast. All stations listen carefully to receive any part of the transmission that Boston may have missed, and transmit it, via teletype circuit, to the Rescue Coordination Center in New York. From then on, planes and various vessels (including boats in the vicinity that may have heard the call) begin to converge on the distressed craft.

If possible, the first mate should give her location, what her problem is, and the size of her boat—hopefully, all accurately. One skipper, stuck on a sandbar, called the Rockaway Coast Guard Station in New York and gave his latitude and longitude. After a moment's calculation, the Coast Guard replied that, according to the information given, the "distressed" captain was right in the middle of Floyd Bennett Air Field.

What to do until help comes depends, of course, on the nature of the problem, and the first mate should not be backward in asking for advice from whoever answers her call. Above all, she should try to keep the boat near the position from which she called, either by throwing over the anchor or by taking the boat in tight circles.

With no radio-telephone aboard, a first mate will have to depend on her own lungs and other people's eyesight. At night, she can begin by sending up flares, if there are any aboard, and blowing the foghorn continuously. During the day, hoisting the boat's American yacht ensign upside down is a time-honored distress signal. And there's always that good old Navy advice:

> When in danger or in doubt,
> Run around, scream and shout.

A first mate is in danger and doubt every time she crosses the street, on land, but she crosses it. She has learned to look right, look left, and to expect reasonable cooperation from automobile drivers. She won't get run down if she doesn't take unreasonable chances. The same is true of a first mate on a boat.

JANE KIRSTEIN

Pressures of Racing

Racing is very exciting, but it often pushes situations to the limit where the exciting may become dangerous. A reasonable skipper will never intentionally endanger his boat or his crew, but he may not be easy on them and he may have to carry them through extreme conditions. In racing, time and course have been set for weeks or months. Weather conditions may be fair or poor; they may or may not delay a race —this is at the discretion of the Race Committee. Once committed, a racing skipper does not often back down unless real danger threatens, and even then he may find that it is safer to go on than to turn back. Most racing skippers

are not incautious or foolhardy and they don't go out looking for trouble, but, admittedly, there are risks and the
skipper and his crew must be aware of them.

The condition of the boat and its equipment and the attitude and skill of the crew are nowhere more important
than in racing, where the boat is being driven and the crew
is under pressure. Gear, rigging, and tackle should be
checked often to avoid accidents caused by worn or faulty
parts. My skipper runs a thorough check before each race.
A chafed sheet that lets go under strain can deliver a ter-
rific blow, as can a block that falls. I was once hit by a small
piece of brass ring from the spinnaker and thought I'd been
hit by the spinnaker pole itself. Had I ducked, I might have
lost an eye, but the piece hit my jaw and laid it open for
half an inch—just enough to get blood all over the sail!

A crew under too much pressure is accident prone. It is
easy to get a hand jammed in a winch or block or take a
blow from a jibing boom or flying clew. A racing crew *will*
be under pressure, but a first mate can help to relieve the
tension by remaining calm, by carrying out her duties as
crew with good humor, and by encouraging jokes, sea
stories, or a coffee break whenever possible, a man at a time
if necessary. A good lunch, when there is time to eat it, is a
great refresher. A tired crew member is a liability, so
relieve him if you can.

If a serious accident happens, and there are very few considering the number of boats racing today, that is the end
of the race for your boat. Do everything you can to make the
injured person comfortable, using your knowledge of first
aid and your common sense, and call for help from the
Coast Guard or a faster boat within range, or head immediately for the nearest port. Except in the largest ocean
races, some of the boats in the fleet are bound to be close by
and will offer assistance the instant they see trouble. One

consolation for the racing mate: she will not be alone to handle the situation. Other crew members can manage the boat while the mate administers first aid or radios for help; there may even be someone aboard better qualified than she to care for the injured person.

MARY LEONARD

Body and
Morale Building
9   Aboard

~~~~~~

A FIRST MATE MAY GO through a lifetime of cruising on small boats and never have a moment of bodily discomfort or sagging morale. Her spirits may invariably lift the minute she steps aboard, and no amount of foul weather or lack of creature comforts can dampen them. She may totter aboard, tired and tense, and spring ashore at the end of a cruise, restored in body and soul, with never an intervening irritable moment. But it's not bloody likely! A normal first mate will have brief fits of fury and despair because she can't (1) get a comb through her hair, (2) fit into her new shorts, or (3) remember when she felt really clean. For no reason apparent to the skipper she may snap when he he asks, "What's for dinner?"

In any case, that's what happens on *Shag* from time to time, and I know, when it does, that I have been neglecting the body-and-morale-building department. Just because I need a shower, shampoo, and a little exercise is no reason to fume and pout. I may be tired of cooking and making up bunks, but I can still be civil to the skipper when he asks a simple question. For a long time and a good many cruises, I didn't realize what was bugging me in such unbecoming moments, and when I did, I was ashamed. Couldn't I rise above such silly irritations? Why just sit there, why not do something about them? For example, the hair problem . . .

Men will never understand why women fuss so about their hair. I, for one woman, wish men would take another look at some of the bushy-topped, tangle-headed young men making the scene nowadays. Do they want us to look like *that?* Not that we care about being glamour girls at sea; we just want to look faintly neat, we don't want to itch and smell, and we want to be able to see. The morale of a first

mate blinded by a mop of gummy hair is in frightful shape.

With the water supply being what it is aboard most small boats, a shampoo is hard to come by. On *Skylark* I had first option on the water drained from the icebox into a bucket for a shampoo. The first time I went to take up the option, I didn't after all; a bottle of white wine chilling on the ice had lost its cork. I must admit that the lost wine was more lamented than the lost shampoo! On *Shag* we have a special funnel-shaped pocket with a detachable hose built into our awning for catching tropical rain showers. When we're at anchor, with the awning in place, I watch the cloud formations, and when a lovely black one comes our way, I rush for the hose and blissfully hold it in the mouth of a plastic jerry can. Sometimes the cloud is big and black enough to give me a shampoo in one try. If not, I just keep watching and rushing when the clouds come along.

If the skipper allows it, a bucket shampoo in the cockpit is the most satisfactory on most small boats. A small wash basin or galley sink doesn't give a girl enough scope. Stripped at least to the waist, or in a bathing suit, a first mate can slosh about to her heart's content in the cockpit, providing the cockpit is self-draining. Hand-bailing a cockpit full of sudsy water would not build morale, especially the skipper's! Don't forget the good old-fashioned virtues of a vinegar rinse to cut the soap and cut down on the rinse water needed. If you're not the shy type and a dock with a hose is somewhere nearby, you can don a bathing suit and shampoo on the dock. This will save the boat's water supply and leave water from the ice chest for other washing (after it is warmed by the sun).

A shampoo ashore is no more of a problem than finding the nearest shower, but that in itself is an art in some cruising areas. In the eleven years I have cruised, great progress has been made in the New York-to-Maine shower route, with new marinas-cum-showers every season, and much of the challenge in tracking down a shower is gone. Northeast Harbor, Maine, now boasts a trim little shower, washing machine, and lounging house always clean and open to yachtsmen at the end of the town dock. I think it's still the only *free* shower, except for those at some yacht clubs, and one of the very few coeducational ones. My daughter will always remember hearing with startled delight (she was fourteen) a male voice in the shower stall next to her calling out, "Can you throw over some soap?" The voice, we found out later, belonged to a young crew member of the winning boat in the Marblehead-to-Halifax Race. He had sailed in fog for the past ten days; he was tired, cold, and dirty, and he wasn't about to stand on propriety.

Finding a shower in marina land is facilitated by having aboard cruising guides, such as the *Waterway Guide*, which is updated annually and published in four editions: for the Southern, Middle Atlantic, Northern, and Great Lakes areas. The guide gives detailed harbor charts, bits of sightseeing and historical background information, and vital facts about a marina's facilities, such as SHOWERS. Or, there is the stop-and-snoop method of finding a shower—the only way once one is out of the marina circuit (short of a friendly yacht club). Mary tells you how to get a yacht club shower gracefully in the chapter "Woman's Role, or What Every First Mate Should Know."

Hotels and guest houses are good shower sources. If approached amiably with the explanation that you are off a small boat, a room with shower, or just a shower, can be rented for an hour and, usually, a dollar. The less sophisticated the atmosphere of the place, the more cordial the reception will be at the desk, if the skipper doesn't appear or if he sits downstairs with a respectable, waiting attitude.

He can have his turn, too. I always bring my own soap and towels and leave the shower as neat as I found it.

I can remember only one unpleasant incident while using this method. After one extremely long, hot, windless day under power on the Gulf of Maine, we turned reluctantly into the tiny harbor of Rockport—reluctantly because it *is* tiny and one must anchor bow and stern to lie free of other boats. The skipper was as eager as I for a shower, so, after considerable maneuvering and playing with anchors, we headed for shore and the nearest hotel—a small one. We not only wanted a shower; we looked as if we had never had one in our lives, and I can't completely blame the lady at the desk for openly turning her back on us. Undaunted, the skipper made our request to her back and then to her adamant front. No, she said, she had only one room with shower free, it was ready for occupancy that evening, and she had no intention of having it messed up. George asked the rate. Ten dollars. He handed her a ten dollar bill, asked for the key, and, in her astonishment, she gave it to him. When we came down half an hour later, she stood silently behind the desk, flanked by three elderly cronies, all unsmiling and shaking their heads. We felt unloved, slightly wicked, but no longer unwashed.

The largest hotel in St. John, New Brunswick, Canada, was something else again, and we will forever think of that city with affection. Four of us this time, looking equally crumby, asked for and were given a room with a shower. The ladies showered first and then went shopping in the colorful and excellent public market. We met the men back at the desk an hour later. An argument was going on between our male crew members and the desk clerk, and money was being shoved back and forth across the counter. The clerk, it seemed, flatly refused to accept anything. We were yachtsmen, weren't we? We had come all this way because we liked sailing in Canada, hadn't we? Well, they were honored to have us there as guests—nonpaying.

A boarding house in Vinalhaven, Maine, a four-room, palm-thatched "club" at Staniel Cay in the Bahamas, a friendly "native" from whom we bought homemade bread in Puget Sound, Washington, all have been delightful shower stops and do-it-yourself beauty salons. I always carry a canvas bag holding shampoo, an extra towel in case there is no bath mat, and a small bottle of vinegar in case there is no hot water. (There never is in the Bahamas, and there seldom is in the Virgin Islands.) Before I cut off my hair to a nubbin, I sometimes put it up in bobby pins and popped a hat over it. Other times, I would postpone the bobby pin bit until I got back to the boat, where I would set my hair and then pop on the hat. A headful of bobby pins or rollers is unattractive enough on land in the dark of night. At sea, it's downright unsightly, I think.

One problem with the shower method of getting a shampoo is that sometimes a wet head doesn't go with the prevailing climate, for example, a cold, wet, spring day in Maine. There are times during a New England spring when one's hair could rot before it would dry! That's the time to settle the skipper in the cockpit or cabin with a drink (cocoa, hot buttered rum?) and a good book and go searching for a beauty parlor. Many first mates do anyway, rain or shine. One I know made an appointment in Northeast Harbor, Maine, for a date two months ahead. She knew she would be going to a party that night, fair winds provided, and she had curly, hard-to-manage hair that had never responded happily to home hairdos.

Speaking of hairdos, I began to notice a strange (?) thing after cruising in the Virgins for a while. All the wives of charter boat captains had tanned, taut bodies and short, gamine haircuts. Before long I spent more and more time on the fantail with a pair of scissors, snipping away, and, with professional help from time to time, I've been there ever since. I don't recommend short short hair to first mates who like their more elegant shore coiffures and are rightly reluctant to sacrifice them to a two-week cruise. Hats and scarves will keep their hair out of their eyes and clear of the winches, and they will probably want to rely more heavily on the beauty salon than the shower method of getting a shampoo. Sets are almost useless, unless very simple, in the breezes and damp. Until recently, Mary had long hair, which she either tied in a pony tail or clipped at the back of her neck. It might have been braided. No problem, she said. (*It still wafted free and into my mouth and eyes!—M.*) But now that the Leonards have *Skylark* and are going on longer cruises than they did on *Prelude,* and are living aboard in the summer while renting their house, Mary has a short haircut, not very different from her boys. She is lucky—on her, both styles look good. (*Well, that's open to discussion. I now look more like a boy than a cocker spaniel, but I can keep my hair clean—my neck, too—and it looks about the same brushed as it does windblown. It's wonderful not to have to scramble around looking for clips, bobby pins, or a whole rubber band, and when my hair gets wet swimming or in a shower, it takes only ten minutes to dry, with no setting needed.—M.*)

In between all-out shower and shampoo stops, I sometimes take boat showers. They are good for morale and for cleaning the head, and they take little water. The recipe is this: Remove everything from the head that you don't want to get wet, including the toilet paper, then strip (you knew that already?) and fill the wash basin with half a tea-kettle of boiling water (reserve the other half). Add only

enough cold water to the basin to avoid third-degree burns. Thoroughly wet a washcloth but don't squeeze it until it is suspended over the body at strategic points. Continue until both you and the head are soaked, then soap yourself generously. Empty the basin, refill with the reserve hot water, add cold water, and repeat the process with clear water and washcloth. You will be left with only a slight film of soap on your body, and by the time you have mopped up the head you may wonder if the whole thing was worth it. It depends on how smelly you were to start with and/or how much the head needed a thorough scrubbing. (*I prefer to do the whole thing in the cockpit, stripped if possible; if not, in a bathing suit. My skipper doesn't like fresh water—not to*

*mention soap—in the bilge, and I don't like trying to dry out
a sopping head in time for someone to use it comfortably,
maybe with the funny papers or a good book.—M.)*

Fingernails take an awful beating aboard a small boat,
so the shorter the nails, the lesser the beating. Even short
nails get broken the minute they connect with a winch
handle or flying line. A nail brush is the best instrument to
get at the grime (where does it come from at sea?) under
what is left of your nails and, on *Shag*, sometimes doubles
as a basin scrubber. Scouring powders are great nail cleaners.

A last-ditch maneuver in the keeping-clean department is
to take a salt-water bath over the side with special salt-water
soap. I have never had a satisfactory salt-water-soap bath,
however; I've always felt gummier when I got out than
when I went in. Plain old detergent works better, but not
much. *(I have always felt very clean after a good swim in
salt water, although my hair needs to be rinsed with fresh
water afterward. To clean grubby knees, elbows, and feet,
a bit of sand works wonders!—M.)*

First mates who sail in fresh-water areas have already
skipped the above section, I assume. All they have to do to
get a bath is find a secluded spot, strip, and dunk, as I did
on Grand Lake off the St. John River in New Brunswick,
Canada. That's all they have to do unless the fresh water is
polluted, as it unfortunately is in so many of our great
fresh-water sailing areas today.

Next to keeping clean aboard a small boat, a first mate
may find keeping fit the greatest problem, strange as it may
seem to landlubbers. People go sailing because they want
to stay healthy as well as get happy, don't they? Experienced sailors, especially long-distance sailors, know there is
an occupational disease of cruising: lower body witheritis.
It is endemic to first mates rather than to captains, because
the latter do more scrambling about than do their mates,

thus activating muscles below the navel as well as those above. No one of either sex has to worry about atrophy of the upper torso on a sailboat, as any sailor can testify; even the most sedentary crew member has to flex an arm muscle from time to time, if only to brace himself when the boat lurches. In any case, muscles in the upper body are in a constant state of involuntary action when the boat is under way, adjusting to the changing motion of the boat through the water. Thigh and lower leg muscles aren't. They just wither. The greatest activity that takes place from the navel down is the hustle and bustle of fatty tissue hurrying to build bulges on the first mate's hips and thighs.

To complete the grisly picture, a first mate's intestines go sluggish, too, lying, as they do, below the navel. I don't need or want to go into the effects of such a physical state on the emotional state of the victim.

Lower body muscles will not wither, nor morale flag, if the muscles are given a little daily attention. The longer the cruise, the more solicitous should be the care. (A cruise under a week may call for no attention at all.) I say *daily* because I remember my first encounter with witheritis.

Suntanned and pictures of health, the captain and I stepped from *Skylark's* dinghy onto a dock crowded with summer visitors in Block Island, Rhode Island, and walked briskly to the bicycle rental shop 50 yards away. Five minutes later we were mounted on two shiny bikes and headed up the country road winding away from the harbor. Twenty-five minutes later we were back, pushing our bikes, out of breath, and barely able to stand on our trembling legs. One loudmouthed visitor who apparently had nothing better to do than spy on us, shouted as we tottered back to the dinghy, "Can't take it, huh?"

No, we couldn't, and I was shattered. This had been a day planned for both body and morale building. We had been sailing blissfully, but continuously, for ten days, with only one brief sortie ashore for shopping, and we were ready for a change of scene and activity. An hour or two of bicycling around the island, a shower and a shampoo, a lobster and blueberry pie dinner ashore, and maybe a movie had been the delightful order of the day. And there we were, back on *Skylark,* collapsed in the cockpit, unwashed, unhappy, and with nothing but beef stew in the canned goods locker.

So, first mates, take it easy with exercise, but take it. Swimming is the obvious, easy, and fun way of getting exercise—unless you're cruising in, say, Maine or Puget Sound, Washington, where you have to be more spartan than I am to enter the icy waters. (I grew up on Puget Sound, and I swam in it, but I learned better later. Mary grew up near Maine's icy waters.) Just a lazy dip isn't enough; twice around the boat, with plenty of arm and leg thrashing, is par for a good workout. If you don't swim well, make it at least to the dinghy, hang onto the transom, and kick as long as you can. When the water or weather is too cold for comfortable swimming, take the dinghy for a row and a little exploring ashore. If you can't get the skipper to go along, go alone. When the boys are aboard, they are Mary's scavenging and exploring companions. If she hopes to find any treasures, she has to keep moving!

I wouldn't advise staying away from the boat as long as I did once on the Tred Avon River, in Chesapeake Bay. I rowed to the end of a narrow lagoon, bordered by sweet-smelling flowering trees and covered with lily pads, to an abandoned mill and an overgrown path leading up from the water. I walked back through time, pre-Revolutionary time, so enchanted by the peace and the smells that I forgot the present. I heard an ear-shattering series of blasts from our foghorn. I knew that sound well. We had just come up the Inland Waterway from Florida and had blown that horn 489 times to open bridges en route! I realized that I was out of sight of *Shag*, I had been away for a long time, and—I was touched by the captain's concern!

Dog walking is the inevitable (and beneficial) by-product of cruising with the family pet, and I miss it now that we have decided that dogs are not for cruising. Skipper, then Nina, then Matey led us up pine-needled paths winding through lovely woods that we might lazily have passed by if we didn't have to walk the dog. Once, on Ile au Haut, Maine, Skipper flushed a deer, and another time a skunk. What saved us all that day was that Skipper weighed a lumbering 160 pounds. He must have looked like a bear, and bears do not bother skunks. The skunk, unafraid, just ambled off with his stink sac still full.

Children have to be "run" just as dogs do, and it's certainly safer to chaperone the party. Besides, lower body muscles don't stand a chance of atrophying if you have to keep up with the children!

Walks, long or short, sometimes take more mental effort than physical. After a day's sail, what is greater bliss than sitting in the cockpit, just doing nothing? People go yachting to get away from demands and commands: go there, come here, sit down, stand up, WALK, etc.

All right. Don't leave the boat, but, just before turning in for the night, walk at least to the bow. There is usually room, except perhaps on the smallest of small boats, to do a few setting-up exercises—or settling-down exercises. First, bend over and let your body hang limp from the waist, arms dangling and fingers reaching (limply) for the deck. Pump up and down eight times, then twist the upper body to the right and to the left as far as is comfortable, and with the feet firmly planted straight ahead pump eight times. Thigh bulges hate that exercise. If there is room to lie down on the bow, do. If not, stretch full length on a cockpit seat or on your bunk and lift your legs 12 inches, hold, count to five, and let them down slowly. Repeat until your stomach muscles object. They are the ones that are being attacked! Jogging in the cockpit, treadmill fashion, or skipping an imaginary rope tones up withering leg muscles.

Shy first mates may not think a crowded anchorage is the ideal setting for exercise under the stars, but I have found that most crews are bedded down, on the bow exercising themselves, or looking the other way. During Block Island Week—that gathering of boats from the Eastern seaboard in the off years of the Newport-to-Bermuda race—Great Salt

Pond was crowded indeed. Yet, early one morning I saw the prettiest young matron in the fleet jogging and jumping rope in the cockpit of the boat next to us. I was doing the same thing and we didn't exchange the usual "Good morning" hail. It reminded me of the first time I was in Manhattan, staying with friends in the window-to-window section of Murray Hill. I was fascinated to find that no one ever closed their blinds. The protocol was: Don't goggle at me, and I won't goggle at you. *(My boys and I can hardly stand sitting in the cockpit doing nothing when the anchor is down, although the skipper, who is a philosopher, loves nothing better after a good sail. I can't stand "exercises" either—I'd rather do* anything *else, even work—so I opt for exploring, swimming, or sailing the dinghy, which* does *take leg muscles! Come to think of it, hauling anchors is great for stomach muscles, too.—M.)*

First mates may have to work at getting exercise aboard a small boat, but without lifting a finger they get all the wind and sun they need. In fact, until I met a certain gallant lady I'll call Betty, I thought there were some women who couldn't take any "weathering" at all, who shouldn't go to sea under any circumstances. They are the ones who have such delicate skin that a day in the sun and wind can be pure misery rather than the delight it is for most sailors. No amount of sun-blocking lotion can keep them from going bright red and peeling painfully away. If they were married to sailors, I was sorry for everyone concerned, but I mentally dismissed all thin-skinned women from first-mate-hood.

Then one day I saw an apparition at the helm of a boat that was sailing into the harbor where we were anchored in the West Indies. In that tropical heat she was wearing a long-sleeved shirt and slacks, but even more noteworthy was the headscarf that she had tied over a deep-brimmed hat and then wound around her face, with only a slit left for her eyes. While her skipper put up the awning, she went below for a few minutes. Shamelessly staring by now, I saw her come back on deck, without the scarf but with approximately an inch of cake make-up and lipstick on her face. We were anchored close to each other—it was a small harbor —and I'll never forget her generous response to my rude, openmouthed regard. She smiled, waved, and pointed to her face with a gloved hand. "Skin trouble," she said gently, as if to a child.

We ran into Betty and her husband often after that, and I learned that she had undergone more than a dozen operations for skin cancer, but had no intention of giving up sailing. Nor did she show the slightest trace of martyrdom. As she said, "I have this little problem."

She also had a great idea for other thin-skinned first mates —pancake make-up for protection, not looks. Betty's brand is both medicated and moisturized, as is her lipstick. I have long been a heavy lipstick user at sea, the gooier the better. Good old camphorated ice gets a workout, too, but I find that ordinary lipstick stays on best and tastes better with cigarettes. Once, when we had misplaced the camphorated ice, I tried to talk the skipper into protecting his poor, sunburned lips with some of my moisturized Hot Pink. He suggested I go on looking for the camphorated ice.

Any first mate can get a painful sunburn if she is not careful, and deal a body blow to morale when she looks in the mirror after the burn simmers down. Those little squint lines at the corners of the eyes may have a certain salty charm, but the dried-out prune effect elsewhere on the face does not. When I remember, I take preventive action with a nongreasy cream before going out into the morning sun. When I forget, I use an extra dollup of Noxema—my own favorite all-purpose cream at sea—at night. (Mary likes Sea and Ski day and night.) During the day I often cool down with a cotton pad slurped with baby lotion. (Smells nostalgically good, too.) Baby bath products are ideal shipmates, I have found; baby powder, baby shampoo, even baby soap. They are gentle in action and in scent, and they are easily obtainable. Nowadays babies are pampered in even the remotest fishing villages. Moreover, baby products come in small packages—just right for small-boat stowage. (And, if you happen to have a baby aboard, you will be consolidating supplies.) Carry the boat's own manicure kit, razor, shaving cream, toothbrushes, and toothpaste if possible—those are the things most easily forgotten in the rush of leaving home. You'll almost never forget the camera, but that certainly won't make your mouth taste any better in the morning!

A well-exercised, well-scrubbed first mate may still have one tiny morale problem: periods of boredom, especially on long passages. She isn't hankering for organized fun and games; she has had enough of organizing or being organized on land. At sea many brief slack periods between her duties as crew are gratefully spent just watching the water go by. Still, once in a while, probably on a long haul and a calm day, even peace and beauty pall and she may wish she had a little more to put her mind to.

Some first mates I know get a lot of reading done during the sailing day. Jean keeps a book of poetry in her lap while she takes her trick at the helm. Poetry has to be read slowly, she says, and reread, to understand its meaning and appreciate its beauty. Keeping one eye on the course and one on the book eliminates any danger of speed-reading! Jean is a painter, specializing in marine scenes, and she carries a sketchbook wherever she goes. On smooth-sailing days she fills the book with quick sketches—not, this time, while she's at the helm. Mary keeps a sketchbook handy, too, and likes to "collect" character boats. She often listens to the Coast Guard on the marine radio and has kept a log of adventures, mishaps, and rescues she heard detailed during lazy sailing periods and evenings in port. She and the boys are fond of pocketbook mysteries, easy plots to pick up if interrupted by sailing maneuvers.

Many first mates do needlepoint or knit. Before I started sailing I hadn't done any knitting since my last child was born, years before, but now my sea-made sweaters fill a bottom drawer in my dressing room. (Someday I may wear them.) I pick easy patterns so I can keep an eye out for buoys, boats, or passing porpoises and still not drop a stitch, but Mary's friend Angie is able to do the fanciest Irish and Scandinavian patterns without a bit of trouble—she has made enough sweaters for her whole family and has some left over for friends! I learned to take extra plastic knitting needles along after I dropped my knitting once and then sat on it.

Fishing from a moving sailboat is fun, although the odds are against catching a fish. We have had some delicious boat-caught fish dinners, but mostly on days when the sailing wasn't good. Neither *Skylark* nor *Shag* is a racing machine, but, with any wind, they move too fast through the water for a fish to get a good look at a lure. Nevertheless, we often trail a heavy line, known as "the clothesline," behind the boat, and one out of every ten or fifteen times pull in a half-drowned fish. I have a box full of lures and a collapsible pole that sometimes catches more than seaweed.

We were just about to take down the sails and turn on the motor off Biddeford Pool, Maine, one day, when we saw

seagulls wheeling and screaming over a huge school of fish breaking the water ahead of us. There was just enough wind left in the dying northwesterly to give us headway, so I rushed for my pole and George maneuvered the boat into the school. The seagulls had better luck than I had, but even so, we snared two handsome mackerel within half an hour and were eating them within an hour. Fun!

Once, in the Bahamas, I hooked into a large, hard-fighting fish and made the mistake of bringing it aboard before I found that it was a barracuda. The problem, then, was getting it back into the water. (George was no help—he claimed he couldn't leave the helm.) I didn't want to fuss around with that toothy, underslung jaw, but I didn't want to lose my lure, either. The barracuda, tired of waiting around while I made up my mind, flopped over the side, lure and all. I just had time to cut the line or he would have taken the pole, too. First mates should try not to catch barracuda!

It's funny how fresh air, exercise, and particularly sailing will give people tremendous appetites. Food cannot be overlooked as an influence on the morale of a crew, the rule being the more, the better. A good mate will try to prepare tempting and hearty meals, of course, but she should be prepared with snacks for every occasion—after-breakfast snacks, coffee-break snacks, before-lunch snacks, after-lunch snacks, tea snacks, cocktail snacks, and midnight snacks. Otherwise the whole crew will grumble as though they were used to eating like that ashore. For those of the crew who should nibble carefully or not at all, carrots, celery, apples, and grapes are the answer (but try to make them stick to that!). For the rest, donuts, peanuts, potato chips, popcorn candy bars, crackers and cheese, etc., will do.

After-dinner entertainment is usually not a problem on a boat. Sea air is a soporific and most sailors have trouble staying awake long enough to finish one game of chess or canasta. But, once in a while, one member of the crew may want to read later than the other, or others, and feels guilty about using the precious electricity, especially if it shines right in the sleepers' eyes. Solution: a portable lamp of the dry-cell or pump-up kerosene type, a couple of cushions, and a blanket, if the night is damp, to make a nest in the cockpit. I have done it often, but usually end up turning off the light and reading the heavens instead of my book.

Not all sailors fall in a heap on their bunks after dinner, especially young sailors, and it is best for everyone's morale that they see a little action. An occasional night on the town, beginning before dinner, gives a first mate a lift, too. Most cruising areas are dotted with towns big enough to support a restaurant, and often a movie. More than once we have gone ashore for provisions and come back with tickets for a local amateur theater production that night as well. Sometimes we run into a real live professional production on summer circuit, and sometimes the performance is no better than the amateur one. Just a soda at the drugstore is a treat and interesting in a new town, and a stroll along Main Street may be all the excitement a crew needs after the day's sail.

JANE KIRSTEIN

Commissioning, Maintenance, and Laying Up of the Boat

10   (Decommissioning)

~~~~~~

Iт's SPRING. The boat is in the water again after its long winter storage in the boatyard. Its outer paint and varnish is all bright and shining. Some sailors will have done much of the work themselves, either because they like to, or because they have to for financial reasons. The first dry spring day—no matter how brisk—in a boatyard is like Old Home Week. Captains, first mates, and children swarm over the yard, greeting friends and workmen they haven't seen since the preceding fall, and thread their way among the boats in the sheds and out in the muddy open, looking for good old *Me Too* or *Compass Rose*. Some come armed with sandpaper and paintbrushes and the great spring spruce-up begins.

Other sailors confine their pre-boat-launching activities to heckling the yard foreman, or if they are knowledgeable enough about what the workmen are doing, the workmen themselves. The warmer the day, the more persistent is the heckling; the pressure to be among the first boats in the

water is in direct proportion to the rising spring tempera-
tures.

Once the boat is launched, it's the first mate who is under
pressure to match the shine of the topsides with that of her
department below deck. She is no slob, so she left the boat
in a reasonable state of cleanliness at decommissioning time
the preceding fall. Nevertheless, the hard-core dirt of last
summer's cruising, plus industrial grime, mildew, and workmen's muddy hand and footprints that have accumulated
over the winter, are all there and must go—*now*. There is no
harm in giving in to the captain's pleading for a short day-
sail to usher in the spring while it is still grubby below deck,
but before the essentials for living aboard are brought on
and stowed, a thorough cleanup is in order. Otherwise, new
grime is added to the old and a depressing dinginess settles
over the whole boat, which cannot be removed by spot-
cleaning while under way.

First mates do not always take kindly to the process, and
with reason. For one thing, it smacks too strongly of the
drudgery of grandmother's day; modern housing and cleaning equipment has all but done away with spring-cleaning,
that primaveral rite in which the entire contents of a house
are moved to the front yard while all the females in the
family and the hired girl fall to with mop and broom. Why
fight progress? Why slip back into the dreary past on a boat?

For another thing, physical conditions for cleaning a boat
are not ideal. There is no hot running water, no all-purpose
vacuum cleaner, and the biggest patch of mildew is always
in the most unreachable spot. Raw hands and strained
muscles may be forgotten while sunbathing on deck in July,
but in April—try telling a first mate that will be the case,
captain.

There are ways to clean a boat, however, without breaking either backs or fingernails. It's been several years now

since I approached *Skylark* in the spring with buckets of
cold water and a pinched look about the mouth. By trial
and error, I organized the cleaning procedure and supply of
equipment so that she seemed to shine brighter each year
and with less pain and strain. Really.

Taking *Skylark* as a trial horse for The Kirstein Method,
as I shall, should be comforting to most first mates; few sailboats built nowadays have her expanse of painted surface
to clean. There is *no* boat that doesn't accumulate some
grime or grease during the sailing season, however, and
proper cleaning equipment contributes just as much to maintaining a happy ship in August as it did to attaining it in April.

First of all—the equipment.

1. *Mop (swab) of macaroni-size strands of synthetic
   sponge*
2. *Whisk broom*
3. *Child-size broom*
4. *Dustpan of hard rubber*
5. *Sponges, large and small*
6. *Rubber gloves*
7. *Scrub brushes, 1 large and 1 small*
8. *Toilet brush*
9. *Toothbrush*
10. *Metal bucket, preferably stainless steel*
11. *Second bucket or waste basket, preferably plastic*
12. *Cleaning powder, preferably white*
13. *Liquid detergent, strong*
14. *Rags*
15. *Paper toweling (lots)*
16. *Stove fuel*
17. *Beer (soft drinks may be substituted)*
18. *Radio (optional)*

Why this particular equipment?

1. A synthetic-fiber swab does not catch as easily on pro-tuberances as a string mop does, nor does it take as long to dry out. Too, it is bound to be the captain's choice for swab-bing the deck during cruising season for the same reasons, so it is a multiple-purpose item.

2. A whisk broom also has multiple uses: cushion clean-ing, corner cleaning, dusting off going-ashore clothes, etc.

3. A child-size broom fits the child-size space of a small boat, from both the cleaning and the stowage viewpoints. I spent much of my first sailing season on *Skylark* on my hands and knees, whisking up crumbs and blanket fuzz. Then I had a small brainstorm and I bought a small broom. I get a new one every year.

4. A dustpan of hard rubber not only bends into odd-size

cupboards, but it also bends back into shape, and it never rusts.

5. Large sponges are for large, dirty areas, and small ones for small ones, of course. But in some cases a small sponge is best for scrubbing really stubborn spots, no matter how large, because you can get your hand around it better, and thus, your back into it. Then, a quick rinse off with a large sponge, wrung out in clean, cold water, and you're done.

6. Rubber gloves need no explanation for first mates who value their skins and finger nails. I like the gloves with coated cloth linings best, simply because they feel less slimy.

7. The scrub brush that the captain will use for cleaning the boat's topsides will do for the big scrub brush, but a junior size of the same model is a blessed addition for below decks. It fits a lady's hand better, as well as the junior-size scrubable areas on most small boats.

8. Toilet brush: self-explanatory. A word of warning, however. To be eschewed at all costs are the plastic-handled ones with disposable paper heads. I tried one once and spent a messy quarter of an hour digging it out of the bowl. Between the toilet brush and the toilet string moplet, opt for the brush. The moplet sheds its strings, again to the peril of the system. Boat heads, unlike their counterparts on shore, can take no solid matter of any kind without clogging up. It is a slow, take-apart job to unclog them.

9. A toothbrush can act like a tiny whisk broom, squeezing into greasy or grimy crevices that are too small for even the human hand. It is also handy for flicking out the last few coffee grounds that spilled in the back of the food locker that windy morning.

10. A metal bucket of stainless steel is standard equipment on our boat. For example, it is used as a garbage bucket; from time to time it is scrubbed thoroughly and loaded with seaweed, salt water, and lobsters to be boiled;

it is used to carry water from shore when there is no dock with hose to tie up to. At spring-cleaning time it gets half-filled with water and is set on the stove to become the scrub bucket. Hot water is a basic requirement for an easy cleaning day.

11. A second bucket of plastic in a wastepaper basket shape is the junior jack-of-all receptacles on a sailboat. Ours normally lives beside my chest of drawers as a wastepaper basket, but it often leads a double life as an extra water bucket. At spring-cleaning time it is filled with clean cold water and follows its stainless steel big brother, rinsing off the muck he has raised.

12. Various cleaning powders have their loyal fans. Some like them white. Some like them green. My allegiance goes to a white-powder product with a high dirt-removing (and probably paint-removing) quality. Sprinkled on a wet sponge or scrub brush and wielded with hearty determination, a cleaning powder beats detergents all hollow for the removal of stubborn winter grime.

13. Detergents do have their place in spring-cleaning, particularly in the head. Again, I opt for a strong detergent, preferably one containing ammonia. Toilet bowls and wash bowls can take it. A detergent is all that is needed for cleaning formica surfaces, usually, as well as the insides of hanging lockers and clothes cupboards that have had little exposure to winter grime, and where a residue of cleaning powder may end up on clothes.

14. Rags have a special compartment on our boat, and I try to have at least six clean ones always on hand. An irreparably torn sheet is a cause for delight because rags made from sheets are soft, seamless, and absorbent. No self-respecting housewife needs advice on what to do with a clean rag.

15. Paper toweling also occupies a big place on our boat,

unfortunately, that's the problem with it—place. I stuff all I can in the housekeeping locker space, and then spread rolls of it around in any niche the captain permits me to use. I use it lavishly all during the cruising season, and at spring-cleaning time I would rather be without rags than paper toweling, beloved as rags are. Grease around the stove area comes off more easily with dry paper toweling than with a wet sponge, thus saving the latter for other uses. Dampened paper toweling doubles as whisk broom and dustpan in small areas, such as food lockers and wells at the back of bunks. Its uses, I find, are legion, and its easy disposability is endearing.

16. Stove fuel is for heating water in the metal bucket (but good, too, for grease spots).

17 and 18. The beer and radio items of equipment are integral parts of spring cleaning. As the captain bends on the sails, or tightens up the rigging out there in the sparkling spring air, occasional waves of self-pity sweep over poor perspiring me. Then I stop, light a cigarette, take a sip of beer, and go up on deck to supervise the captain for a spell. Sometimes I just have a sip of beer and go on working. The radio is for background music.

The line of cleaning attack varies, of course, according to the boat. Many modern boats, particularly those of fiber glass, have little or no painted surfaces below deck. A swipe of a damp cloth over the cabin's plastic inner skin or a dusting off of the wood paneling is all that is necessary. Heads, lockers, and drawers will, of course, need a going over on any type of boat. And the care and cleaning of the teakwood decks and paneling on old, and even more so on new boats is a problem. There is no need to rely solely on the classic soap-stone-and-elbow-grease method for cleaning teak now that commercial teak cleaners are sold in every marina, but there is no harm, either, in having a bit of these in reserve.

Spring-cleaning in any form may be no more than an item on your boatyard bill; some sailing friends of ours have a wooden boat the same length as *Skylark,* with approximately the same cabin area to be cleaned, but their boatyard in New England follows the admirable custom of shining up the inside as well as the outside of the boat before it is turned over to the owners in the spring. (The "custom" has a price, of course, but not an outrageous one.)

Not so in our boatyard. We live in a suburban town, twenty-five miles from New York, and our busy boatyard houses hundreds of sail and power boats in the winter. In the spring bustle we consider ourselves blessed if ours is among the first boats in the water—dirty below decks or not. The secret of our early exit, incidentally, is that we are one of the last boats into the yard in the fall. We officially close the sailing season with an October cruise, just as the leaves are turning red and yellow on shore and, the days are getting brisker and shorter, and we have the sea almost to ourselves. It is definitely what we call "Shipmate weather" then, as it is when we open the sailing season with an early spring cruise.

"Shipmate" is both the official and the loving name given to a cast-iron coal stove. Its contribution to both high morale and the superior quality of the cuisine aboard a boat is considered in the chapter "Choosing a Boat," but at commissioning time, it must be admitted, it is a problem—the captain's problem.

If you have a Shipmate, the captain must be pressed into removing the grease remaining from last season's cruise and the rust accumulated during the winter storage. Be sure he takes a wire brush, stove polish, a small paintbrush, and paper toweling along with him on one of the days he goes to the boatyard for pre-sailing-season foreman-heckling or do-it-himself work. The Shipmate must be cleaned with a wire brush, the stove polish must be applied and dry and the excess wiped off with paper toweling, before the portable fair-weather, alcohol cooking stove can be placed on its top, ready to heat water in the galvanized bucket for the first mate's clean-up day.

Then, with the Shipmate black as new, the captain out on deck where he now belongs, and water heating on the stove, the first mate is set to do some, or all, of the following:

1. Whisk out all the small areas: cupboards, drawers, lockers, etc. Use the toothbrush, as recommended above, for crevices. Collect the debris with either the dustpan or dampened paper towels. Dump it all on the cabin sole.

2. Sweep the entire cabin sole with a child's broom, dump debris overboard, and smile at the captain. He is already feeling sorry for you.

3. Add detergent to the now-warm water, fill the plastic bucket with clean cold water, take sponges, scrub brushes, cleaning powder, and water buckets to the forepeak, and wipe off—or scrub—the overhead, or cabin ceiling. No matter how little cleaning up your boat requires, the overhead is bound to have collected some fly specks, sooty film, and industrial grime. A sponge, dipped into the detergent water and wrung dry, will take care of most of it, but sometimes cleaning powder and sponge or scrub brush are needed. Rinse off with clean sponge and water. It is a good idea to wipe dry the areas where you have found mildew traces.

4. Now, repeat the same process for any washable area in the cabin, ending with the bunks, denuded of their mattresses, of course! Have a cigarette and a sip of beer before you take on the other cabin—if there is one.

5. Next comes the whisking and wiping out of closets, cupboards, drawers, etc.

6. Then, the head. *Skylark's* sink and toilet bowl are of enamel, so I always gave them the same treatment as their landlubber equivalents. Metal fixtures take kindly to an added swipe with a metal brightener.

7. Now, the galley counter-space, be it of Monel metal, like ours, or of formica, like many others. I use a metal cleaner on our Monel metal, and then shine it up with glass wax. Formica girls need only a damp sponge and a little detergent.

8. Finally, a floor mop-up and a mirror and porthole shine-up, and then, according to your stamina, your spirit, and your captain, you can go home and take a bath—or begin to bring aboard the things that make a boat a home. You are in shipshape condition to provision the boat with permanent boat gear, the essentials of happy sailing.

On our boat, the most *essential* essentials of living aboard come on as soon as possible after spring-cleaning day—if not that very day. Blankets, pots and pans, bed linens, bath accessories, and cleaning equipment are needed for even the shortest shakedown or weekend cruise, and might as well be in place and ready to go to Maine or Miami when that happy day comes. Pre-cruise provisioning is thus reduced to fresh food, clothing, unread books, unfinished knitting, and other odds and ends.

I regard these essential essentials as "permanent boat gear" and do not shuttle them back and forth between boat and shore during the sailing season. Once the season is over, the boat gear is cleaned, repaired, or mended, and sent into hibernation in a dry spot at home until the following spring. If budget and home storage space permit the first mate to have separate supplies for home and boat, she has a head start on boatkeeping fun. She can choose things especially adapted to boat use—and there are many—instead of having to make do with equipment that may work like a charm on shore but loses its magic at sea.

There is no need, to be sure, to insist that all boat gear be virginal. Slightly tired towels and sheets, for instance, can finish their lives with dignity at sea instead of ending up prematurely as rags or in the garbage can. (Sheets, by the time they are of boating age, are usually blissfully silky in texture.) Most shoreside blankets, however, are not good shipmates, for reasons to be gone into while expanding on the following list of basic equipment for living aboard a small boat:

Blankets
Pillows
Towels, bath and dish
Bed linens
Pots and pans
Kitchen tools
Flatware and tableware
Cleaning-up equipment

Blankets come in for harder use at sea than they do on shore. Except in rare and luxurious instances, bunks are made up each night and disassembled the next morning. As a result, blankets are handled a lot, so they must be sturdy. During the day they are stowed in close quarters, so they must be as unbulky as possible. They get a constant, though usually inadvertent, bath of salt spray, so they should have at least a modicum of water repellency. Because stowage space is at a premium, one blanket at sea should, ideally, do the job of two at home, so they must have a high heat-making potentiality. Since their nap gets a good work-

ing over in the twice-daily handling of them, they should be
of long-staple wool if blanket fuzz is not to become a nuisance. Long-staple wool, in fact, allows a blanket to comply
with all the above "musts"—*virgin* long-staple wool, that is.
Blankets that have reworked wool woven into them not
only shed nap shamelessly, but also take on a boardlike
quality that can best be described as unlovable. Blankets
of lovable, virgin, long-staple wool fold and stow easily,
shed water instead of nap, and cooperate readily with body
heat to keep the sleeper warm and snug. If you have such
unused treasures at home, fine, bring them aboard—providing they are of single- or three-quarter-bed size. Trying to
tuck a double-bed blanket under a bunk mattress less than
single-bed size is not good for the nerves at make-up time
or for lump-free sleeping later on. Dark colors are best, for
obvious reasons. The number of blankets, of course, depends
on the size of the crew and the degree of warmth that keeps
it happiest. On *Shag* we keep aboard three blankets
apiece, but seldom use more than two. Usually one on the
bunk and one in the bin above it, within reach, are enough
comfort, physically and psychologically. If stowage space is
truly limited, a man can be happy, my captain tells me,
rolled up in one blanket sans sheet. If they are warm, some
people apparently don't care if they itch. As an extra blanket, sports stores sell a waterproof blanket of vinyl lined
with a warm, soft synthetic material. It is marvelous for
sleeping on deck or as a leg covering in the cockpit on a
cold, wet day. Waterproof side up, it also frustrates leaks
over the bunk in a rainstorm.

Pillows on our boat, as on many boats, double as bedpil-
lows at night and backrests in the daytime. We have four,
covered in the same sturdy blue duck as the bunks—with
foam-rubber insides—that we slip into pillowcases at night.
We also have one feather pillow (mine) that refutes all my

captain's predictions that it would mildew, shed feathers constantly, and take up too much space. *My* head bounces on foam-rubber pillows, and it also drips perspiration on a hot night. I air my feather pillow from time to time (it stuffs unobtrusively into the blanket cupboard during the day) so that it doesn't acquire mildew, and two protective pillow covers of ticking, with their zippers at opposite ends from each other, keep feathers from annoying the captain (who just hates feathers, I guess), and I haven't heard another word from him in the subject.

Towels come aboard in quantities, as hands get dirtier the farther away we get from a water-supply stop. Our

towels are of all sizes and colors, and all are old. The same is true of our washcloths. Both items have tapes sewn across one of their corners to keep them safely on hooks above the toilet instead of, disastrously, in it. One of my less pleasantly memorable mornings on my maiden cruise was spent handing tools to the captain while he undid inaccessible screws and pipes in pursuit of a sneaky washcloth that I had failed to hang from its tape; it had fallen in and I had unsuspectingly pumped the flush handle—vigorously. Neither pipes nor captains of small boats take kindly to that treatment.

Dishtowels and dishcloths come aboard in liberal quantities, as they are easy to stow and have a fast turnover—especially when the captain washes the dishes. ("Scraping" the dirty dishes with paper towels before handing them over to the dishwasher helps somewhat, but in the end, it's the dishcloth that takes the rap.)

Bed linen—lots of it—is a freely used item of household equipment on *Shag*. Every three days, whether we need it or not, we have a complete change of bed linen. Many a salty sailor will sneer at our sybaritic ways, but clean-sheet night is a happy night aboard *Shag*—no yesterday's wrinkles to smooth out, and though I don't like to sound as if we never wash or swim, no yesterday's grime, either. If clean-sheet night happens to coincide with shower-ashore day, the purrs cannot be distinguished from the snores when the lights are out. Granted that *Shag* has unusually ample linen stowage shelves in the head, people with less space aboard can still luxuriate as we do, without necessarily having to stuff clean sheets into the sail locker. The sheet supply can, of course, be cut in half by using one folded-over sheet instead of two—one top and one bottom. I found that system highly unsatisfactory because of the straightjacket effect I always managed to achieve by morning. Then some bright fellow in the sheet business thought up the split-sheet idea, and I am sold on his product. For those who don't know about it, the split sheet is merely a standard-size double sheet folded down the middle, then cut down that fold to a depth of 36 inches from the top hem, with the slit firmly bound to prevent it from ripping into two sheets instead of one. The fold is tucked under the bunk mattress at the back, the bottom half under the remaining three sides, the top half left free, and you are ready for the blanket layer. Because of the middle slit, the top half's hem folds neatly over the blankets, and there you are—all set for beddy-bye. No danger of straitjacketing, as in the folded-over sheet method; no double effort, as in the two-sheet method. And, dirty or clean, half as many sheets to stow. Split sheets have two minor disadvantages: (1) they are not readily available, though some large department stores and a few posh sporting goods stores carry them, and (2) they are not what my broad-shouldered captain considers to be generous enough in width. Both those difficulties can be overcome by a little home industry: the first mate buys king-size sheets at White Sale time, slits them part-way down the middle herself, binds them in the wounded section, and everyone—with the exception of the commercial split-sheet manufacturer—is happy.

If sheet stowage space is a problem, why not make pillows of the sheets in the daytime? Many a small boat keeps its blanket supply in small, zippered cushion covers during the day. Fold the blankets, I say, *under* the bunk cushions in the daytime, instead, and stow excess clean sheets in the cushion covers. Blankets usually have to be liberated from any stowage place every night anyway, whereas clean sheets emerge only as the need or fancy dictates.

Soiled linen need present no more of a problem than that of shipping it home from the nearest post office. If other first mates dislike wrapping packages as much as I do, they will supply themselves with a heavy canvas duffle bag complete with small padlock and shipping label, thus eliminating the brown-paper-and-twine bit. A strategically timed stop at a Laundromat in one of the shiny new marinas that are burgeoning nowadays along with the yachting industry can also clean up the laundry situation neatly. Few marina Laundromats, however, have ironing facilities, so anti-wrinkle people will not be entirely happy with clean sheets done that way.

A final word about boat linens: Give each piece some mark of distinction, whether it is to be considered as permanent boat gear, and thus segregated from the other items in the linen closet at home, or gets year-round use. Otherwise linens get mixed up in the wash and it is a nuisance to sort them out afterward. The boat's name inked into one corner, or a whipping of colored thread, saves much toil and trouble at boat-provisioning time. For some reason, one undersized sheet (unmarked) always slips into the pile of regulars on *Shag*, evoking roars of anguish at bed-making time from the captain, who, of course, always happens to get it. He happened to once too often, and *Shag's* rag supply skyrocketed overnight.

Pots and pans are as personal with first mates as clothes; each first mate knows what suits her best. Some like pressure-cookers. Others are frightened to death of them. Some like percolators; others, dripolators. Everyone, however, has to consider the limited space on a small boat for stowing her pet pots, so let them be multipurpose. And rust-proof. I wouldn't think of frying bacon in anything but a heavy iron skillet at home, so foolish virgin-sailor that I was, I brought it along on my first cruise. For the first few days I kept the faith, working away at the new rust each morning. Then we made a truce, the skillet and I. It could just sit there and rust until we got home, and it wouldn't have to go on any more cruises. A square, stainless steel, two-faced griddle has taken its place, and I have grown so fond of it that I have a brand new replacement stored away against that day when Happytime Grill's handle comes off for good. (I do not trust "progress," as manufacturers term the seasonal changes they make in their products. For the same reason, I am also thinking of hoarding a case or two of the few remaining colorless cleansing powders.)

Nondentability and nonchipability become obvious requirements in the pots-and-pans department the minute the boat is taken on a beat to windward. No matter how snugly I have stowed the pots and pans after the morning washup, the banging and crashing sounds from the cooking-utensil bin rise and fall with *Shag* as she rides the wind and the waves. Enamel pots would soon chip away, so they are not good sailors. Soft aluminum pots acquire dents and lose their shape, a matter of importance when the bottom of the pan is affected, and they corrode quickly; even stoves hung on gimbals have a hard time keeping on an even keel in a head sea, and if a pot with an uneven bottom is added to the generally unstable situation, the cook is likely to spill the beans. Copper-bottomed cookware is a good choice and, incidentally, responds brightly to the same liquid we use for cleaning the brass on our boat, so there's no need to carry a special copper-brightener.

So, rust-proof, chip-proof, and dent-proof the pots should be, and the more multipurpose, the better. A stainless steel, copper-bottomed double boiler has earned more service stripes aboard *Shag* than any other cookware. Potatoes boil in its bottom half while red cabbage to go with the pork chops heats in the top. It breaks into two flat-bottomed sauce pans at times, and has even served as a water bowl for the dog and as a bilge bailer. (If that seems unsanitary as well as multipurpose, remember that our stainless steel garbage bucket is also our lobster boiler, packed with sea-weed and a little sea water. The double boiler is, of course, scrubbed and rinsed out with boiling water *after* dog or bilge use, and the garbage bucket *before* it takes on the lobsters. We haven't lost a member of the crew through ptomaine poisoning yet.)

The shape and size of a first mate's pots and pans depend on the number of stomachs aboard and what keeps them happy. If, as has been suggested elsewhere in this book, the first mate has a few menus planned in advance of the cruise, she will know what cookware she needs aboard for their preparation. She may need an oddball pan or two for some special gourmet recipe—a one-purpose pan that a dog would shun or that wouldn't fit in the bilge—but the fewer pieces she has to stow and care for, the more carefree a first mate she will be. And come dinnertime, she always has a perfect excuse for the simplicity of the fare: "I would have made sauce Béarnaise, but I didn't have the right equipment."

Flatware of stainless steel is the answer to a first mate's prayer aboard a small boat, as it is increasingly on shore; no tarnish, no rust, no metallic taste. Add a set of steak knives, and there will be no comments about the tenderness of the steak. (I found the steak-knife box an unwieldy thing to stow, so I transferred the knives to a flannelette, pocketed wraparound.)

Tableware is a fighting word to many first mates: some like it made of disposable paper, others are plastic lovers, still others have a childlike attachment to their white enameled plates with blue rims—just like the ones mother used to pack in the picnic basket. Even china is laid on some boats—though I must admit I am only reporting hear-say. *Shag* has metal dishes, bright and shiny and silvery. They are ancient and show a knife slash or two, but we find them a delight to eat from. I've never seen them on another boat, or in a store, for that matter, and my captain can't remember when they came aboard. We don't even know what metal they are made of. But none of that matters, of course. What does matter on *Shag*, as it will on any boat, is that they are the tableware that suits our taste and resists our destructiveness. Each first mate will know what will do the same for her and her crew. She has a wide choice.

Cleaning equipment has usually been brought aboard, on spring-cleaning day at the beginning of the season, so need only be checked again for possible replacement. I try to keep one can or bottle ahead of each item of cleansing product, and I also try to have a virgin sponge or two tucked away.

Now to the larder, first mates. Every can of soup that can go aboard at commissioning time is one less that will have to go into the provision hamper at cruising time—a hamper already overflowing with fresh food. Prudent captains insist that there be always aboard a week's supply of nonperishable food, in the unhappy (and unlikely) event that the boat is blown to sea and out of sight of supermarkets. For less dramatic reasons, forehanded first mates keep at least a skeleton supply of canned, short-order hot meals aboard; shopping day ashore is sometimes postponed by weather or itinerary changes, and canned beef stew is just what the captain orders. Staple canned goods on *Shag* are noted on a "permanent" list that I keep filed away during the winter in a folder with other important documents, such as passports and birth certificates, and the same number of old favorites (including condiments) come aboard year after year at commissioning time as automatically as do the sails. Some items, such as canned beef stew, somehow lose their savor when opened on shore, so any leftover cans from the sailing season are packed in labeled cartons and stowed with the permanent boat gear in our storeroom at home. Come spring, they are checked with the list, which is adjusted to any change in size or taste of the crew, and the supply is amended accordingly.

True, many small boats simply do not have storage space for anything more than is needed to fill the immediate demands of the crew, and canned goods can be brought aboard only as fast as they may be expected to go overboard— empty. The classic place for stowing canned goods on a small boat—in the bilge—can be used, but I think the procedure is more of a nuisance than it is worth; the labels must be removed from the cans and identifying symbols painted on instead. Too, there is something unappetizing about fishing a can of food out of rusty, oily water slopping around in the bowels of the boat. I am sure that if I were provisioning a boat for an ocean crossing, I would pop cans into the bilge with appreciation and abandon. But then I would also be writing another kind of book.

One admirable first mate I know stows her canned goods, lists them, Scotch-tapes the list to the cupboard, and checks off items as she uses them. I tried it, but the system broke down, and I now limit my orderliness to stowing all juices, fruits, and soups in one compartment, and meat-containing foods, coffee, and other various and sundry goodies in a second cupboard. Thus, I have at least a head start on finding the right can with the reach-and-feel method and, with practice, have developed a most sensitive touch for snagging a can of consommé instead of black bean soup at the first try.

Whatever else can be brought aboard at commissioning time, or in staggered dribbles on weekends as the boat rocks at its home mooring, should be brought. However, I urge first mates to refuse to take the sole responsibility for the captain's "professional" gear. Charts, sail-mending equipment, protractors, current and tide tables, etc., should be checked off *his* list by *him*. If he needs more marlin and hasn't time to go to the marine hardware store, fine—first mates can get it for him. But, I say, it should then be put in his hand and what he does with it is his responsibility. Incidentally, my captain heartily agrees with me. He knows what he wants, and he wants to be able to find it when he wants it.

Commissioning time is happy time. The future is full of lengthening, bright days and that cove in Maine is just around the corner. But what goes on the boat then has to come off in the fall, and by that time all the fun is over until another year. Nevertheless, it must be done, and if the impulse is resisted to just jumble the whole unsightly, beat-up mess into a likely corner at home and forget about it until spring, a first mate will have a leg up on the next commissioning time. There is no need to repair the summer's damage in one day, true. But little by little, a stitch here, a scrub there, and then a winter pack-away—of items considered as permanent boat gear—is to be recommended.

No matter how neat a boatkeeper a first mate is, her pots and pans can usually take a bit of brightening up at the end of a cruising summer. Galley stoves leave their sooty mark, and before the equipment is returned to the kitchen cupboard or wrapped in newspaper and sent into hibernation with the rest of the permanent boat gear, a going-over at home with a metal cleaner and hot, running water is recommended. Bunk and cockpit cushions may have accumulated Bloody Mary stains or a split seam or two, and need a scrub and a stitch. If their insides are damp, they should be left to dry before storing. Blankets should be aired—if not cleaned—before beginning their winter sojourn on land. Perhaps none of this will come as news to other first mates, but as for me, it was only after my second cruising season that

I was sadly convinced that unremoved dampness in December is mildew by May.

Shag, denuded of its summer plumage, gets a final sweep-out and wipe-out below deck before it goes forlornly into winter storage. Though the custom is motivated largely by sentimentality, there is also a practical reason: less scrubbing in the spring. Suburbanites though we are, industrial grime is everywhere in our village air, and when it settles on a base of bacon grease over the stove or cookie crumbles in the cupboard, it acquires a tenacity that is discouraging. We leave drawers and lockers open, as well as the icebox—cleared of its last melon seed—so that air can circulate freely. We even clean the last bit of soot from the brass kerosene lamps. But, as I say, we are mighty sentimental in the fall about *Shag*.

During the winter we go over to the boatyard to pat her occasionally, and there, high on her winter cradle, she seems to promise us that there will be another spring and time to commission again.

JANE KIRSTEIN

Women in the Boatyard

There are three types of people who own boats: those who can afford a boat, those who shouldn't afford a boat, and those who can't afford a boat. Those in the first and second groups generally keep their boats right up to snuff and looking spiffy. Those in the last group make a stab at it but never come out on top of the situation. The first group have their boats maintained in a boatyard and putter around the boat and its equipment only for the pleasure of it. The second group may have some work done by the yard, but they try to do as much as possible themselves for economic reasons. The third group do all their own work with whatever materials can be scrounged up when it's absolutely necessary, also for economic reasons.

Most people would say we are in the second category, but I'm not sure—every season when the boat is launched I know what hasn't been done and decide we're in the third group. We just keep trying to do better every year, and John wouldn't be worth having without a boat anyway. He's a dyed-in-the-wool sailor. He should have been born a hundred years earlier, in time to command that finest of racing machines, the Clipper.

There is a lot more expense to a boat than the cost of sails, and for a woman there is nothing more motivating to do-it-yourself work than the sight of an average yard bill! The jobs that require the least skill are the ones that cost so much in labor (which is time!), so women in the "shouldn't" and "can't" groups had better think of joining the team in the yard. It takes absolutely no skill to wield a scraper, putty knife, sandpaper, wire brush, or sanding machine. It takes very little skill to use a paintbrush and ninety-nine women out of every hundred are better painters than their male counterparts. (After a little practice, I could paint *Prelude* with one quart of topside paint whereas it took John two; it went on better, stayed on better, and was shinier. At least half a quart of his went on the ground, his pants, and his hands.)

Most women who decide to help out in the yard in the spring will find it a pleasant experience. There is a comradeship among skippers and crews in the yard as on the water. The yard workers, too, admire a willing worker and will be glad to help out in a sticky situation. The job of commissioning a boat is a satisfying one—you can see every bit of improvement.

Children love boatyards and can spend hours making their own toy boats out of various yard scraps, fishing along the shore, or staging battles among cradles and behind sheds. There is a certain courtesy to be observed where children are concerned, of course—no playing on the docks or boats, no kicking sand into paint or varnish, no tying cans to the tails of boatyard cats, etc.—but most mothers are used to dealing successfully with similar protocol elsewhere. We started our boys in playpens and graduated them to leashes before they were allowed to take off freely. Most children like to help—they particularly like to paint. As terrible as this may sound, encourage every bit of it because they'll soon grow big enough to be really useful! Last year we gave

Nate a can of red lead and a ratty brush and set him to work on the keel, figuring this couldn't possibly hurt and might even help. If a child is too young to paint with paint, give him an old brush and a coffee can full (half full?) of water and set him to "painting" the cradle. Children soon become interested in other boats or people in the yard and will gather all manner of information, which most boat owners are glad to pass out. A boatyard can be the very finest yacht club to be found!

Because we're all working for a good cause and "saving money," we often buy lunch at the boatyard—nothing more than sandwiches and soda, but it's a treat for me and always pleases the children. (Lunch Out!) A picnic is fun, too.

I'm not the world's champion housekeeper. I was brought up right and I know how to do things properly, but I don't happen to like that occupation best. I find that working on boats gives me a very good excuse to let things slide at home and get away with it. The way to a skipper's heart is through his boat, as I discovered very early in the game. Chances are, too, that I will get dinner out more often because I didn't get home from the yard in time to put the roast in.

A woman will come to know her boat well and will become very ingenious about certain repairs and maintenance problems. There is, of course, the right way to do every job, but I've found that the "right" way isn't always the best way. Every can of marine paint you buy will carry instructions stating that the paint should be used as it comes from the can (after stirring thoroughly). Scratch that! If you followed those instructions, the boat would have to be wooded (cleaned down to the bare wood) every two or three years, and that's one of the longest, grimmest, and grimiest jobs I know—we've done it to two boats and are about to start on the third. Besides, the paint manufacturers *do* mention, on the bottom of label, that the paint *may* be thinned. Most bottom paint in the can has the consistency of putty—and it can't be used in that state. Thin with brushing liquid, turpentine, or kerosene (whatever is recommended) to the consistency of condensed mushroom soup or mud. Bottom paint wears away some, so needs to be thick, and the bottom should be well sanded every year to avoid paint buildup. I won't say the job is any aid to beauty, but a woman is as good as a man at it.

Topside paint can be thinned almost 50 per cent if you're not trying to hide a bad preparation job. Thick paint is good only for covering layers of thick paint and it always looks *bad*. It peels, chips, and cracks easily, too. We thin topside paint with Penetrol, an extender and brushing liquid that

gives paint more working time without making it runny. Marine paints dry quickly and laps are hard to avoid, especially in very hot or very cold weather. I use the best 3-to-4-inch brush I can afford on topsides. Use any big brush on the bottom and brush the paint well into seams and cracks. Racing skippers fuss more over the bottom than any other part of the boat—a very good, smooth preparation job is mandatory there. It pays to use high-quality paint. Never use house paint—boats take lots of wear and tear from the elements and marine paints are made for the job. (I find they're best for porch furniture and bathrooms, too!) You may have to wood your boat to get a good start—it's really worth it, horrible job that it is—but if you sand surfaces well and thin your paints each season thereafter, you should never have to do the job again and your boat will look like the classiest of yachts.

The right way to paint a hull, I've been taught, is from the rail down—topsides first, boot top next, and then bottom painted up to the boot top. There is good reason for this; it's hard to paint a straight line along the water line upside down. And it's hard not to splatter paint on a finished surface below the one you are working on. We don't do it this way, however. Because our boat is wooden, we work like crazy to get the bottom cleaned up and painted first so that it won't dry out. We then proceed to topsides. Deck and brightwork come last and aren't finished when the boat goes into the water because we're rushing so to keep her from drying and opening seams.

It's very handy to be at a dock, while the boat swells or awaits her mast, to do your varnish jobs. There's less dust and no one is sanding topsides upwind. Seagulls don't care whether the boat is ashore or afloat, but watch out for ducks!

Varnish should be applied with the finest of brushes. And when the manufacturer states that varnish should never be thinned, believe him! Varnish should be put on as it comes from the can (do not shake or stir) with a very clean brush, allowed to dry thoroughly, and sanded lightly between coats. Horizontal surfaces, which are exposed constantly to the sun, take the hardest wear and usually require at least two coats of varnish. Vertical surfaces in good condition may be sanded lightly and given one coat of varnish. New wood requires at least four coats. We prefer a chilled varnish that has proved to be even tougher than the new synthetics.

Clean your brushes yourself and hide them. Skippers don't clean brushes ("woman's work") and always grab your best ones for any old job. Some brushes aren't worth cleaning, but the kind you should use on topsides and brightwork should be treasured.

While women do a good job of painting and varnishing masts and booms, skippers are automatically riggers. There are few men who sail who don't know all about every stick, block, and line they carry. They check standing and running rigging and all tackle before the mast is stepped and they tune it all after. Very few women and not many skippers are engine mechanics, so that is a job best left to the yard. Leave them the radio-telephone and Fathometer, too, unless someone in the family is an electronics engineer. Those are things that must be serviced thoroughly and properly, no fooling!

Fiber-glass boats save the boat owner much time on maintenance. Detergent, Babo, and wax clean the topsides, sanding and painting take care of the bottom. There may be brightwork, but not much, and it may be weathered or oiled teak or varnished mahogany. But fiber-glass boats cost a lot more to buy than wooden boats of the same size. Weigh your needs against your pocketbook to determine what boat you can afford to keep.

A dinghy can be transported atop your car from or to anywhere and stored in your own backyard, cellar, or garage to be sanded, painted, or polished. That may be all the yacht your family needs. *Cantie* was the last boat we trailed home and she was 26 feet long with a keel and draft of 5 feet. Even larger boats, in this day of fiber glass, can be hoisted by crane or lift, in their cradles, onto trailer or flatbed for transport to your backyard if you live a reasonable distance from the water and can get a few hefty friends to help get the boat off the trailer. This is done with planks, a crowbar, and a tackle. It's quite a sight, but an even better sight is your boat on the road. (Whew!) If you have a small or shallow draft boat, you might want to invest in a trailer with a winch in order to haul, portage, and store your boat yourself. (As did Bill Robinson, of *Yachting* fame, who has trailed and sailed his Amphibette over most of the country.) It's very similar to (but better than) trailing a camper.

You have a tremendous advantage toward superior maintenance if your boat is stored at home. Many and major projects can be undertaken without organizing a safari. Tools, food, coffee, and bathrooms are handy without lengthy interruption to progress. Little jobs can be taken care of in little pieces at a time, and the dust that blows around boatyards won't settle in your paint and varnish. You won't need a baby-sitter and there won't be any excuse for you not to work on the boat if it's right at home all day!

If the you-haul-it, you-store-it plan doesn't suit you or isn't feasible, or if you don't like to work that hard, you need to find a boatyard that will let you do all or any necessary work; one close enough to home for you to commute to, of course! If you have to spend every weekend in a motel (fun though that would be), it will cancel your savings on maintenance. You will be required to buy all paints and most hardware through the yard, and that's only fair because the plot is to keep the yard from charging all that *labor* to your boat! Yards are not happy about imported labor, whether it be expert or neighborly, so you must ask the yard to do whatever you can't handle yourselves.

A mate can make or break a boat's status in the yard. I have learned that there are friends, tolerable customers, and "people who won't be back next year." The boats belonging to those in the "won't be back" class are usually on the bottom of the work sheet because of some breach of yard etiquette. Many times, it is an overzealous mate who has reduced her boat's status. A skipper should have all business dealings with the yard (short of picking up another quart of paint). He should list jobs to be done by the yard and apply pressure if pressure is necessary (diplomatically!). If a mate is working on the boat and needs advice, she may ask for it from the yard boss, but she must be careful not to impose on yard time or personnel. The yard workers will be glad to talk during coffee break or between jobs. Much can be learned just from observing, and other boat owners love to give advice. Try to check all advice with the skipper and get his approval before using new products. Many new "miracles" won't work with or over whatever you have already.

Boatyard owners are, to a man, independent types. They don't like being pushed, they don't like being told how to do a job, and they don't like bossy women. Seventy-five per cent of their work is done in the spring and they must schedule their time and manpower accordingly. Given reasonable warning, a boatyard will do as much or as little as the skipper instructs. If he asks the yard to "paint the bottom and put her in," that's just what the yard will do—no more. If the skipper asks that the boat be well scraped, sanded, painted, and varnished to perfection, they'll do that too, at five to ten dollars per hour. Boat owners often quibble about the cost of labor or the amount of labor charged to their boats. That isn't fair, as you will learn if you do any work on your boat yourself. The labor rate must include some percentage for overhead, insurance, and social security, and a good job takes time. I know of one man who refused to pay for labor on an engine servicing job—he thought, apparently, that that was supposed to be included with the

4 quarts of oil and spark plugs. Obviously, no boatyard could survive that way! The cost of marine hardware is harder for me to understand (it might as well be gold-plated), but boat owners seldom argue about that—if they want it, they easily justify the cost. Everything for hardware, nothing for service—that's another way boats lose status in the yard.

After twenty-five years of boat maintenance of one sort

or another, I was hired as an able-bodied yard worker. It wasn't that I didn't have enough to do, nor was it any civil rights protest on my part; we found ourselves in the embarrassing position, due to an emotional decision the fall before, of owning and having to commission two 40-foot boats. We all worked on weekends and I worked all week on our fleet. When *Prelude* was slick and shiny, ready for a buyer, a buyer hove into sight. Great! Except for the fact that his finance company insisted the boat be refastened. The yard was already working overtime, John couldn't leave his job to refasten the boat, and it was a job I couldn't handle myself even had the finance company trusted me to do so. (I did bung the holes and chip the bungs, which I'd done before on *Cantie.*) So I went to work for the yard in the hope that they could find time to refasten *Prelude* before we lost our buyer—and they did!

My partner in the yard was a retired town policeman, a party boat skipper, a fisherman, and a native of Noank—a pure Yankee, tough and taciturn, named Palmy. Undoubtedly, I cramped his style and affronted his sense of the fitness of things, but he never said so. Luckily, he had a sense of humor. I thought we made a good team and I'm sure the yard boss and owner took some pleasure from his planning. Not only could he leave Palmy to deal with a female yard worker, but he could put *me* to the test. He knew I was used to maintaining a sailboat as a yacht. The first boat we were assigned to was a far cry from anything I'd ever dealt with. It was an old cruiser, 42 feet long, three stories high, and 6 inches off the ground. The biggest part of our job was to putty seams and paint the bottom, no mean trick with 6 inches to work in! After that we moved to a sailboat, but one that hadn't been loved for many years—a minimum maintenance type. It broke my heart, for she had once been a nice Hinckley sloop. The third boat I had all to myself and it was a vacation after the other two! A spanky little runabout that only had to be polished and washed before the bottom was sanded and painted. I got the first paycheck I'd ever earned in my life, John got a good laugh and a buyer for *Prelude,* and the boys got to spread the rumor around school that their mother worked in a boat-yard.

Before we left the yard, I started work on the yard tug, a very snappy craft named *Little Toot.* She was snappy except for her cabin, that is. The red had peeled and faded to pink, and no tug should appear in pink! I didn't get the job finished because *Skylark* was sailing by then, but I hope to get the second coat of red on this spring—after all, we'll only have one 40-foot boat, three dinghies, and a kayak to get ready this time!

MARY LEONARD

For Husbands Only: The Care and Training
11   of First Mates

~~~~~~

Dress a woman up in foul-weather gear from head to boot and it's easy for her captain to forget there's a difference between boys and girls. But, if he's wise, he remembers.

He remembers if only to assure himself of a steady crew. Joshua Slocum, on *Spray*, may have sailed around the world alone at the end of the last century and many a single-hander may have followed in his wake, but, by and large, sailing is a family affair. True, many small boats go to sea with an all-male crew, splitting family units right down the middle for a spell, but those are temporary arrangements. Rare are the sailing cronies who can get away from office and home at the same time, time after time. The captain's most available crew is usually right in his own backyard—a ready, willing, and able first mate. If she isn't at least ready and willing, the captain has mostly himself to blame. He has slipped up, somewhere, in her care and training.

Most women sailors are good sports. They go to sea because they love sailing and/or their husbands, and they

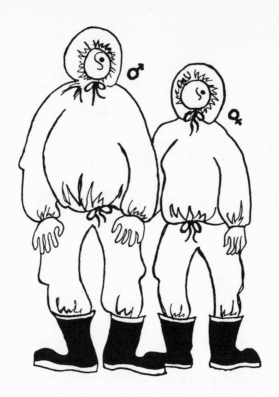

earnestly want to be competent first mates. Competent first mates are made, not born, just as are first-class cooks. There *are* natural-born sailors, men or women who take easily to the sea and its ways, just as there are people who have a special flair for cooking, but experience in both areas is the basic ingredient for flawless performance. (Remember that first roast beef when the honeymoon was over?) Experience in cruising aboard a small boat is acquired under unfamiliar and sometimes uncomfortable conditions, and the boat's narrow confines breed an intimacy that can get on one's nerves—male or female—if little problems are allowed to grow into big ones.

Problems had apparently reached giant proportions on a small boat we saw one day in Great Harbor, Wood's Hole, Massachusetts.

It was one of those hot, humid summer days when Vine-yard Sound is laced with low-lying fog banks, and out of the blue we ran into one, just south of the powerful horn on Nobska Point. Though it had been clear when we left our anchorage at Vineyard Haven that morning, the captain forehandedly had taken off compass courses from the horn to the zigzag of buoys that mark the tricky, narrow passage between rocks, past the Wood's Hole Oceanographic Insti-tution, with Great Harbor next to it, and into Buzzard's Bay, where the fog often lifts over the land.

Most Buzzard's Bay sailors are an indomitable lot who never let a little thing like zero visibility keep them at their moorings, and we came unnervingly close to some of them. A breeze was coming up, likely to blow the fog away before long, so the captain, who dislikes fog and knows I *hate* it, decided the whole thing would just be more fun if we turned into Great Harbor, had a drink and an early lunch, and waited for the soupy mess to blow away.

We were not alone in our decision. Wood's Hole yacht harbor was crowded with visiting boats, most of them with their crews in the cockpit already having a drink and an early lunch. We picked up an empty mooring, probably belonging to one of the indomitable Buzzard's Bay crowd whom we had just "grazed" out there, and as the captain busied himself coiling lines in the cockpit, I lingered on the bow to watch a young couple on a nearby sloop who were struggling with a dragging anchor. What rivetted my atten-tion on them was that they also seemed to be struggling with each other. Apparently there was a divergence of opinion as to how the thing should be handled, and tempers were audibly rising.

He hit her. To my utter astonishment, the young man on the bow of the sloop swung a long arm toward the young lady at his side, and I not only saw the blow, I heard it.

There was a brief, stunned silence on both boats before we first mates caught our breath; then the stricken lady let out an outraged whoop that drew every eye in the harbor to the embattled craft, ran 25 feet to the stern of the boat, and jumped into the trailing dinghy.

"George," I hissed in a stage whisper, "did you see that?" But my captain was busy calculating how soon the sloop would be drifting into our immediate vicinity and hull, and he was shouting advice to the young man who was working desperately to get his dragging anchor to hold before that unsailorly eventuality occurred. Fifty feet from impact, the anchor caught on an unoccupied mooring line, and though fouled, it held. The emergency over, my captain looked at me, and I looked at him, and we both shook our heads sadly. That was not a happy ship.

When we left, an hour later, the young man was still trying to free his hopelessly entangled anchor from the chain of the mooring and the young lady was still slumped in the dinghy, her head in her arms. There were no oars or motor in the dinghy, and it was a long, cold swim to shore. We wondered how long it would be before *that* cruise was resumed. Most of all, we wondered how long the tensions leading to the incident had been building on that craft.

A wise captain will not allow tensions to build. At the first sign of mutiny, he will find out what is bothering his first mate and see what he can do about it. He does at home, after a door slam or two. Why not at sea?

What, a captain may ask, can he do about conditions at sea? He has no control over the weather. He can't add another wing onto the sailboat to make more room. If trouble is brewing, he would *like* to ease the situation. He loves his wife and he loves sailing, or he never would have bought the boat in the first place. What can he do?

He can begin at home, with the charts spread out on the

living room floor. Keeping in mind the probable weather
conditions at the time of the proposed cruise, and with a
rough idea of the area to be covered in the time available,
the captain *and* his first mate should block out an itinerary.
It is astounding to me to find that this is seldom done.
Instead, the general cruising area may be agreed upon as the
sailing season nears, and from there on the captain is on
his own. He probably assumes that his first mate is with
him mentally, every nautical mile of the way, up the coast,
into the bays, and home again, but most of the time she
isn't. She reasons that the captain is the navigator. He will
get them to their destination and back. Her job is to see
that the gear they will take is in good shape and proper
quantity, and she leaves the rest of the planning up to the
captain.

She may well leave it up to him if they have sailed over
much water together and he knows and respects her likes
and dislikes on sea as well as on land. The captain who
plans, without being told, to include a layover day at Old
Barrington because there is an antique shop on the water-
front there that his wife likes to explore, or who remembers
to favor picturesque fishing villages over glossy marinas

because his wife paints, doesn't need to hunch on the floor with her over charts. (Actually, such a sailing couple will be hunched there together anyway, shouldering each other out of the way, at cruise-charting time. It's a delightful way to spend an evening, particularly a winter evening.) He is a captain who can tell a girl from a boy, even in foul-weather gear, and he is willing to make concessions to the difference at sea, just as he does on land. He has also tacitly exacted a few concessions of his own, just as he does on land, and has traded equally: an antique shop for a great spot for mackerel fishing the following day, and maybe the day after.

Captains may point out that such amiability has nothing to do with sailing, that a man goes to sea because he is a salt, not a tourist. He longs for brisk winds, above all, and doesn't much care where they will take him. He can't govern their direction nor the schedule they will dictate. (One of the most impossible questions to answer precisely aboard a sailboat is "When will we get in?" My captain tries this: "You tell me from what direction and velocity the winds will be all day, and I'll answer your question.") True, no captain, however experienced, can chart a cruise over water as he can a motor trip on land; a sea chart cannot be used like a road map. But the spirit with which both sorties are planned should be the same. Superhighway or back roads? Motels on the edge of town or hotels in midtown? Beaches or mountains? Decisions on all such choices are negotiated on land, usually without a cross word. Coves or marinas? Long sails or short? Antiques or mackerel? These are negotiable, too, and first mates should be urged to voice their preferences. A captain who heeds them, wind and tide willing, has a good chance of finding a happy woman under that foul-weather gear on a long boat to windward, when he is headed for his mackerel-filled cove.

He has an even better chance if he has helped her acquire

at least a basic knowledge of seamanship early in their sailing life. Most captains, I have found, have a head start on their first mates in seamanship. As boys, they raced dinghies, or as men, they crewed on other captains' boats, whereas their brides' previous experience aboard a small boat, if any, may have been limited to making Bloody Marys or handling an occasional line.

Seamanship, the art—or skill in the art—of working and piloting a vessel, is, of course, what sailing is all about. Captains who think one skilled sailor—the captain—is all that is necessary aboard a small boat, and who neglect that part of the training of their first mates, make a mistake for two reasons: (1) First mates who know something about seamanship are almost never peevish; the more they know about the problems in handling a small boat, the more understanding they will be of the captain's role. (2) The more they know about seamanship, the sooner will come the unique rewards of sailing as a team—the freedom and the pride, and so, the fun.

Too many captains do not realize that the real fun of sailing, whether cruising or day-sailing, begins for the first mate only when she becomes a sailor rather than just a passenger. So as not to frighten their brides away from the

sea before they even get them there, captains often sing the praises of long, sunny days aboard a pleasure-luxury-yacht (be it ever so small or so bare!) and promise their novice first mates that they will not have to lift a finger.

My captain was, apparently, one of those. True, it was my shakedown cruise—my first cruise on a sailboat—and it was our honeymoon. The captain, who had sailed most of his life so far and hoped to sail out the rest of it, planned to break me in easy.

To my surprise, I found that just being a body—a passive passenger—on a small boat wasn't the fun I had expected it to be, after the first few lazy days. The beauty of the sea palled. The sun either seemed to beat down relentlessly, or not enough. I was always in the captain's way, no matter how I shifted position, and most of all, I felt so inadequate. I wanted to help but I didn't know what to do.

Then my captain, a wise man, knew the time had come to teach me some seamanship.

My training began by taking the helm, and almost from that moment on I was "hooked" on sailing. I say almost, because terror dimmed my enjoyment for many a turn at the helm: terror that I would get off course, endanger the boat, accidentally jibe, or just look foolish. But the captain was relentless. He sat me down, refused to take over unless disaster seemed imminent, and—from time to time offering instructions in gentle tones—waited for that moment of truth to come when the boat and I would "communicate." At last, I gave her what she wanted in the way of wind in her sails, and she gave me a feeling of exhilaration that only sailors can understand. Of soaring like a seagull in an updraft of air. Of galloping a fresh horse over an endless plain. Of catching a whisper of a new and lovely truth. You will excuse the expressions; that's just the way it is.

As I say, my seamanship began at the helm, but for other

first mates it may well begin in the family bathtub at home. A full tub of water, a toy sailboat, and an electric fan or a powerful set of lungs can be the classroom equipment for a cram course in winds and how they affect a sailboat. I spent more than one evening on my knees beside the bathtub, with a portable fan in one hand and an illustrated book for junior sailors in the other. Now, old salt that I am, I can't remember why it was so difficult for me to figure out such a simple thing as the difference between "coming about" and "jibing." We were turning in another direction from the one in which we had been going, with either maneuver. What difference did it make what it was called? I will admit that I still have to think, sometimes, which way I should turn the wheel when the captain calls "jibe-o," and because he cares for me as well as tries to train me, the captain also adds, if he sees me hesitate, "wheel down—to the left," or "to the right," as the case may be.

In fact, sailing terms were in minimum use until I learned my way around the binnacle. Once I could tell a halliard from a sheet, the use of marine nomenclature was stepped up a bit and operations unquestionably went more smoothly. No longer was it necessary for the captain to use ten words to do the work of two or three and, more important, I didn't have the mainsail fluttering down over our heads when what he really wanted was for me to let it out a bit. As I say, though, I still need mental nudging from time to time, and am grateful that my captain gives me time to acquire salt gradually. Though I recommend like patience to other captains, it may be that lessons in seamanship—from nomenclature to navigation—should come from an instructor outside the family circle. Any captain who has tried to teach a Loved One to drive a car will know what I mean.

Lessons in seamanship used to be a hard thing to come by, but now, with the growth in the number of new sailboats and sailors, classes in the handling of small boats are being offered with increasing frequency.

Membership in a yacht club that has sailing classes as part of its activities is one entree to the academe of seamanship. But there are several others: (1) Yachting magazines carry advertisements of sailing classes given by experienced sailors. (2) A few municipalities, near the water, return part of a salty taxpayer's dollars in the form of sailing lessons. Our village owns a fleet of five small day-sailors, and they are the busiest boats in the harbor all summer long. (3) National organizations, such as the Red Cross, Boy Scouts, and YMCA, offer sailing instructions as part of their safety or outdoor programs. (4) The American Sailing Council, a group of sailboat builders and manufacturers of sailboat equipment devoted, they say, to furthering the sport of sailing, will supply beginners with lists of places where sailing instruction is available. (For information, write to American Sailing Council, 420 Lexington Avenue, New York, New York.) (5) The U.S. Coast Guard, which has a big stake in the campaign to encourage proficiency in boat operation and adherence to safe boating practices, works through its Auxiliary to assist in the education of the newcomer to the sport. (6) The United States Power Squadrons, who hold classes similar to those conducted by the Coast Guard, concentrate on such subjects as: piloting (use of charts and compass), recognizing and utilizing aids to navigation (buoys, lighthouses, etc.), rules of the sea, safe motorboat operation, and accident prevention—all essential elements of seamanship, even if they don't have to do with the wind in the sails.

If, as it happens in rare cases, a captain has a reluctant scholar on his hands, he personally can help her through the classroom door. Captains and first mates who study together, stay together, as the saying goes. During the ensuing bull sessions the captain will find the area in which the first mate excels and thus be better able to capitalize on her potentialities for being a helpful member of the crew. A first mate who can take off a new compass course on a chart while the captain concentrates on keeping temporarily on the present course is a whole lot better than any old port in a storm. A first mate who has the eyesight to distinguish buoys on the horizon, and also the wit to locate same on the chart, not only pulls her weight on a sailboat, she is worth it in gold. What is more, she is happy; she is needed and she is adequate. A girl likes that feeling at sea, just as much as she does on shore.

A word of warning on that score, however, captains: Don't give her more than she can handle, either physically or mentally, or she will mutiny, sooner or later. I, for one, am both amiable and expert while picking up a mooring buoy with a boat hook, but ask me to throw over the anchor, and I would balk. I *like* to take off compass courses on a clear day when any mistake I might make would not seriously endanger life or boat, but when a thick o' fog settles in, it's the captain who mans the protractor and I take the helm. It may turn out to be quite different on another boat, with another captain and another first mate. I've seen many a first mate easing the anchor over the side or bringing it up as the captain handles the helm, and I may have been wrong in thinking that either the captain had a heart condition or the first mate was put upon. That may have been the way they both liked it. After all, lifting a 20-pound Danforth is within a girl's capacities. Whatever the division of labor on a small boat, it should be happily agreed upon, each task according to the strength and ability of the parties involved. Smooth teamwork is the goal, no matter how it is arrived at.

Teamwork frees the sailing couple from the necessity of taking on extra crew just to help handle the boat. Guests may be great, and some couples wouldn't be without them on a cruise. But there comes a time in every captain's and every first mate's life when they want to get away from it all—alone. A small boat gets smaller with every added body aboard, and strains increase as space diminishes, love your friends as you do. Moreover, friends who sail are not always available at the chosen cruising time, nor do they always like antique shops or mackerel coves as well as the first mate and her captain do. In any case, a sailing couple that is self-sufficient is free to take guests or leave them behind. They are also free to choose their guests just because they like them, and not because they have strong backs or are wizards at navigation.

A smooth-working team of captain and first mate is a pretty sight coming into a harbor. If they bring the boat in under full sail, they are downright handsome. Even if they come into a deserted harbor, with no one watching and no sails up to complicate the business of anchoring, they are beautiful unto themselves. There is a pleasant feeling of smugness that comes to a proficient team of captain and first mate that is one of the great rewards of sailing. Sails up or down, fair weather or foul, crowded anchorage or not, they can cope, and they can do it alone.

There is no rule of thumb by which to know what a first mate can best do on a team. Each boat differs in its demands from the crew, and each captain will have to find out for himself whether to handle the jib sheet while his wife, at the helm, brings the boat around on a tack, or vice versa. Trial and error will show the way to teamwork, and captains who are indulgent towards errors will find their first mates making them less and less often. I repeat: A first mate is made, not born.

Helmsmanship is one facet of seamanship that a first mate can handle easily, and usually very well. And a captain should encourage her to do it. Some first mates I know are never given a whack at it until the captain has to go forward to throw over the anchor or go below for a minute, and so they not only miss much of the fun of sailing, but are too inexperienced and tense to do a good job. Teamwork begins at the helm, and I will wager that in every proficient sailing couple you will find a first mate who can steer as well as cook. Seamanship, of course, is made up of many elements and will be practiced in varying forms or combinations on different small boats.

The training of a first mate in seamanship, whether beside the family bathtub, in a sailing class, or at the helm itself, is only part of the recipe for a happy, well-sailed boat. There's the tender, loving care part, the recognition, for instance, that a clean body and a clean head of hair lie close to every woman's heart—no matter how salty a sailor she is. If, as is true on most small boats, the water supply is limited, the captain should get her to a shower on shore from time to time.

Actually, it was a total stranger and not my captain who got me to one in Georgetown, Maryland, which is up the Sassafras River from Chesapeake Bay, but a shower *was* on our schedule. We were watching our boat being treated for some minor wound inflicted on the way down, by a submerged log in Manhattan's East River, when the captain off a ketch in the harbor joined us. That gentleman offered the keys of his car to me and said, "If you are like my wife, you might want to go find a shower in town while you wait."

While I was gone, my captain learned that this man and his wife sail every possible moment of his semi-retirement, that his wife insists they live on the boat after he finally retires, and that—there is no need to add—they were a devoted sailing couple.

The moral of my story is that the aforesaid gentleman-captain knew his wife was a lady, and he wasn't fighting it. Getting her to a shower was undoubtedly only one of the ways he showed he knew, and cared. We didn't go into it, but I'm sure their cruise itineraries were always negotiated. That they were a proficient team was unquestionable; I saw their 40-foot ketch, and it needed two to make it go. Moreover, I would bet my bottom dollar that he wasn't what I call a "hero" type of captain.

A "hero" captain is one who goes out in all weather—ignoring ominous weather reports and lowering skies—even though he is not racing or in a hurry to get anywhere. He carries too much sail in the face of an impending storm, and then prefers to "run it out" rather than put into a nearby protected harbor. Or he insists upon groping through thick fog, willy-nilly, though he can't see his hand before his face, let alone hazards or tankers on a collision course. He will beat into a blustery head wind, soaking gear and the freezing crew in the process, even though time is not of the essence and a layover day or a more leisurely pace would be easier on both the crew and the boat. A "hero" is not only unattractive. He is dangerous.

Having said all that, I would like to mitigate it a bit. If sailors throughout history had waited for fair weather before putting out to sea, and then hightailed for home again the minute the sun went behind the clouds, a lot of real estate would still be on the open market. Today, men who go to sea for pleasure are no less masculine than their hardy forebears. In fact, one of the reasons they go to sea today is to prove that to themselves; a slippage of a few hundred years back into history, and they might well have been crew on the *Santa Maria* or the *Golden Hind.* And what, a captain may ask, is so dreadful anyway about cold winds, high seas, and fog? A man who spends his working hours in an air-conditioned office and steps out of it into the smog not only welcomes wind and rain in his face, he needs it. Above all, if there were no challenge from the elements to be met, most of the fun of sailing would be gone. There is no trick to handling a sailboat on a sunny day with a light wind abeam.

True, all true. And I would add that the majority of the memorable sails we have had have been when the seas were high, or the fog was down, or there was so much wind that even with the mainsail furled, and running under jib and jigger alone, we seemed to be carrying too much sail. We may have been wet and cold, but those are the sails we remember—and with pleasure—more than the endless succession of fair days in a normal sailing season.

But, captains, there is a difference between "making do" with bad weather and going out *looking* for it, as far as first mates are concerned. There isn't a sailing couple worth their salt who haven't had to reach, at one time or another, for their foul-weather gear, and I doubt if many of the first mates complained. When we cruise from the harbor at Mamaroneck, New York, to St. John, New Brunswick, Canada, I do not throw myself down on the cockpit floor and kick and scream if a storm comes up on an overnight passage. Nor when coming back from Maine do I jump ship because I know that we will be wet and cold much of the week or ten days if the seasonal prevailing wind is, as usual, from the southwest and right on our nose. In other words, I am not a sissy, nor are other first mates. They take the foul winds with the fair, and have fun, knowing it is all part of sailing. They will brew up hot consommé in the middle of the night and they will take the midnight-to-dawn watch with the best of captains, without snivelling, providing they are persuaded that there is a reason for it.

I, for one, didn't need much persuasion to leave Boothbay Harbor, Maine, one morning late in August to go out in what threatened to be more than a comfortable wind for our size boat. We had been fog-bound in that lovely but now tiresome harbor for three days and were itchy to go farther to the west and home. For two weeks we had been following the jagged Maine coastline, and a delightful two weeks it had been. Fog—Maine's summer problem—had dogged us little, and the few times it came down we went up the widemouthed rivers, where the nasty stuff dissipated over the land. The time had come, though, as it does on all cruises, when our duties at home were calling us back, and we decided that the first moment the wind shifted from the fog-making, southerly quadrant, we would be off and running.

We knew the wind was bound to shift before long because at that time of year, in the Northeastern part of the United States, what I call the "Battle of the Highs" is resuming, and the Arctic High always begins to win out over the Bermuda High. I will explain this, though meteorologists may think I oversimplify.

For my purposes, it is enough to know that a high (short for high-pressure system) is synonymous with fair weather. Where we live, there are two highs that govern our outdoor lives, the cold Arctic High and the warm Bermuda High, and they are engaged in a constant fight. When the weatherman begins to talk about Bermuda Highs, in the spring, I know that warm air from the southern hemisphere is not just sitting there near the equator, but is flexing its muscles and beginning to push its way north. Summer, and sailing, is just around the corner. For a while, its opposition—the Arctic High—puts up strong resistance and successfully pushes its cold air masses on down from the North Pole, occupying and holding the battlefront—us, that is, the temperate zone. All summer there are skirmishes between the two highs, with the Bermuda winning most of the time for a few weeks. Then, reluctantly, the Bermuda High retreats, a few days at a time, and ultimately surrenders to the Arctic High, and winter. There is no question in my mind which side I am on; the Bermuda High believes in the same things I do—sailing, swimming, and sunbathing—but it mixes its blessings with fog at times, in most parts of the Northeast, and most of all, in Maine.

When we left Boothbay Harbor, however, even I was plugging for the Arctic High to win. Not only would it melt away the fog, but it would also bring north winds with it, and we could *use* those winds, going south as we were.

The night before the weatherman had said the magic words. A Polar High was on its way toward us, and it was a massive one. The wind was expected to shift in the night, when the cold front arrived, bringing first rain and then north winds—50- or 60-mile-an-hour winds, the man said. The captain and I had a little talk. That was a lot of wind for our boat. Oh, she could handle it all right—had many times. But, she hadn't deliberately gone out looking for such a wallop; it had just happened to her in the course of twenty years' cruising in fair weather and foul. There turned out to be more pros than cons in our discussion, however, so after checking over our foul-weather gear and thermal underwear (we had been provisioned up to our ears with food, water, and gas for days), we turned in and waited for the polar air to come charging in.

It did, about midnight, with a whoop and a holler of thunder and a torrent of rain that washed every grain of salt from the decks and every droplet of fog from the harbor.

The next morning the wind velocity was as advertised and there were few boats other than ours moving in the harbor. True, it was still dawn. Too, the red flag that warns small craft to stay put was flying. One sloop, with, of all ill-advised things, a large Genoa jib set, poked her nose out of the harbor with us, but apparently her captain didn't like what the wind and waves were doing so he turned tail and, with difficulty, headed back for home. Running under jib and jigger alone, with the mainsail prudently furled, we headed for Gloucester, and as the captain said, we had a sleigh ride; those two small sails carried us ahead at hull speed—the maximum speed she had been designed for.

The storm in the night and the high wind had played games with the sea, and the waves were tall and confused. But, when we rose from their troughs, the visibility was endless. We could see the conical red nun buoys as far as the horizon and had Sequin Island Lighthouse in sight for hours—ahead, abeam, and astern. And there on land, around noon, we could see Mount Agamenticus, our standing joke. If Easterners will permit, Mount Agamenticus is a *hill* to a girl from Seattle. Anyway, *I* always laugh when we pass Mount Agamenticus. My husband grew up in Boston.

The waves, I will admit, were mountainous, and quite often we found they were cold as they pounded against the wind and sprayed over the bow and the stern. As to the wind—remember, it was from the Arctic. There were moments during that day when I wondered why we were in such an all-fired hurry to get home, and others when I even wondered, foolishly, if we *would* get there. There seemed to be a certain amount of wonderment, too, aboard a turquoise-blue Danish freighter we saw close by when we rose momentarily from the trough of a wave. Binoculars were trained on us—apprehensively, we fancied—until we waved sturdily and flew cheerily on.

We flew so fast that we almost missed Cape Ann. It *looked* like Cape Ann, but it just couldn't be. According to our reckoning, it should still lie well ahead. We almost missed Gloucester, too, for the same reason, though night had fallen and you would think we could tell where we were by the characteristics of the light on Thatcher's Island. By that time we were wary, however, and mighty weary, so we accepted the fact that we were off Gloucester, entered the harbor, picked the first likely spot inside the breakwater, and threw over the anchor. Wet, cold, dog-tired but happy, we had a warm-up nightcap of three large fingers of bourbon and turned in. The next morning we woke up to find that we had anchored almost in the middle of Gloucester's large outer harbor, and though dozens of fishing boats must have passed close by on their way out to sea, we hadn't heard a thing. It was a fine morning—bright, warm sun and a gentle wind. Before long we set sail and went back to leisurely port-to-port sailing, hugging the shore. We could afford to, now. The back of the homeward trip had been broken.

So there was a reason for ignoring the small-craft warnings in Boothbay Harbor. My captain was not acting like a "hero," but like a reasonable man, as any first mate could see.

"Heroes," or unreasonable men, go out in the wind and the rain just for the ducks of it. First mates of "heroes" should not be hog-tied and slung on board just because their captains feel an urge coming on and need a crew. There is an alternative. Other men can be found—men who furtively read adventure magazines in their offices when their secretaries are out of the room and who will spring to the tiller at the first sound of a foghorn. The all-male cruise under the best of conditions is wonderful fun, and even under the worst it can be fun for "heroes." They will drive into head winds all day, and talk about it half the night. They will ghost past the *Queen Mary's* bow in a thick o' fog, and laugh boisterously about it afterwards. And they will come back to their first mates exhausted but happy. Do it, "hero" captains—and first mates, let them. Boys will be boys, but girls don't have to be. Maybe they will get "heroism" out of their systems and take you on a lady-liking cruise later.

One final word for captains: DON'T SHOUT AT YOUR FIRST

MATE. Of all the complaints registered by sailing wives, being shouted at is the most prevalent, and the most resented. Shouting in public—in a crowded anchorage—is the most heinous crime of all, but an overly raised voice packs trouble even on the broad reaches of the open sea. Not only does a shout raise the female dander; a shout is likely to panic the lady right out of action, when action is what the captain is yelling for. Unfortunately for happy cruising, there are more shouting captains than one would think.

Captains may argue that there is good reason to shout at sea. Things have to be done in a hurry on a small boat, or worse things will happen. There is no time to say "please" when the first mate, at the helm, is about to allow an accidental jibe. Nor will soft tones carry above the sound of the wind or the motor. An angry first mate is preferable to going aground or ramming a dock. Anyway, a captain may say, he isn't shouting at her because he hates her. Women are too sensitive.

That the captain is absolutely right doesn't help matters at all. The fact still remains that women don't like to be shouted at, and he might as well face it. Fortunately, there are ways of keeping shouting to an acceptable minimum, and casualties, ditto.

Hand signals are the answer much of the time. They should be clear and the crew well-rehearsed in them, or they can cause more trouble than a raised voice. Generally, the instinctive gesture is clear enough to get the message across, but a practice session or two is good therapy for nervous first mates. "Go left, go right, ahead, reverse, neutral"—all can usually be transmitted by hand signals that are agreed upon ahead of time.

If shout you must, shout *away* from the wind, not into it —an obvious but oft-forgotten maxim. Look at your first mate, captains, not at the object you want her to miss. By the time she has said, "I can't hear you," it may be too late. It's anti-instinctive to point one way and look the other, but it keeps voices and accidents down.

Self-control is, of course, the key to the whole problem of shouting, and self-confidence is the master key to self-control. A nervous captain, a man who isn't sure what he or his boat is or should be doing, is likely to be short on self-control. He has enough things to worry about without having to remember to keep his voice down. There is no short-term solution to this problem. Self-confidence comes with experience, but remember, captains, that experience comes only with more and more sailing, and for that, you need a crew. Remember, too, if you think you're nervous, you should have a look inside your first mate's stomach: butter-flies the size of seagulls. A jaunty smile, strained though it may be, will go a lot further toward quieting flutters than a shout.

The recipe for a happy ship is not hard to come by, really. Pre-cruise consultations, lessons in seamanship, a fair distribution of duties, no "heroics," an occasional shower, and a bit of self-control don't seem too much to ask of captains. If he thinks they are, he'd be best off looking into the game of golf as a sport, now. He'll have to, sooner or later, because he won't be yachting much longer.

JANE KIRSTEIN

The Other Side of the Coin

Dropping and hauling anchors is old hat to me—I've done it from Sag Harbor to Nantucket, from New London to Sakonnet. I must admit that since Jane happened to mention that in ten years she's never had to touch the anchor, things have improved for me. It may also have helped that I couldn't get the dragging Danforth up in a heavy westerly in Great Salt Pond not long after Jane's comment. Anchors can be a nasty business, but I wouldn't have given you ten cents for the helm in Great Salt Pond that day! Or the night in Cuttyhunk when the wind swung 180 degrees and half of the boats there broke out. Or when the squall hit in Nantucket and we took off through the fleet. As mate, you're likely to find you have to put up with the job at your feet— especially if you're the only crew. Often it's a choice between dog-work and responsibility. Take the one you can handle best.

Shouting is impolite, frightening, and grudge-making. Unfortunately, I find, it's completely necessary in many instances. In a local race several years ago I was assigned bow watch. We were on starboard tack, heading for the starting line, when another boat in our class, on port tack, adjusted her course so that she was heading right for us. Both skippers were unable to see under their Genoa jibs (which is the reason I was on the bow), but on the other boat the bow watch was clearing lines or otherwise occupied. I may not have shouted—I think I *screamed*—"HEAD UP!" Instantaneous reaction. And then our whole crew shouted, "RIGHT OF WAY." Well, too late for right of way, but just in time for safety—we were about and had lost any advantage we had over port-tackers on the line, but *Tomadrus* had fallen off and disaster was at least postponed until the next mark!

John is from Rhode Island and speaks the native patois. When he first called me for a date, I couldn't understand what he was saying. I asked "What?" a few times, and when I couldn't say that anymore, I laughed. Somehow, we solved the communication problem. He shouted. Anyway, I did agree to a date. Ever since then I've been trying to figure out why I could understand him better when he shouted.

I think that when one shouts, one concentrates on enunciating clearly. When I'm on the bow and John is at the helm and *asks* me to do something, I have to walk aft to get my instructions, but when racing or in tight situations, we communicate instantly—we shout!

A loud voice, a shout, in adverse circumstances is not to be taken personally. The skipper wants action, now, and no misunderstanding. He is directing *crew*, not you. If he is reasonable, as John is, and you haven't sabotaged the boat with premeditated action or put her on Middle Ground in spite of the compass, you will find that all is friendly and relaxed when the anchor is dropped. But don't forget the lunch. That would get a rather unreasonable shout.

MARY LEONARD

Glossary

~~~~~~

Abeam: at right angles to the keel of the boat; from or to the side of a boat as "Cape Ann abeam" or "wind abeam."

Above: above decks or on the decks (upstairs).

Aft: after-section of a boat; that part of a boat behind the mid-section.

Afterdeck: that part of the deck aft of or behind the mid-section of a boat or, more commonly, that part of the deck aft of the helm.

After Life Rail(or Lines): safety railing or lines on the after-section of a boat.

Aftermast: mizzen mast or hindmost mast on a ketch, yawl, ship, brig, barkentine, etc. On a schooner, the aftermast is the mainmast.

Anchor (or "Hook"): (n.) shaped piece of iron or steel used to hold a boat in place; (v.) to drop anchor.

Anchorage: a place to anchor; that part of a port or harbor designated as the place to anchor or moor a boat (in United States waters, determined by the Coast Guard).

Anemometer: wind speed indicator.

Astern: (1) at or toward the stern of a boat; (2) behind a boat or off the stern.

Backstay: a supporting rope or wire from the back of the mast and running to an after-section of the deck or hull.

Ballast: (1) weight carried in or built into a boat to balance and steady it; (2) the keel.

Ballooner (or Balloon Jib or "Drifter"): a large, light headsail carried when sailing in light air off the wind or before the wind if a spinnaker is not used.

Batten: (n.) a strong, flexible strip of wood or plastic used in the leach of a sail to keep it from sagging or folding; (v.) (batten down) originally, to nail or tie planks, boards, or battens over hatch covers or companionways to keep them closed, protected, or in place during a storm. To "batten down" commonly means to secure all loose gear for heavy weather sailing.

Beam: the width of a boat measured at its widest part.

Beat: to sail against the wind in zigzag fashion; to change direction while sailing as close as possible to the direction from which the wind is coming.

Below: below decks; the cabin area or hold (downstairs).

Bilge: that section of the hull that is below the floorboards in cabin or cockpit.

Binnacle: the compass box or housing and its stand, which is placed in front of the helm on many boats.

Block: a pulley (see diagram).

Block Pad: a pad or mat, often woven of light rope or line, used to protect deck, cabin top, or brightwork from a moving block.

Boat Hook (or "Gaff"): a long pole with a metal hook at one end used to catch mooring line, dinghy, etc.

Boom: that spar or pole along which the bottom of a sail is stretched and, usually, clipped or tied.

Boot Top: a waterline stripe between the bottom and the topsides of a hull (see diagram).

Bottom: the underside of the hull; that portion of the hull that is in the water (see diagram).

Bow: the front of a boat.

Bowman: man on the bow who may handle anchor, jibs, or serve as lookout, etc.

Bowsprit: pole or spar projecting forward from the bow of a boat which extends the sail area forward.

Break Out: (1) to rig or hoist a sail; to free or open a sail that has been hoisted in stops; (2) to free an anchor from the bottom; to dislodge an anchor (by mistake or intent!).

Brightwork: oiled or varnished wood such as that used for seats, rails, or trim on or in a boat.

Broach: to turn broadside to the waves, an uncomfortable and sometimes dangerous position.

Bulkhead: wall or partition below deck in a boat.

Bulwark: a raised coaming or solid railing around the decks of a boat.

Bung: (n.) a wooden plug used in drain, scupper, or screw holes to close the hole or finish the surface; (v.) to insert a bung.

Bunk: the bed on a boat.

Buoy: (1) a navigational aid such as a nun or can used to mark a channel; (2) a float or marker on a mooring or lobster pot.

Cabin (or "House"): (1) the living quarters on a boat; (2) that part of the deck that is raised to allow light and headroom in the living quarters; (3) a structure built upon the deck of a boat as the pilot house.

Cabin Trunk: the vertical section of the cabin that is above the deck.

Capsize: to turn over, to upset.

Capstan: a machine for lifting or pulling that stands upright; a large winch. A capstan is used to hoist anchor, to haul lobster pots, and to haul fishing nets.

Carling: a fore and aft member supporting a deck of a ship or the framing of a deck opening or hatch.

Catboat: a shallow draft, centerboard vessel with mast at the extreme bow and fore and aft sail (see diagram).

Celestial Navigation: navigation by the stars; establishing one's position by determining the altitude of certain stars, the sun, the moon, etc., with a sextant.

Centerboard: a board or plate in a watertight centerline slot which may be lowered to prevent side-slipping (leeway) when sailing to windward or raised to increase speed when sailing before the wind (see diagram).

Chain Plate: a metal (usually brass or iron) bar or plate on the side of a boat bolted into ribs or frames to which the shrouds are attached.

Chart: a nautical map showing the shoreline, depths of water, navigational aids, and hazards. Charts of United States waters and adjacent waters are prepared and published by the Coast and Geodetic Survey, which was authorized in 1807.

Chock: a fitting with two arms curving inward for a rope to pass through.

Chop: short, steep waves, often breaking, caused by the wind or tide; "white caps."

Class (of Boat): type or design of boat or a division of a race.

Cleat: (n.) a piece of wood or metal shaped like a small anvil used to secure ropes or lines; (v.) to fasten to a cleat (see diagram).

Clew: (n.) the lower, outer corner of a fore and aft sail, the bottom corners of a square sail, or the fittings in those corners of the sail; (v.) (clew up) to wind up into a ball, as clew up a sail (i.e.,

SIMPLE RIGS

Hull forms will vary and boats may be gaff or jib-headed rig. To distinguish the type of boat, note particularly the number and position of masts.

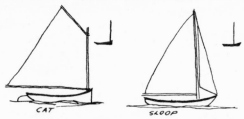

CAT: One mast far forward, one sail.

SLOOP: One mast forward, one headsail (jib or Genoa) and mainsail.

CUTTER: One mast just forward of amidships, one or more headsails, and mainsail.

YAWL: Two masts, one main, one mizzen. Mainmast is forward as on sloop, mizzen is far aft, **behind** the helm (wheel or tiller). One or more headsails, mainsail and mizzen or "jigger."

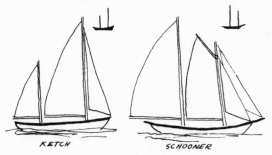

KETCH: Two masts, one main, one mizzen. The mizzen is positioned **ahead** of the helm. One or more headsails, mainsail, mizzen.

SCHOONER: Two (or more) masts, one (or more) fore, one main. The foremast is shorter and forward of the mainmast. The mainmast is positioned aft of amidships and ahead of the helm. The foresail is gaff or staysail and the mainsail may be either gaff- or jib-headed. Topsails may be carried on either mast. Two or more headsails, foresail, mainsail.

tie up by its clews); (clew down or out) to tie down or out through a clew or clews.

Club: a small boom used with a jib.

Coaming: a raised edge, bulwark, or rail around a hatch or cockpit to prevent water from running or splashing into cabin or cockpit.

Cockpit: a well in the deck where crew or passengers may sit. The helm is usually in the cockpit of a sailboat.

Come About: to head into the wind and cross it in order to change direction, filling sail on the opposite side of the boat.

Commissioning: according to Webster, the hoisting of the ensign, after it has been laid up, thus formally beginning the season on a yacht; according to yachtsmen, the same, but also the activity of getting the boat ready for the season before the ensign is hoisted.

Companionway: stairway or ladder from deck into cabin or hold.

Compass: an instrument indicating the magnetic meridian used aboard a ship or boat to aid in directing the vessel on a straight or proper course.

Compass Course: (1) a path or course between two points laid out on a chart with the aid of a compass; (2) the compass reading or bearing while on a plotted course as, "The course is 128 degrees."

Cotter Pin: a split pin with bent ends that has been inserted through a slot or hole to hold parts of machinery or tackle together.

Crosstrees: spreaders (usually on square-rigged vessels).

Cruiser: a boat fitted out for cruising, or (by sailors) a power boat.

Cutter: a single-masted fore and aft rigged vessel that has the mast a third of the length from the bow (see diagram).

Danforth: a type of anchor that folds flat and has wide, flat flukes. It is reputed to hold well under some circumstances (see diagram).

Deck: the planking or molding over the top of a boat. The deck is built over the top of the hull to make cargo or living space within the hull. In the cabin, the deck or flooring is called the sole (see diagram). (N.B.: In nautical language, floors are structural members fastened to the keel and are braces and supports, not floorboards.)

Dinghy: a small rowboat or tender for a larger boat.

Ditty Bag: a small drawstring bag resembling a sailbag for odds and ends of boat gear or sail repair equipment.

Dory: a narrow, flat-bottomed, and very seaworthy rowboat that has a pointed bow and a narrow, triangular transom.

Downhaul: a rope or small tackle from boom or spinnaker pole to a cleat or winch to hold the boom or pole down and steady.

Drag: (1) (n.) nets and gear used by a fishing boat (dragger) to drag for fish; (v.) to fish by dragging nets behind a boat; to search for the water's bottom by dragging a grapple, net, etc.; (2) (v.) to slip or become dislodged; if an anchor does not hold, it will drag; (3) (n.) wife, child, or dog aboard.

Draught (or Draft): (1) the depth of a boat from the waterline to the bottom of the keel; the amount of water a boat "draws" or requires in depth; (2) the amount of wind caught or held in a sail.

Drifter: a balloon jib or large, lightweight headsail for use when reaching in light air.

Ensign: a yacht's national emblem, flag, or banner. Documented yachts of the United States are authorized to fly the U. S. Yacht Ensign, which shows thirteen stars surrounding an anchor on the field. The ensign is flown between 8 A.M. and sundown on sailboats at anchor or under power, or may be flown from the peak of a gaff mainsail. When cruising in foreign waters, a yacht will fly her ensign in the proper place (on a staff or line at her stern) and, in courtesy, the flag of the other country on her starboard flag halliard (see diagram).

Fair Wind: anything short of a gale and other than a head wind; a wind that will allow a boat to make direct progress toward its destination under safe conditions.

Fall Away: to drift back or away (from a dock, mooring, boat, etc.)

Fantail: deck behind the helm or at the stern of a ship or boat.

Fathom: a unit of length equal to 6 feet, used for measuring the depth of water.

Fathometer: depth finder; an electronic sounding device.

Fend: to protect, to push off.

Fender: a soft strip or cushion on boat or dock to protect the boat from bumps, bruises, or abrasions. Standard boat fenders are corkfilled canvas, inflated rubber, or plastic.

Fill (or Fill Away): to fill the sails with wind and move forward.

Flare Kit: a kit containing flare signals for use in an emergency, particularly at night.

Flying: (1) free; not stopped or bagged; (2) any boat speed in excess of 5½ knots.

Fore and Aft Sail (or Rig): sails set in line with the keel.

Foredeck: forward part of the deck; that part of the deck in front of midships (see diagram).

Forepeak: the forward section of the cabin or hull under the foredeck.

Foul: (n.) unfavorable, stormy weather; (adj.) tangled (lines); (v.) to hit, tangle with, or obstruct (marks or boats).

Frostbite: to race dinghies or small boats during frost seasons.

Furl: to roll or fold a sail along a boom. (Buzz describes this as an "organized way to bunch up the sail.")

Gaff: (1) spar or pole extending along the upper edge of a fore and aft sail; (2) a boat hook.

Gaff Rig: a fore and aft sail plan in which the mainsail is attached along the upper edge to a spar (gaff) (see diagram).

Galley: the kitchen on a boat.

Gear: equipment necessary for a boat and its crew.

Genoa (or Genny): a large jib cut close to the deck and reaching far aft, used for power and speed when working to windward.

Grab Rails: hand rails, generally found on cabin top or along inside of cabin trunk to provide a hand hold when working in a heavy wind or rough sea.

Green Running Lights: the lights on the starboard, or right-hand, side of the boat that Coast Guard regulations require be kept burning, along with the portside (left) red light, while the vessel is under way between sunset and sunrise.

Ground Swell: broad, deep waves caused by distant storm, etc; the steady rolling waves often found offshore (seasick-making rollers).

Ground Tackle: anchor, mooring, weights, and chains used to anchor or moor a boat.

Guy: a line attached to the windward end of a spinnaker pole to control the position of the spinnaker.

Hail: to call loudly to, to shout at.

Hailing Distance: the distance within which one may hear a call or shout.

Hailing Port: home port, a boat's regular mooring place; the place referred to when a boat "hails" or calls her identity as, "*Skylark*, out of Stonington."

Halliard (or Halyard—from "haul yard"): rope or line used to raise or lower a sail, gaff, yard, or flag.

Hand Grips: generally, anything one can find to hang onto, but some boats have handles or cutouts in useful places to provide a hand hold when working in heavy weather.

Hanging Locker: closet or cupboard for hanging clothes.

Haul: (1) to pull or drag with force, as "haul anchor"; (2) to turn a boat nearer to the direction of the wind; (3) to change course (wind or boat may haul).

Head: the toilet facility, or bathroom, on a boat.

Headroom: room made available for one's head in a cabin or hull.

Headsail: any sail set forward of the foremast; a jib.

Headway: forward progress.

Head Wind: wind blowing against the front of a boat, in fact, blowing from the direction in which you are trying to go!

Heel: to lean with the wind.

Helm: wheel or handle by which a boat is steered; (2) the entire steering apparatus, i.e., wheel, gears, and rudder.

Helmsman: the man (or woman!) who steers a boat.

Helmsmanship: (1) the art of steering a boat; (2) fine maneuvering.

Hot Bunking: using a bunk immediately after someone else when standing watches and bunks are limited (common practice on yachts when ocean racing).

Hull: the main body and frame of a ship or boat exclusive of masts, house, sails, or rigging.

Hull Speed: maximum speed of which a boat is capable as determined by the design of her hull. (Exception: a boat may exceed hull speed if it is capable of planing.)

Jib: a triangular headsail attached to headstay or forestay above the bow (see diagram).

Jibe (or Gibe): to change sails from port to starboard or vice versa in a following wind; to change tack when sailing before the wind.

Jigger: mizzen; the sail on the aftermast of a yawl or ketch (see diagram).

Keel: outside ballast on the hull of a boat; the center bottom strip or plank on a small boat without ballast (see diagram).

Ketch: a two masted vessel in which the mizzenmast is placed forward of the helm (see diagram).

Knock Down: (v.) to lay over very far until the spreaders touch the water; (n.) any sudden leaning over at an extreme angle due to a gust of wind.

Knot: a nautical mile equalling approximately 1⅛ statute miles.

Landside (or **Shoreside**): on land.

Lay: to stay or rest, as "we lay at anchor."

Lay Over: (1) to stay at anchor for some time; (2) to heel or lean with the wind.

Lazarette: cupboard or locker; place where supplies are kept, generally those lockers under a bunk.

Leach: the outer edge of a sail (see diagram).

Lead: (v.) to lay out a line from sail, boom, anchor, etc., through or to the place where it is to be controlled (pronounced *leed*); (n.) the weight on a lead line (pronounced *led*).

Lead Line: a sounding line; a long line marked off in fathoms with a lead weight for measuring the depth of water.

Lee: out of the wind, away from the wind; a sheltered place.

Leeward: direction away from the wind (pronounced *lu'ward*).

Light Displacement: light weight and shallow draught, thereby displacing little water.

Lightship: a Coast Guard vessel permanently anchored at or near an obstruction, shoal, or reef which serves the same purpose as a lighthouse. A lightship is bright red with large white letters identifying it on each side (i.e., *Nantucket, Breton Reef, Ambrose, Portland,* etc.).

Line: a rope or wire.

Lloyd's Register: *Lloyd's Register of American Yachts,* published annually by Lloyd's Register of Shipping, 17 Battery Place, New York, New York; a list of most yachts over 25 feet long, giving the year they were built, the particulars, and the names and addresses of owners. It also contains a list of yacht clubs and shows burgees and private signals.

Luff: (n.) the inner or leading edge of a sail or that edge of a sail that is attached to the mast or stay (see diagram); (v.) (1) to spill wind out of the sail, which causes the sail to flap and billow along the luff; (2) to force a competitor up into the wind, thus causing his sail to spill wind or "luff."

Mainsail: formerly the largest working sail on a sailboat, but today many Genoas exceed in square footage that of the mainsail. The mainsail is attached by its luff to the main mast of a boat (see diagram).

Mark: a buoy or race-course marker.

Marlin: heavy twine treated with creosote to prevent rotting.

Marlin Spike: (1) a pointed metal implement used by sailors to separate strands of rope in splicing; (2) a spike often attached to a yachtsman's pocket knife.

Midget Ocean Racer: a racing sailboat approximately 25 to 35 feet in length equipped for offshore racing and cruising.

Mizzen: the after- or hind-most mast on a ketch, yawl, ship, brig, etc.

Moor: to secure by lines and anchor or weights.

Mooring: (1) the chains, weights, or anchors laid at the bottom of a harbor to which a vessel may be secured; (2) (n.) the place where a vessel is moored or anchored; an anchorage; (v.) the act of securing a vessel to a particular place.

Nun: a red can buoy with a conical top that suggests the habit of a nun.

Oarlock: a notch, pegs, or U-shaped metal support in which an oar rides when rowing.

Ocean Racing: offshore racing as opposed to racing in bays, sounds, and harbors.

Offshore: (1) at sea, or away from the land; (2) blowing from the land, as "an offshore breeze."

Oilskin: a foul-weather suit or raincoat originally made of oiled skins or canvas, now made of rubber- or plastic-coated fabric or plain plastic.

Onshore: blowing toward the land, as "an onshore breeze."

Overhead: that part of the deck or cabin top that is overhead when "below," or in the cabin area of a boat.

Patent Log: a device with a finned metal drag towed on a long line behind a boat. As the drag spins, the revolutions are recorded by a gauge that shows the distance, in nautical miles, a boat has traveled. A log is of great assistance in determining a boat's position when navigating blind (in fog, at night, or out of sight of land).

Pennant: (1) a small triangular flag such as a yacht club burgee; (2) a short piece of line, rope, etc.; the line on a mooring with which the boat is tied to the mooring.

Port: (1) a harbor or mooring place; (2) left; on the left-hand side, facing the bow of a boat.

Port Tack: a boat is on port tack when the wind is blowing from the port (left) side and the sails are set to starboard (right).

BASIC HARDWARE

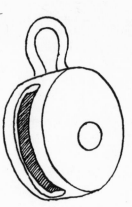

BLOCK
ON MAST, BOOM &
DECK - HALLIARDS
AND SHEETS RUN
THROUGH BLOCKS ON
ROLLER (SHIV)

CLEAT
ON MAST, BOOM, DECK
-LINES ARE SECURED
ON CLEATS

SHACKLES
TO ATTACH SAIL
TO HALLIARD OR SHEET,
CHAIN TO ANCHOR,
BLOCKS TO MAST, BOOM, OR DECK

CLIPS
OR
SNAPS

USED TO CLIP
JIB TO HEADSTAY, SHEETS TO JIB
OR SPINNAKER, ETC.

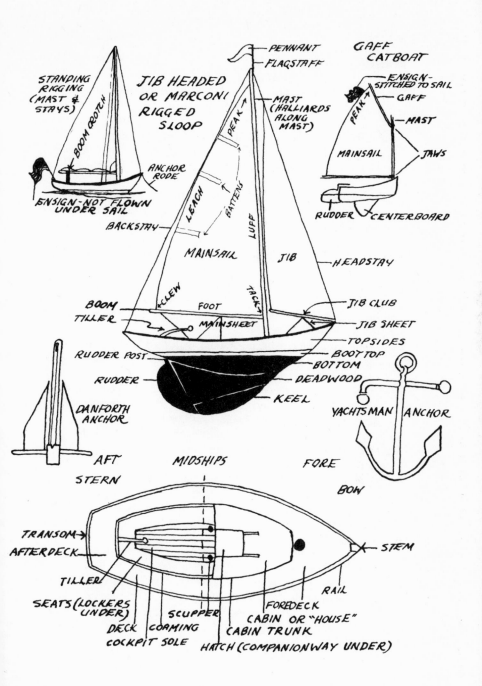

STANDING RIGGING (MAST & STAYS)

BOOM CROTCH

ENSIGN—NOT FLOWN UNDER SAIL

JIB HEADED OR MARCONI RIGGED SLOOP

ANCHOR RODE

PEAK

BATTENS

LEACH

LUFF

BACKSTAY

MAINSAIL

JIB

CLEW

FOOT

TACK

BOOM
TILLER

MAINSHEET

RUDDER POST

RUDDER

DANFORTH ANCHOR

PENNANT
FLAGSTAFF

MAST (HALLIARDS ALONG MAST)

GAFF CATBOAT

ENSIGN—STITCHED TO SAIL
GAFF
MAST

PEAK

MAINSAIL

JAWS

RUDDER   CENTERBOARD

HEADSTAY

JIB CLUB
JIB SHEET
TOPSIDES
BOOT TOP
BOTTOM
DEADWOOD
KEEL

YACHTSMAN ANCHOR

AFT   MIDSHIPS   FORE

STERN   BOW

TRANSOM
AFTERDECK

STEM

TILLER

RAIL

SEATS (LOCKERS UNDER)

DECK   COAMING
COCKPIT SOLE

SCUPPER

FOREDECK
CABIN OR "HOUSE"
CABIN TRUNK
HATCH (COMPANIONWAY UNDER)

Protractor: instrument for measuring angles, used for taking off a compass course on a marine chart or map.

Punt: (n.) a small, flat-bottomed, square-ended rowboat; (v.) to push a boat along with a pole.

Quadrant: (1) quarter section of the circle of the compass as North-east quadrant; (2) instrument used in astronomy, navigation, and survey for measuring altitudes.

Radio-Telephone: a ship-to-shore radio that has those frequencies monitored by marine telephone operators so that a boat's radio call may be transmitted over regular telephone lines to any telephone.

Raft: (n.) boats tied together to swing from one anchor or mooring (rafting); (v.) to tie boats together.

Rating: time allowance in racing, figured by a complicated formula accounting for sail area, displacement, length, and beam, which, presumably, makes all boats equal under the same sailing conditions.

Red Lead: an orange paint pigmented with lead that is used to protect iron from rust and wood from rot. Bilges and keels are often painted with red lead.

Reef: (1) a narrow ledge of rocks at or near the surface of the water; (2) to shorten or reduce the size of a sail by rolling and tying a section of the sail to the boom (yard, gaff, etc.).

Refasten: to re-screw or re-nail planks to the frames of a hull.

Rig: (n.) the arrangement of masts and sails, as "a cat rig"; (v.) to equip with masts, sails, shrouds, and spars.

Rigger: one who equips and arranges the masts, shrouds, spars, and lines on a boat.

Rigging: ropes, lines or wires used to support the masts.

Rode: an anchor line.

Round: to go around.

Rudder: a hinged, flat piece of wood or metal at the rear end of a boat by which it is steered (see diagram).

Running Backstay: an adjustable backstay. Backstays run from the upper part of the mast to an after-section of the deck to counter forward thrust of the mast. Running backstays, with block and line, may be "taken up" or "let off" depending upon the force of the wind and the direction of the tack.

Running Rigging: halliards and sheets; lines used to hoist or control sails, booms, gaffs, etc., which are regularly "run" or moved when a boat is sailing.

Samson Post: a strong post around which ropes or lines may be tied.

Schooner: a fore-and-aft rigged vessel having two or more masts with the mainmast aft (see diagram).

Scope: the amount of anchor line necessary to allow a boat to swing or ride properly on her anchor without picking up or dragging the anchor.

Scratch Boat: the first boat on the racing sheet or handicap list, which must give every other boat in the race a time allowance. The scratch boat may be first to finish but lose the race on corrected time.

Scupper: a drain or hole that allows water to run out of a cockpit or off the decks.

Sea Anchor: a cone-shaped drag of canvas that may be dragged behind a boat to slow her progress or hold her before the wind (a bucket may serve the same purpose).

Seam: (1) a stitched connection of panels in a sail; (2) the space between planks in a deck or hull.

Seamanship: the art of working or piloting a vessel.

Seaworthy: fit for sailing on the sea; safe, sound, able.

Self-Bailing Cockpit: a cockpit with watertight sole above the water-line and scuppers or drains through the hull. If filled with water, the cockpit will drain without allowing water into the bilge.

Serve: to bind or wind a rope, line, or rail with small cord to strengthen, protect or beautify it.

Set: (1) to hoist and trim sails; (2) to be swept back or to the side by tide or current; (3) to hook an anchor firmly to the bottom.

Sextant: instrument used by navigators, surveyors, etc., for measuring the angular distance between two objects. Sextants are used at sea to measure the altitude of sun, moon, and other stars, in order to determine longitude and latitude.

Shackle: (1) a metal link with removable pin used to attach a line to a block, chain, sail, or an anchor to a chain (see diagram); (2) wife, child, or dog (see diagram).

Shakedown: (1) trial run; the first sail of the season; (2) "I can't cash a check in Nantucket; give me your allowance."

Shallow Draft: requiring little depth of water; not deep.

Sheer: (n.) the curve of a boat's deck or lines from the middle toward each end; (v.) to turn from a course.

Sheet: (n.) a line attached to a boom or sail to control the angle and draft of the sail; (v.) to adjust or control the angle of a sail.

Shipmate: an iron, wood, or coal stove used for cooking or heating aboard small boats.

Shoal: (adj.) shallow; (n.) a sand bank or sand bar that makes the water shallow.

Shoot: to bring a boat head-to-wind some distance from a mooring or dock and downwind of it so that the wind will slow the boat's momentum and she will coast to a stop at or near the mooring.

Shoreside: on land.

Shroud: a stay; a rope or wire from a mast to the side of a boat to help support the mast.

Skiff: a flat bottomed rowboat with pointed bow and flat stern.

Skipper: an affectionate term for the Captain. If you are annoyed with the captain, address him as Sir.

Slicker: a long raincoat of rubber- or plastic-coated material, traditionally black or bright yellow and worn with a Sou'wester.

Slip: (v.) to drift or be swept sideways; (n.) a docking space between two finger piers or pilings where boats may be tied perpendicular to a main pier.

Sloop: a fore-and-aft rigged vessel with one mast well forward of midships (see diagram).

Small Craft: vessels under 65 feet in length.

Sole: the flooring of a cockpit or cabin.

Sound: (n.) a body of water between the mainland and an island or a passage between two bodies of water; (v.) to measure the depth of water or determine the characteristics of the bottom.

Sou'wester: (1) a waterproof hat having a broad brim behind to protect the neck, worn especially by seamen ("A Nor'easter calls for a Sou'wester"); (2) wind from the southwest.

Spars: masts, booms, gaffs, or poles used to support or extend sails.

Spinnaker: (from sphinxer, after *Sphinx,* the America's Cup challenger on which it was first carried): a large, bellied and lightweight three-cornered sail carried forward and on the side opposite the mainsail when sailing before the wind. Originally a racing sail now gaining popularity in cruising.

Splice: (v.) to join two pieces of rope by weaving the untwisted ends together; (n.) such a joint in a rope.

Spreaders: horizontal arms on a mast to hold shrouds away from the mast and stretched tight.

Spring Lines: lines rigged between bow and stern lines from boat to dock or another boat to adjust for rise and fall of tide, wind, and current.

Standing Rigging: masts and stays; the fixed rigging on a boat.

Starboard: right; on the right-hand side facing toward the bow of a boat.

Starboard Tack: a boat is on starboard tack when the wind is blowing from the right side and the sails are set to left (port).

Stay: a shroud; a rope or wire from mast to the side of a boat used to support the mast.

Steerage Way: motion necessary to allow a boat to be steered.

Stem: the main piece of the bow of a boat to which the planking or sides are fastened.

Step: (n.) the hole or blocks into which a mast fits (the mast step); (v.) to set the mast into the boat.

Stern: the after-section of the hull or deck (see diagram).

Stock: to provide and stow food and gear necessary for boat and crew.

Stop: to tie a sail in sections, usually with rotten twine, so that the sail will break free easily when hoisted without becoming tangled or caught in the rigging.

Stores: provisions; food or clothing.

Stowage: space in which to store things.

Swab: mop.

Swamp: to fill with water.

Sway: to heave and hold a rope or line repeatedly in order to raise a heavy object (sail, gaff, etc.).

Swell: a long, rolling wave that is not breaking, caused by a distant storm, etc.

Tack: to come about—also define tack as a *direction* relative to boat.

Tackle: ropes and pulleys for lifting, lowering, and pulling; halliards, sheets and blocks.

Tail: (n.) the end of a rope or line; (v.) to hold or pull the end of a rope being hauled in by a winch.

Tiller: the handle by which a boat is steered (see diagram).

Topping Lift: a line running from top of mast to boom to keep the boom from dropping in very light air or when the sails are lowered.

Topsail: the second sail above the deck on a mast or a boat, carried above the main or foresail on a schooner, etc.

Topsides: (1) on deck (upstairs); (2) that part of the vessel's side which is above water when she is afloat.

Transom: the sternboard of a boat on which the name and hailing port are often printed.

Traveler: a metal bar, track, or wire on the deck of a boat to which one end of a sheet may be attached enabling a sail on a boom or club to swing ("travel") over to the proper angle without tending when coming about.

Trim: to adjust to the proper angle or draft.

Turkshead: a fancy knot often seen on wheel spokes, rails, and lately, wrists.

Under Power: using engine rather than sails.

Under Way: in motion, moving under your own power (sail or engine).

Wake: the trail of waves left by a boat.

Watch: (1) the crew on duty; (2) a lookout; (3) a four-hour period of time. Maritime watches run from midnight to 4:00 A.M., 4:00 A.M. to 8:00 A.M., 8:00 A.M. to 12 noon, etc., and ships crews traditionally stand four hours on watch and eight hours off, or "watch and watch," which is four hours on and four hours off duty.

Waterline: (1) line where the water touches the side of a boat; (2) a painted line indicating the depth to which a boat will sink into the water when properly loaded.

Way: motion; "Way is off my ship" means "This vessel is not moving."

Weather Helm: tending to head into the wind.

Wheel: (1) a steering wheel used instead of a tiller; (2) the helm.

Wheel Down: to turn the wheel; actually, to push a spoke of the wheel down, thus turning the wheel and rudder.

Whip: to wind fine line or thread around a heavier line to keep the ends of that line from raveling or fraying.

Winch: (n.) a revolving drum around which sheets, halliards, or other lines may be coiled to pull those lines taut, adding mechanical advantage to the force exerted; (v.) to pull a line with the help of a winch.

Winch Handle: the crank used to turn a winch.

Windward: toward the wind; the side from which the wind is blowing.

Wood: to clean down to the bare wood.

Work Ship: to perform those labors necessary to sailing a vessel, such as handling the sails or lines.

Yachtsman Anchor: a very good stock-type anchor for general use (see diagram).

Yardarm: the spar from which a square sail is flown.

Yaw: to become unsteady, to swing back and forth without control.

Yawl: a vessel with two masts in which the mizzen is stepped aft of the helm or rudder post (see diagram).

Index